# José Martí
# Revolutionary democrat

# JOSÉ MARTÍ

Revolutionary democrat

Edited by
CHRISTOPHER ABEL
and NISSA TORRENTS

Duke University Press
Durham
1986

Copyright © 1986 by Christopher Abel, Nissa Torrents

Published by The Athlone Press Ltd
44 Bedford Row, London WC1R 4LY
Published in the United States of America by
Duke University Press
6697 College Station
Durham, North Carolina 27708

Library of Congress Cataloging-in-Publication Data

José Martí, revolutionary democrat.

Bibliography: p.
Includes index.
1. Martí, José, 1853–1895.   I. Abel, Christopher.
II. Torrents, Nissa.
F1783.M38J67   1986          972.91′05′0924          86–11519
ISBN 0–8223–0679–4

# Contents

# Acknowledgements

The editors and the publisher wish to acknowledge the generous support towards the publication of this book, received from the Manuel Pedro González José Martí Fund of the University of Florida Foundation and from the Latin American Publications Fund of the Institute of Latin American Studies, University of London.

# Introduction

José Martí (1853–95), Cuban revolutionary, poet and journalist, needs no introduction in the Americas and Spain. Elsewhere he is little known. This book arises from a seminar that was intended as a corrective to neglect of him in the United Kingdom.

The seminar was held in 1983 at the Institute of Latin American Studies, London, and directed by teachers based in the Spanish and History departments of University College, London. The meeting formed part of a continuous programme of post-doctoral and post-graduate seminars. These included comparable meetings on Simón Bolívar, Andrés Bello and Rómulo Gallegos, as well as regular workshops on Latin American culture and Caribbean societies. (Two volumes of selected seminar papers from the Caribbean societies' meetings were published by the Institute of Commonwealth Studies, London, in 1982 and 1985.)

We have to thank Professors John Lynch, Maldwyn Jones and J. S. Cummins, for the encouragement they gave us. The seminar was made possible by the Nuffield Foundation, the University of Florida Manuel Pedro González José Martí Fund, Dalhousie University, Nova Scotia, and the Centro de Estudios Martianos in Havana. Scholars attended the seminar from Cuba, Canada, the United States, France and the United Kingdom. The gathering of scholars from such backgrounds was greatly assisted by Dr Hermes Herrera, the Cuban ambassador to the United Kingdom and former Rector of the Universidad de la Habana, and by Mr David Thomas, then British ambassador to Cuba. We have a particular debt of gratitude to Professor Ivan Schulman for his advice and encouragement throughout.

The aim of the seminar was to reappraise the significance of Martí in a non-partisan and dispassionate manner. Literary scholars and historians from different intellectual and ideological backgrounds were invited to contribute. The seminar papers gave rise to vigorous discussion of the continuing significance of Martí as an interpreter of US–Latin American relations, as a social critic, and as a nationalist thinker and man of letters whose influence permeated the entire continent. The debate contributed further to the reappraisal of Martí. Among numerous discussants, Professor Gordon Brotherston,

Professor C. A. M. Hennessy, Dr John King, Professor Evelyn Picón-Garfield and Dr Robert Pring-Mill, played an active role.

The translations of quotations from Martí in chapter 2 by Gerald Poyo, are by the author. The translations of the chapters by the Cuban scholars; and the translations and the transliterations of most other quotations from Martí are the responsibility of the editors.

Annie Shone provided indispensable administrative support before and during the seminar and during the preparation of the volume. We want also to thank Cristina Weller for her typing and for her most helpful suggestions.

CHRISTOPHER ABEL   NISSA TORRENTS

# Notes on contributors

**Roberto Fernández Retamar** is director of the Centro de Estudios Martianos in Havana and vice-president of Casa de las Américas, whose periodical *Casa de las Américas* he directs. He is a poet and critic known throughout the Spanish-speaking world who has written extensively on Martí, especially *Introducción a José Martí* (Havana, 1978) and contributions to the *Anuario del centro de estudios martianos*. His book *Calibán, apuntes sobre la cultura en nuestra América* (Havana, 1971) has been a seminal influence on a generation of literary scholars.

**Gerald Poyo** researches and teaches at the Institute of Texan Cultures at San Antonio, Texas. He has contributed articles to the *Anuario del centro de estudios martianos* and the *Florida Historical Quarterly*.

**Antoni Kapcia** is a lecturer in the School of Modern Languages at Wolverhampton Polytechnic. He has studied Cuban literature and history for several years, contributing to such journals as the *Bulletin of Latin American Research* and *Problems of Communism*, and also to C. Abel and M. Twaddle (comps), *Caribbean Societies, Volume 1, Collected Seminar Papers No. 29* (Institute of Commonwealth Studies, London, 1982).

**Jackie Kaye** is lecturer in the Department of Literature at the University of Essex at Colchester. She has written extensively on Caribbean and US literature and edits a series of occasional papers in cross-cultural studies published by her department. She has contributed to a volume entitled *Modern American Poetry* (ed. H. Butterfield, London, 1984).

**Jorge Ibarra** is a member of the Instituto de historia of the Academia de Ciencias, Havana. He has published on a wide range of Cuban historical topics, in such works as *Ideología mambisa* (Havana, 1967) and *Aproximaciones a Clio* (Havana, 1979), and on Martí in *José Martí: Dirigente político e ideólogo revolucionario* (Havana, 1980).

**John Kirk** teaches Hispanic Studies at Dalhousie University in Nova Scotia. He has recently co-edited *Cuba, Twenty-Five Years of Revolution, 1959–1984* (New York, 1984) and is currently engaged in a project on religion in Nicaragua. He has authored *José Martí: Mentor of the Cuban Nation* (Tampa, Florida, 1983).

**Christopher Abel** is lecturer in Latin American history at University College, London, where he specialises in Caribbean and Andean history, and was previously junior research fellow in Cuban studies at St Antony's College, Oxford. He is co-editor with Colin M. Lewis of *Latin America: Economic Imperialism and the State* (Athlone Press, London, 1985).

**Ivan Schulman** is professor and head of department of Spanish, Italian and Portuguese at the University of Illinois (Champaign-Urbana). He has been president of the José Martí Foundation and Director of the Center of Latin American Studies at the University of Florida. A leading scholar on Martí, he wrote *Símbolo y color en la obra de José Martí* (2nd edn, Madrid, 1970) and co-authored both *Martí, Darío y el modernismo* (2nd edn, Madrid, 1974) with Manuel Pedro González and *Las entrañas del vacío: ensayos sobre la modernidad hispanoamericana* (Mexico, 1984) with Evelyn Picón-Garfield.

**Nissa Torrents** lectures in Latin American literature and cinema at University College, London. She has co-edited *Spain: Conditional Democracy* (London, 1983) with C. Abel, has contributed a paper on Cuban cinema to *Caribbean Societies: Volume 1* (noted above) and writes regularly for *La Vanguardia* of Barcelona. She is currently working on women's questions in contemporary Cuba.

# Chronological guide

| Life of Martí | Political events | Cultural context |
|---|---|---|
| | | 1842 Stéphane Mallarmé is born. |
| | | 1846 Joaquín Costa is born. |
| | | 1851 Publication of *Moby Dick* by Herman Melville. |
| 1853 Born in Havana of Spanish parentage. | | |
| | | 1854 Publication of *Walden, or Life in the Woods* by H. D. Thoreau. Arthur Rimbaud is born. |
| | | 1855 Publication of *Leaves of Grass* by Walt Whitman. |
| | | 1857 Publication of *Les fleurs du mal* by Charles Baudelaire. |
| | | 1859 Manuel Gutiérrez Nájera is born. Publication of Darwin's *The Origin of Species*. |
| | 1860 Garibaldi's landing in Sicily. Lincoln is elected President of the USA. | 1860 Jules Laforgue is born. |
| | | 1862 Publication of *Les Misérables* by Victor Hugo. |
| | | 1863 Julián del Casal is born. |
| 1865 Comes under the influence of Rafael María de Mendive. | 1865 Prohibition of slavery in all the states of the USA. | |

| Life of Martí | Political events | Cultural context |
| --- | --- | --- |
| | | 1867 Publication of Marx's *Das Kapital*. Rubén Darío is born. |
| 1868 First poem published. | 1868–78 First (abortive) Cuban war of independence ('Ten Years' War). | 1868 Ricardo Jaimes Freyre is born. |
| 1869 *Jan.* First political articles published. Edits *La Patria Libre*, where his poetic drama *Abdala* is published. *Oct.* Imprisoned. | 1869 Opening of Suez Canal. | 1869 Publication of *Les Fêtes galantes* by Paul Verlaine. |
| | 1870 Franco-Prussian War. | 1870 Amado Nervo is born. G. A. Bécquer dies. Lautréamont dies. |
| | 1870–7 The Septenio: first administration of Antonio Guzmán Blanco in Venezuela. | |
| 1871–4 Deportation to Spain; in 1871 publishes in Madrid his leaflet *El presidio político en Cuba*. | 1871 Establishment and defeat of the Commune. | 1871 José Enrique Rodó is born. |
| | 1873 Abdication of King Amadeo of Savoy and declaration of First Republic (Spain). | 1872 Publication of *Martín Fierro* by José Hernández. |
| 1874 Graduates. | 1874 Fall of First Republic. | 1874 First Impressionist exhibition in Paris. Leopoldo Lugones is born. |

xv

| | Life of Martí | | Political events | | Cultural context |
|---|---|---|---|---|---|
| 1875 | Arrives in Mexico and collaborates with press. | 1875 | Restoration of Bourbon monarchy in Spain. | 1875 | José Santos Chocano is born. Julio Herrera y Reissig is born. |
| | | 1876 | Coup of Porfirio Díaz against Sebastián Lerdo in Tejada (Mexico). Beginning of Porfiriato. | | |
| 1877 | *Jan.* Brief appearance in Havana using only matronym. *Feb.* Arrives in Guatemala; teaching. *Dec.* Marries Carmen Zayas Bazán in Mexico City. | | | | |
| 1878 | Leaves Guatemala for Havana. | | | | |
| 1879 | *Sept.* Second imprisonment and deportation to Spain. *Dec.* Escapes to France. | 1879–80 | *La Guerra chiquita.* | 1879 | Publication of *Progress and Poverty* by Henry George. |
| | | 1879–84 | The Quinquenio; second Guzmán dictatorship in Venezuela. | | |
| 1880 | *Jan.* Leaves for New York; immediate engagement with press and politics. *Mar.* Acting leader of Comité Revolucionario. | 1880 | *Feb.* Moret Law abolishing Cuban slavery. | 1880 | Publication of *Azul* by Rubén Darío. |
| 1881 | *Jan.* Travels to Venezuela; journalism and teaching. *July* Returns involuntarily to New York. | 1881 | De Lesseps begins building of Panama Canal. French take Tunis. | 1881 | Publication of *Braz Cubas* by Machado de Assís. |
| 1882 | *Apr.* Publication of book of poems, *Ismaelillo.* | | | 1882 | Ralph Waldo Emerson dies. Longfellow dies. |

| Life of Martí | Political events | Cultural context |
|---|---|---|
| 1882 *July* Works for *La Nación* of Buenos Aires in New York. | | 1882 Publication of *Cecilia Valdés* by C. Villaverde (definitive edition). |
| | | 1883 Publication of *Les poètes maudits* by Verlaine. |
| 1884 Breaks publicly with Maceo and Gómez over what he perceives as their militarism. | 1884–6 General Joaquín Crespo, President of Venezuela. | 1884 Publication of *La Duquesa Job* by M. Gutiérrez Nájera. Publication of *A rebours* by J. K. Huysmans. |
| | | 1885 Publication of *The Adventures of Huckleberry Finn* by Mark Twain. Victor Hugo dies. |
| 1886 *Dec.* Gives *Madre América* speech. | 1886 Last slave freed in Cuba. | |
| | 1886–8 The *Aclamación*; third Guzmán administration in Venezuela. | |
| 1887 Becomes Consul of Uruguay in New York. | | |
| | 1888 Pan-American Conference. | 1888 Domingo Faustino Sarmiento dies. Publication of *Looking Backward* by Edward Bellamy. |
| 1889 *July* Begins publication of *La Edad de Oro*, a monthly magazine for children; 4 issues only. | 1889 Benjamin Harrison, US president. | |
| 1890 Appointed Consul of Argentina and Paraguay in New York and representative of Paraguay at International Monetary Conference. | 1890 Sherman Anti-Trust Act. | |

| | Life of Martí | | Political events | | Cultural context |
|---|---|---|---|---|---|
| 1891 | Resigns consular positions. Publishes book of poems, *Versos sencillos*. | | | 1891 | Herman Melville dies. |
| 1892 | *Jan.* Proposal for Bases del Partido Revolucionario Cubano and Estatutos Secretos approved. *Mar.* First issue of *Patria*. *Apr.* Elected delegate of PRC. *Sep.* Meets Gómez in Dominican Republic. | 1892–7 | Second Crespo administration in Venezuela. | 1892 | Walt Whitman dies. |
| 1893 | *June* Further meeting with Gómez in Dominican Republic. *July* Supposed meeting with Maceo in Costa Rica. | 1893 | Maura's projected reform of Cuban administration. Grover Cleveland, US president. | | |
| 1894 | Campaigns in Cuban émigré centres in USA. Travels in Central America, Jamaica and Mexico. | | | 1894 | Publication of *Wealth against Commonwealth* by Henry Demarest Lloyd. |
| 1895 | *Jan.* Decides to maintain independence struggle despite betrayal of planned invasion; co-signatory of order for uprising; leaves for Dominican Republic. *Feb.* Lands in Cuba. *Mar.* With Gómez signs Manifiesto de Montecristo. | 1895 | (*Feb.*) Second War of Cuban Independence begins (Spanish–American–Cuban War). | | |

| Life of Martí | Political events | Cultural context |
|---|---|---|
| 1895 *Apr.* With Gómez leaves again for Cuba; proclaimed Mayor General del Ejército Libertador. *May* Meeting with Maceo and Gómez. *19 May* Killed in battle at Dos Ríos near Santiago. | 1895–8 War. | |
| | 1896 *Feb.* Lt-Gen. Valeriano Weyler made Governor General of Cuba. *Dec.* Death of Maceo in battle. | 1896 Publication of *Prosas profanas* by Rubén Darío. |
| | 1897 Assassination of Cánovas (Spanish prime minister). William McKinley, US president. | |
| | 1898 *Apr.* US intervention in war. *Dec.* Treaty of Paris by which Spain loses Cuba, Puerto Rico and Philippines. | |
| | 1899 Establishment of US military government. | |

# 1 The modernity of Martí

## ROBERTO FERNÁNDEZ RETAMAR

Rubén Darío wrote in an emotional outburst at the death in battle of Martí:

> ¡Oh, Cuba! ¡Eres muy bella ciertamente, y hacen gloriosa obra los hijos tuyos que luchan porque te quieren libre . . . más la sangre de Martí no te pertenecía; pertenecía a toda una raza, a todo un continente; pertenecía a una briosa juventud que pierde en él quizá el primero de sus maestros; pertenecía al porvenir![1]

> Oh, Cuba! You are certainly very beautiful and those of your children that fight for your freedom, perform a glorious task . . . but the blood of Martí was not yours alone; it belonged to an entire race, to an entire continent; it belonged to the powerful young that loses in him the first of its teachers; he belongs to the future.

⌐It is difficult to contradict these painful words. Martí does not belong to Cuba alone, nor even to 'an entire continent'; he belongs more to 'the future', part of which we are becoming; he belongs to the whole of humanity.⌐ For reasons similar to those mentioned by Darío, Martí cannot be understood with exclusive reference to the history and literature of Cuba, although it was the pivot of his life. This is the reason why this chapter extends beyond Martí's lifespan. Cuba itself cannot be understood without reference to the rest of the world or at least to a good part of it.

Let us begin by pointing out a crucial influence upon Martí – that of Simón Bolívar. And let us recall a famous passage from Martí:

> Cuentan que un viajero llegó un día a Caracas al anochecer, y sin sacudirse el polvo del camino, no preguntó dónde se comía ni se dormía, sino como se iba adonde estaba la estatua de Bolívar. Y cuentan que el viajero, sólo con los árboles altos y olorosos de la plaza, lloraba frente a la estatua que parecía que se movía, como un padre cuando se le acerca un hijo. El viajero hizo bien, porque todos los americanos deben querer a Bolívar como a un padre.[2]

They tell how a traveller arrived one day at Caracas at dusk. Without shaking off the dust of the road, he did not ask where he could eat or sleep, but how he could find the statue of Bolívar. And they tell how the traveller, amidst the tall and sweet-smelling trees of the square, wept before the statue, that for him seemed to come to life, moving just as a father when his son comes near. The traveller did well, because all the people of the Americas must love Bolívar as a father.

This well-known scene occurred in January 1881, and was narrated eight years later in the magazine for children and young people, *La Edad de Oro*, by the protagonist himself, José Martí, the most enlightened and affectionate of Bolívar's disciples. Every word Martí wrote about the man he most admired was that of a loving son writing of the father whose bicentenary we celebrated in 1983 along with the one hundred and thirtieth anniversary of Martí's birth. Martí called Bolívar 'father of the Americas',[3] of whose 'sword we are all born',[4] 'prince of liberty',[5] 'solar man',[6] that 'burns and cradles',[7] and upon whom 'it is impossible to heap excessive praise'.[8] If it can be affirmed that the Cuban poet and schoolmaster, Rafael María de Mendive, was the spiritual father of Martí, it should be added that, without diminishing the influence of Benito Juárez, Simón Bolívar was his political father. It is important to bear in mind that, although Martí was endowed with literary greatness, he was above all a political creature in the fullest and most elevated sense of this so widely despised word.

Martí showed equally delicate and tender sentiments to one man other than Bolívar; and that was his only son to whom he dedicated the poems written in Caracas in 1881, in which he symbolically called the boy *Ismaelillo*.[9] In this slim but seminal volume, the child is addressed as 'tiny little prince', 'monarch of my sentiments', 'my gentleman', 'son of my soul', or named with untiring sweetness as 'my little one', 'my little rider', 'my naughty little muse', 'my little king' and 'fresh rosebud'. Let us not leave this point without mentioning that Martí had not only called Bolívar father but called Darío son,[10] which gives an idea of the scope and complexity of his spiritual world.

The Bolivarian ancestry of Martí was never denied by him. In Guatemala, in 1877, he affirmed, 'The soul of Bolívar breeds life into us,'[11] while in New York in 1880, Martí described Bolívar as 'greater than Caesar, because he was the Caesar of liberty'.[12] As proof that he saw himself as an heir of the Liberator, Martí said again, in Caracas in 1881: 'It is known that the poem of 1810 lacks a strophe, and I, when the real poets had vanished, wanted to write it.'[13] Because that poem was still unwritten, on writing his outstanding speech on Bolívar in 1893 in New York, Martí began by excusing himself with the words, 'With the contrite head of those Americans that have still been unable to enter their America . . .'[14] Two years after this speech, Martí, faithful to the Liberator, died in battle.

It is precisely this self-image as heir of Bolívar that moved Martí to bring up to date the pioneering work of the Liberator. He succeeds to the extent that Carlos Rafael Rodríguez, in his speech 'Martí and the new Ayacucho', could say in 1983 of Martí's contemporary relevance, 'His advice and example are so fruitful and his lesson so valid that we can consider him as the greatest among us, never distant, always at our side.'[15] To this belief in the modernity of Martí in the socio-political order, as in the literary,[16] this chapter, without claiming originality, is addressed. Such a process of updating does not imply a divorce of Martí from the essential teachings of Bolívar, in the genesis of a new world, in the aspirations to continental unity that lay at the root of the basic *martiano* concept of *nuestra América*, used repeatedly by Martí after 1877,[17] in his projects to liberate the Antilles from Spanish rule: plans that were to move Martí, the Antillean, so profoundly. It is important to point out that although Martí shared much with Bolívar, he belonged to another era and another environment. Bolívar was forced by the extraordinary circumstances in which he lived, as Martí said, to take advantage of every single moment.

Two further differences between Martí and Bolívar merit attention: first, that Martí was a citizen of the Caribbean, and it was not by accident that the verse missing from the 1810 poem was still unwritten there; and secondly, that nearly three decades of Martí's exile were spent in the United States during a crucial phase of its history. These two facts, taken together, were to prove decisive, inescapable for the modernity of Martí.

The first intense social experience of Martí, who had been born in Havana in 1853, to humble, petit bourgeois parents, took place at the age of nine when he accompanied his father to work in Matanzas, a prosperous sugar-cane-producing zone. Martí was suddenly overtaken by a terrifying scene, which thirty years later he described in a poem:

> El rayo surca, sangriento,
> El lóbrego nubarrón:
> Echa el barco, ciento a ciento
> Los negros por el portón.

> El viento, fiero, quebraba
> Los almácigos copudos;
> Andaba la hilera, andaba,
> De los esclavos desnudos.
>
> El temporal sacudía
> Los barracones henchidos:
> Una madre con su cría
> Pasaba, dando alaridos.
>
> Rojo, como en el desierto,
> Salió el sol al horizonte:
> Y alumbró a un esclavo muerto,
> Colgado a un seibo del monte.
>
> Un niño lo vió: tembló
> De pasión por los que gimen:
> ¡Y, al pie del muerto, juró
> Lavar con su vida el crimen![18]

Lighting ploughs a bloody furrow through the gloomy storm clouds and the boat spills out through the gate, by their hundreds, the blacks.

The fiery winds were breaking up the bushy plantation trees; and the line of naked slaves was moving, moving.

The thunderstorm was beating against the crowded slave barracks, a mother with her child passed by, howling.

Scarlet as in the desert, the sun rose in the horizon: it shone upon a dead slave, hanging from a mountain ceiba.

A child saw him and shook with passion for those who suffer. And beneath the dead man he swore to expiate with his life the crime.

The sensitive nine-year-old had come up against the most sombre aspect of the society into which he was born: slavery, the worst horror of the plantation system that was the vertebral column not only of his motherland but of the whole Caribbean. In that same year, 1862, J. E. Cairnes, subsequently professor of political economy at University College, London, published *Slave Power*, a book that became a classic. He wrote:

It is in tropical culture, where annual profits often equal the whole capital of plantations, that negro life is most recklessly sacrificed. It is the agriculture of the West Indies, which has been for centuries prolific of fabulous wealth, that has engulfed millions of the African race. It is in Cuba, at this day, whose revenues are reckoned by millions, and whose planters are princes, that we see in the servile class the coarsest fare, the most exhausting and unremitting toil, and even the absolute destruction of a portion of its numbers every year.[19]

Of course, the boy Martí was unaware of the complexities of his discovery. Horrified, he was confronted with the bloodiest feature of his society. The moral reaction that was to guide him throughout life made him take his most seminal decision. Without understanding his complexity little can be comprehended of the burning modernity of Martí's proposals and his thinking upon the Antilles.

Let us return to Cairnes. In the early nineteenth century in Cuba 'planters [became] princes' by turning their island into the sugar-bowl of the world after the unprecedented Haitian revolution, and by exploiting slave labour in the most brutal fashion. The addition to the poem of 1810 of the strophe that Martí envisaged – the independence of Cuba and Puerto Rico – would not but be rejected by planters, who feared that rebellion against the metropolis could have the same consequences as in Haiti.

The non-Spanish-speaking Antilles remained backward in the process of national emancipation within the Latin American and Caribbean context. When finally in 1868 the most radical and least slave-dependent fraction of the Creole landowning class unleashed in eastern Cuba the war of independence against Spain, they confronted the hostility of the richest slave-owning landowners in the west. To a considerable extent the slave-owners' opposition contributed to the failure of the struggle, which at this stage lasted a decade. This was not a complete failure. For one thing the rebels had decreed the abolition of slavery, which encouraged Spain to decree abolition in 1880. For another, during the war, while the hegemonic role of the landowners was being eroded, leaders of popular extraction like the Dominican Máximo Gómez and the Cuban mulatto Antonio Maceo, who were later to play a leading part, came to the fore.

José Martí, who was only fourteen years old when the war broke out, was profoundly marked by it. His irreducible commitment to the independence cause took him in his adolescence first to prison and then into exile. Martí's class origins were also important in making possible his links with those groups headed by Gómez and Maceo, who were to lead the next phase of the struggle for national liberation. As such authors as Ricaurte Soler[20] and Paul Estrade[21] have underlined, the 'delayed' independence of the Hispanic Caribbean, explained by the refusal of the sugar oligarchies to back a struggle that would threaten their privileged position, meant that when the struggle did occur it acquired a far more 'advanced' character. In consequence, the leaders of the Hispanic Caribbean struggles were not conservatives, like the Venezuelan *mantuanos* that disavowed Simón Bolívar when he challenged their privileges, as Miguel Acosta Saignes has so lucidly recalled,[22] but belonged to the popular classes, like Betances and Hostos in Puerto Rico, Luperón and Gómez in the Dominican Republic and Maceo and Martí in Cuba.

José Martí was thus not unique among a cohort of Antillean combatants and thinkers (to whom Haitian figures of the calibre of Antenor Firmin must be added) that in the nineteenth century, for specific historical reasons, overtook the dependent liberalism of most of the major leaders of *nuestra América*, and took up positions which, in the circumstances, were extremely radical. It is customary to describe as revolutionary democrats these spokesmen not of the large landowners and the vacillating and insecure native bourgeoisies, but of the popular classes.[23]

The long exile of Martí in the United States, with few breaks (1880–95), is crucial to the understanding of his modernity. In those years the United States underwent the transition from the competitive capitalism of the self-made man and the rags-to-riches myth to monopoly and imperialist capitalism.[24] In numerous newspapers Martí gave an impressive analysis of the United States of the time. He identified and denounced the characteristics of what we now recognise as the beginnings of the last stage of capitalism: the rise of the monopolies ('The monopoly', says Martí, 'sits like an implacable giant at the door of all the poor'[25]); and the fusion of banking capital with industrial in a financial oligarchy ('those iniquitous consortia of capital'[26]). According to Martí, these processes gave rise to 'the most unjust and shameless of oligarchies',[27] which he also called the 'monied aristocracy'.[28] He referred to the export of capital: 'Chain-ganged, shoeless and with shaven heads, those evil people that make their fortunes by exploiting the anxieties and inflaming the hatreds of peoples, should be paraded through the streets . . . They are not bankers, but bandits!'[29] Martí described how the international monopolies carved up politically and militarily weak territories and condemned Samoa (1889) and Hawaii (1890) as well as the Americas to US expansion. Hence, José Cantón Navarro[30] and Angel Augier[31], among other scholars, have correctly stated that Martí realised a pre-Leninist analysis of imperialism, even before imperialism displayed those mature features that Lenin diagnosed in his classic work, *Imperialism – the highest stage of capitalism, a popular outline*, twenty-one years after Martí died.[32] Martí's exile in the United States was, indeed, very fertile.

Bolívar himself had warned in the early part of the century of the danger posed to the continent by the United States;[33] and Martí, at least during his stay in Mexico (1875–6), came to know well how the United States had appropriated half of Mexican territory. Yet it is certain that at the beginning of his first long stay in New York, in 1880, Martí had had a positive vision of what was, after all, the most progressive country in the world and seemed an example to all liberals to follow.[34] But very soon, without denying the virtues of its people and while praising many of its great men, Martí was more and more aware of the negative features of US society.

In 1881 Martí began to write what became his 'Escenas norteamericanas' for *La Opinión Nacional* of Caracas. But in May 1882 the editor informed him that many of his articles had not been published and asked Martí 'to abstain in his criticism from bitter remarks on the vices and habits of that people [North Americans]'.[35] Martí stopped writing for the newspaper. A few months later he sent his first article to *La Nación* of Buenos Aires, then a leading Spanish-language newspaper, where the majority of the 'Escenas' appeared over ten years. Martí's first article was mutilated by the editor, Bartolomé Mitre, who wrote to Martí on 26 September 1882, as follows:

> La supresión de una parte de su primera carta, al darla a la publicidad, ha respondido a la necesidad de conservar al diario la consecuencia de sus ideas . . . Sin desconocer el fondo de verdad de sus apreciaciones, y la sinceridad de su origen, hemos juzgado que su esencia, extremadamente radical en la forma absoluta de las conclusiones, se apartaba algún tanto de las líneas de conducta que a nuestro modo de ver, consultando opiniones anteriormente comprendidas, al par que las conveniencias de empresa, debía adoptarse desde el principio, en el nuevo e importante servicio de correspondencias que inaugurábamos. La parte suprimida de su carta, encerrando verdades innegables, podía inducir en el error de creer que se abría una campaña de 'denunciation' contra los Estados Unidos como cuerpo político, come entidad social, como centro económico . . . Su carta habría sido todo sombras, si se hubiera publicado como vino . . .[36]

The suppression of a part of your first article from the newspaper responds to the need to retain coherence in its ideas . . . Without denying the element of truth and the sincerity of your views, we have deemed it necessary, given the extremely radical form of their conclusions, to [remove part of your article. This is because your article] differs to some extent from the lines of policy that we have established, and which should be followed in the new and important service of foreign correspondents that we have just started. The suppressed part of your article, although containing undeniable truths, could lead our readers into the error of believing that we were opening a campaign of denunciation against the United States as a body politic, as a social entity, as an economic centre . . . Your article would have been all darkness, if it had been published as sent . . .

The content of this first article of Martí for *La Nación* will never be known. Thus Martí confronted a bitter dilemma as be began elaborating his critique of US society: either to lose a forum that had resonance throughout the Hispanic world, or to proceed in an indirect manner. Naturally, he opted for the second.

From· then on Martí's criticisms had to become more subtle, but they did not disappear. On the contrary, as the 1880s progressed, Martí was increasingly anxious as he saw problems grow. At the end of the decade, his last illusions about the United States vanished. He saw inequality and rampant racism all around him.[37] He saw also the 'legal' assassination of the Chicago workers.[38] And, horrified, he reached the conclusion that as part of the grand design of those whom he himself called the 'imperialists',[39] it was now the turn of Latin America to be devoured by what the fiery Chilean intellectual Francisco Bilbao called, years before, 'the magnetic boa'.[40] Imperialism was the principal aim of the first Pan-American Congress held in Washington (1889–90), whose legatee was the Organization of American States.[41] Taking advantage of the imperial rivalries between the United States and Britain and the fact that Argentina was moving into the British orbit, which turned the Argentine delegation and its press against the congress, Martí gave vent to many of his worries in his articles for *La Nación* which were written in the form of letters at the time of his death:

Cuando el famoso Congreso Panamericano, sus cartas fueron sencillamente un libro. En aquellas correspondencias hablaba de los peligros del yankee [*sic*], de los ojos cuidadosos que debía tener la América Latina respecto a la hermana mayor; y del fondo de aquella frase ('América para el mundo') que una boca argentina opuso a la frase de Monroe ('América para los americanos').[42]

During the famous Pan-American Congress, his letters were quite simply a book. In those articles he talked about the yankee dangers, of the careful vigilance with which Latin America must watch her elder sister, and of the meaning of that phrase ('America for the world') that an Argentine proposed as an alternative to the expression of Monroe ('America for the Americans').

It would suffice to quote probably the best-known paragraph of those articles:

Jamás hubo en América, de la independencia acá, asunto que requiera más sensatez, ni obligue a más vigilancia, ni pida examen más claro y minucioso, que el convite que los Estados Unidos potentes, repletos de productos invendibles, y determinados a extender sus dominios en América, hacen a las naciones americanas de menos poder, ligadas por el comercio libre y útil con los pueblos europeos, para ajustar una liga contra Europa, y cerrar tratos con el resto del mundo. De la tiranía de España supo salvarse la América española; y ahora, después de ver con ojos judiciales los antecedentes, causas y factores del convite, urge decir, porque es la verdad, que ha llegado para la América española la hora de declarar su segunda independencia.[43]

Never in America, from its independence to the present, has there been a matter requiring better judgement or more vigilance, or demanding a clearer and more thorough examination, than the invitation proposed by the powerful United States. [The United States], glutted with unsaleable merchandise and determined to extend its dominions in America, is inviting the less powerful American nations to arrange an alliance against Europe and establish a trading ascendancy in the rest of the world. Spanish America knew how to save itself from the Spanish tyranny; and now, after viewing with wise eyes the antecedents, motives, and ingredients of the invitation, it is imperative to say, for it is true, that the time has come for Spanish America to declare its second independence.

In 1891 a second Pan-American Congress addressed itself to the theme of creating a unified currency for the entire continent that would cause a definitive rupture of our trade with the European nations and tie it irrevocably to United States interests. Martí, who attended the second congress as the delegate of Uruguay and played a

decisive role in opposition to the US proposal, which was finally
defeated, wrote about the ruling classes in the United States:

> Creen en la necesidad, en el derecho bárbaro, como único derecho:
> 'esto será nuestro, porque lo necesitamos'. Creen en la superiordad
> incontrastable de 'la raza anglosajona contra la raza latina'. Creen en
> la bajeza de la raza negra, que esclavizaron ayer y vejan hoy, y de la
> india, que exterminan. Creen que los pueblos de Hispanoamérica
> están formados, principalmente, de indios y de negros. Mientras no
> sepan más de Hispanoamérica y la respeten más . . . ¿pueden los
> Estados Unidos convidar a Hispanoamérica a una unión sincera y
> útil para Hispanoamérica? ¿Conviene a Hispanoamérica la unión
> política y económica con los Estados Unidos?[44]

> They believe in necessity, in the barbaric right as the only law:
> 'This will be ours because we need it.' They believe in the invincible
> superiority of 'the Anglo-Saxon race over the Latin'. They believe
> in the inferiority of the black race, whom they enslaved yesterday
> and denigrate today, and of the Indians, whom they are
> exterminating. They believe that the Spanish American nations are
> made up principally of Indians and blacks. As long as the United
> States remains as ignorant about Spanish America and as
> disrespectful as at present . . . can the United States invite Spanish
> America to a sincere and useful alliance? Is it convenient for
> Spanish America to enter into a political and economic union with
> the United States?

Martí's comprehension of processes that he observed in the late
nineteenth century has still not lost its validity today; because the
historical path followed by the United States aggravates, rather than
lessens, inequalities amongst men, a different path has to be found for
his America. He wrote in 1891 that Spanish Americans in the first
wars of independence had to make common cause 'against the system
of power and of interests of the oppressors'.[45] He continued that
Spanish America had freed itself almost entirely from its first
metropolis, but that a new and much more powerful metropolis was
overtaking it under the guise of economic penetration, and by
diplomatic, political and, where necessary, military means. Martí
added that those Antilles that had not obtained their independence
from Spain, and particularly his beloved Cuba, would be the
immediate prey of the new 'system of colonization',[46] as he described
what we now call 'neo-colonialism'. He concluded that the rest of
*nuestra América mestiza* would be the next victims.[47]

In order to be effective in opposing the ambitions of the United States, Martí dedicated himself wholeheartedly to the political struggle. He resigned as consul for Argentina, Uruguay and Paraguay, and to a large extent he stopped writing for the press, with exceptions, for revolutionary reasons, like his articles for the New York newspaper *Patria*, which he founded in 1892. In today's terminology Martí became a political cadre, trying to build a bulwark in the Antilles against the rapacious avalanche. After travelling around the country inspiring the communities of Cuban and Puerto Rican émigrés and writing tirelessly on the heroes of the war of 1868–78, Martí founded the Partido Revolucionario Cubano (PRC), whose principal support-base was among the exiled tobacco-workers, 'the wretched of the earth', with whom, in a famous poem, he had decided to 'share his fate'.[48] The first article of the 'Bases' of the PRC stated: 'The Partido Revolucionario Cubano is founded to achieve with the united efforts of all men of goodwill the complete independence of the island of Cuba, and to encourage and assist with the independence of Puerto Rico.'[49] Martí's aim in conceiving this party, the first to be created by Latin Americans and people from the Caribbean, was to prepare for a revolutionary war, from which an authentically democratic republic was to be born. Martí's project was to put an end to Spanish colonialism in the Americas and to check the advance of incipient US imperialism. Frequently Martí indicated clearly that he did not merely foresee independence from Spain. Far from it, his commitment to national liberation struggles across the world was evident from 1889. In the 1880s Martí had censured British colonialism in Egypt and India[50] and in Ireland,[51] and French in Tunisia[52] and Vietnam[53]; and now he began to speak of 'the balance of the world' which he believed would be decided in *nuestra América*, and, in particular, in the Caribbean.

For a time I believed that the concept of the 'balance of the world' had its origins in Saint-Simon, who also used it, if not always in the same sense.[54] But, more recently, following the analysis of Julio Le Riverend,[55] I have come to recognise that its origins are to be found in Bolívar, the source of so much of Martí's thought. To cite a report of the ministry of external relations of Nueva Granada, written in 1813 at the instructions of Bolívar:

Yo llamo a éste el equilibrio del Universo y debe estar en los cálculos de la política americana . . . Este coloso de poder que debe oponerse a aquel otro coloso (al europeo), no puede formarse sino de la reunión de toda la América Meridional, bajo un mismo cuerpo de Nación, para que un solo gobierno central pueda aplicar sus grandes recursos a un solo fin.[56]

I call this [concept] the equilibrium of the universe, and it must be present in all the calculations of the policy of the Americas . . . This colossus of power that must confront that other colossus (the European), cannot be formed except by the unification of all meridional America, under the same national body, so that a single central government can apply its large resources to a single end.

Many years later Martí accepted the essentials of the Bolivarian thesis, but he could not repeat it literally. For Martí, the Antillean colonies were uniquely vulnerable; and their place in the equilibrium of the continent and even of the world was obvious owing to their location between the powerful United States and Central America, where the construction, at least, of an interoceanic canal – perhaps in Panama, perhaps in Nicaragua – was imminent. Martí wrote extensively on this subject. One of the most famous articles on the subject was published in *Patria* in April 1894, with the title 'The Third Year of the Cuban Revolutionary Party', and carrying the revealing subtitle 'The soul of the revolution, and the duty of Cuba in America'. Martí put it thus:

En el fiel de América están las Antillas, que serían, si esclavas, mero pontón de la guerra de una república imperial contra el mundo celoso y superior que se prepara ya a negarle el poder, – mero fortín de la Roma americana; – y si libres . . . – serían en el continente la garantía del equilibrio, la de la independencia para la América española aún amenazada, y la del honor para la gran república del Norte, que en el desarrollo de su territorio . . . hallará más segura grandeza que en la innoble conquista de sus vecinos menores, y en la pelea inhumana que con la posesión de ellos abriría contra las potencias del orbe por el predominio del mundo . . . Es un mundo lo que estamos equilibrando: no son sólo dos islas las que vamos a libertar . . . Un error en Cuba, es un error en América, es un error en la humanidad moderna. Quién se levanta hoy con Cuba se levanta para todos los tiempos.[57]

At the pivot of America are the Antilles that, if slaves, would still be willing to contest the power of the imperial republic, and, if free, would be the guarantee of equilibrium, of the independence of the still threatened Spanish America, and of the honour of the colossus of the North. [The United States] will find a more certain greatness in the development of its own lands than in the ignoble conquest of its lesser neighbours or the inhuman struggle for world leadership that seizure of the Antilles would unleash . . . . We are not only trying to liberate two islands, we are trying to balance the world . . . One error committed in Cuba is an error for all America and for modern humanity. Those who fight with Cuba against oppression today fight oppression for all time.

On 25 March 1895, Martí, on his way to the war which had resumed on 24 February, wrote to the Dominican politician Federico Henríquez y Carvajal:

The free Antilles will save the independence of *nuestra América*, and the doubtful and wounded honour of English-speaking America, and will possibly establish the balance of the world.[58]

That same day he wrote to Máximo Gómez, supreme military commander of the Cuban Liberation Army (Ejército Libertador), the Manifiesto de Montecristi (named after the town in the Dominican Republic where it was written), in which the reasons for the war were analysed:

La guerra de independencia de Cuba, nudo del haz de islas donde se ha de cruzar, en plazo de pocos años, el comercio de los continentes, es suceso de gran alcance humano, y servicio oportuno que el heroismo juicioso de las Antillas presta a la firmeza y trato justo de las naciones americanas y al equilibrio aún vacilante del mundo. Honra y conmueve pensar que cuando cae en tierra de Cuba un guerrero de la independencia, abandonado tal vez por los pueblos incautos o indiferentes a quienes se inmola, cae por el bien mayor del hombre, la confirmación de la república moral en América y la creación de un archipielago libre.[59]

The war of Cuban independence, located at the core of the Greater Antilles archipelago, which in a few years will be the crossroads of the commerce of two continents, is an event of the greatest human importance. The well-judged heroism of the Antilles loans an opportune service to the strength and just treatment of the American nations and to the still uncertain balance of the world. It honours us and moves us to think that when a warrior of independence falls on the land of Cuba, maybe abandoned by unwary or indifferent peoples to those that died, he falls for the greater good of man, for the reaffirmation of the moral republic in America and the creation of the free archipelago.

In his famous letter to the Mexican Manuel Mercado on 18 May 1895, left unfinished on the eve of his death in the battle of Dos Ríos, Martí expressed clearly his agony at the grave menace hanging over the islands. Martí wrote:[60]

Mi hermano queridísimo: Ya puedo escribir; ya puedo decirle con qué ternura y agradecimiento y respeto lo quiero, y a esa casa que es mía, y mi orgullo y obligación; ya estoy todos los días en peligro de dar mi vida por mi país, y por mi deber . . . de impedir a tiempo con la independencia de Cuba que se extiendan por las Antillas los Estados Unidos y caigan, con esa fuerza más sobre nuestras tierras de América. Cuanto hice hasta hoy, y haré es para eso. En silencio ha tenido que ser, y como indirectamente, porque hay cosas que para lograrlas han de andar ocultas, y de proclamarse en lo que son, levantarían dificultades demasiado recias para alcanzar sobre ellas el fin.

My beloved brother: I can now write to you and tell you with what tenderness, gratitude and respect I love you. [I want to tell you too] how much I love your home, which is my pride and responsibility. I am every day at risk of giving my life for my country and for my duty . . . and with the independence of Cuba to prevent in time the expansion of the United States in the Antilles, and their descending, with their additional strength, upon the lands of America. What I have done up to now, and shall continue to do, is towards this goal. In order to achieve certain aims, it has been necessary to be both silent and indirect. To proclaim them openly would raise such problems that my objectives would not be attained.

Martí continued by stressing that while Cuba was sacrificing itself to prevent the annexation of the rest of the continent by the 'brutal and disturbed North', the same minor and public duties of the (American) peoples prevented them from providing 'obvious assistance to a sacrifice made for their immediate benefit'. 'Viví en el monstruo, y le conozco las entrañas; – mi honda es la de David.' 'I lived in the monster, and I know its entrails; and my sling is that of David.'

The rest is well-known. Martí died in 1895 and Maceo in 1896, both on the battlefield. The fears of Martí were to prove more than justified. In 1898, the United States used as an excuse for declaring war on Spain a self-inflicted explosion aboard a US warship, the *Maine*, anchored in Havana; ratings lost their lives but no officers were killed. At this moment Spain was virtually defeated by the

Cuban armies of independence, from whom victory was snatched after thirty years' struggle. The United States converted Cuba into a protectorate or neo-colony for six decades, and seized as booty, up to the present day, the sister-island of Puerto Rico.

Overwhelmed by the First World War and incapable of understanding the events around him, the great French poet Paul Valéry exclaimed, in his essay 'The crisis of the spirit': 'We, the civilizations, now know that we also are mortal',[61] a sentiment that has Gobineau as a precursor. Later in the same essay Valéry wrote: 'The circumstances that could make the works of Keats and Baudelaire join those of Menander are no longer inconceivable. They are all over the press.'[62]

These words are recalled here not only out of respect for the pure poetry of the author of *Le cimetière marin*, nor because I share his pathetic bewilderment as I confront a much more serious problem than faced Valéry. I would like to borrow from Valéry a few words with which to answer those who require proof of the modernity of Martí, proof that is not to be found in this text or in much wiser works or even in the will or devotion of any man. If I may beg the indulgence of Valéry, who may be displeased or simply bored by the plebeian use of his spiritual terminology, the proof of the modernity of Martí is 'all over the press'. Let us go out into the street and read the papers; and the modernity of Martí, if we are not totally insensitive, will overwhelm us. From 1898 to the present day the validity of the admonitory words of Martí has retained its force. If asked to state in a few words the main problems confronting *nuestra América* since the 1880s, we would answer without vacillating: those foreseen by Martí. The intervention of the United States in Grenada indicates that the Big Stick policy resurges like the spell of the sorcerer's apprentice. So too does Dollar Diplomacy.

# 2 José Martí: Architect of social unity in the émigré communities of the United States

GERALD E. POYO

Efforts to gain a thorough understanding of José Martí's political and socio-economic thought have been hampered by the failure to consider him in the context of the émigré communities within which he worked. While Martí's activities in the Cuban immigrant centres from 1880 to 1895 are well documented, his impact on the communities, as well as their influence on him, are not well understood, in part because scholars have disregarded the political, social and economic traditions and characteristics of the exile colonies themselves.

Traditional considerations of the centres provide a simplistic, romanticised vision that obscures the focus and substance of much of Martí's writings. The classic works on the émigré centres by Castellanos, Deulofeu, Rivero Muñíz and Casasus in general characterise Cubans in Key West, Tampa and New York as exclusively committed to separatist activism and divided only by strategic considerations.[1] These studies rarely mention the socio-economic dynamics that greatly influenced the communities and their political perspectives. As a result, Martí's socio-economic writings have never been analysed within their appropriate context; a situation that unwittingly contributed to the view that Martí was a romantic and an idealist, out of touch with the realities of his day. As a recent study of Martí aptly notes, 'One of the most characteristic features of the traditional approach to Martí was the constant reference to him in idealised, reverential, and semi-mystical terms.'[2] Without the proper socio-economic context, it is not surprising that some have considered Martí as a visionary rather than as an insightful, practical revolutionary organiser whose writings were directed at dismantling very specific barriers to an effective separatist movement.

While it is primarily studies written prior to mid-century that characterise Martí in 'semi-mystical terms', even the more recent works that emphasise his socio-economic dimension tend to overlook the daily realities of émigré life that influenced Martí's thinking.[3]

16

Their focus on Martí's concern for social issues, however, does point to a logical next step in Martí studies, which is the purpose of this paper: to understand the relationship between Martí's ideals and the socio-economic realities of the Cuban communities. This analysis would be quite difficult without the availability of considerable research on the demographic, economic and social evolution of the émigré centres, produced since the 1960s.[4] Authored by North Americans interested primarily in Florida's ethnic and immigration history, these studies emerged independently of any concern for Martí, but do provide a useful framework from which to build an understanding of the communities he led.

## Social tensions in the émigré communities

Detailed study of the Cuban centres reveals that they were not only exile enclaves interested in the political destiny of their homeland but socially diverse communities deeply involved in the daily struggles of immigrant life. In addition to separatism, Cubans had to grapple with the class and racial tensions that permeated North American society and their own communities. Indeed, these factors played an important role in dictating the political and socio-economic organisation of the communities, often at the expense of weakening practical, if not ideological, support for the nationalist movement.

Beginning in the late 1860s, Cuban immigration to the United States reflected the social stratification and racial composition of the island's urban society. New York émigrés included members of Cuba's socio-economic élite, middle-class professionals and a multiracial working-class community employed primarily in the city's cigar trades.[5] In Florida, a centre initially relatively undifferentiated socio-economically in the 1870s gave way to a more socially stratified community during the next two decades as a dynamic cigar industry produced a group of prosperous, primarily white Cuban manufacturers, merchants and professionals. The centres in Florida, however, were primarily of working-class character, with blacks in Key West comprising some twenty-one per cent of the Cuban community. Cuban blacks always represented a distinct social group within the Florida centres, with their own leaders and institutions.[6] Since the 1870s they had suffered discrimination not only at the hands of the increasingly racist Anglo-American society but within their own community as it integrated into North American life. Throughout the final third of the nineteenth century Cuban workers and blacks in the Florida communities consistently struggled to defend their interests. They organised in Key West during the 1870s and 1880s and established an activist tradition that was carried to Tampa after 1885.[7]

Socio-economic concerns deeply influenced community affairs. The contradictions between the unifying force of nationalism and the divisive impact of class and racial conflicts served as the central dynamic in the Florida communities during the decade after 1885. Cubans were faced with the dilemma of defending their day-to-day social and economic interests, or placing their time and resources exclusively at the disposal of the separatist movement. Always eager to avoid in the communities class and racial strife that could affect the flow of funds to the rebel cause, the nationalist leadership and press sought quick compromise solutions to labour-management disputes and battled with ideologies that encouraged divisions among Cubans.

The moderating influence on labour of the separatist leadership was, of course, advantageous to the cigar capitalists; a fact that caused many workers to suspect the movement was manipulated by the factory owners to advance their interests. As a result, while most of the traditional labour and black leaders co-operated with the political activists, by the late 1880s a new generation of militants influenced by socialist and anarchist thinking took charge of the workers' movement in Florida. Some embraced the anarchist proposition that all political movements were contrary to workers' interests, while others merely made a pragmatic decision to back union instead of patriot organising, noting the nationalist leadership's lack of sensitivity toward workers' issues. These conflicts culminated in divisive debates in the émigré press and in bitter strikes led by anarchist activists that isolated the separatist movement within the Florida communities during 1887–90.

During late 1889 an extraordinarily long and bitter work stoppage in Key West caused deep divisions in the émigré centres that virtually paralysed nationalist organising initiatives. In October the cigar-makers at the Eduardo Hidalgo Gato factory walked off their jobs demanding that the manufacturer honour a contract signed the previous February guaranteeing a wage increase of $1 per thousand cigars rolled. The Manufacturers' Association responded with a general lock-out and by the end of the month the entire cigar industry was at a standstill. Leading the workers were anarchist organisers from Havana, which gave credence to the factory owners' charges that outside agitators were responsible for instigating the conflict. Hoping to break the strike, local officials deported one of the anarchist leaders, Enrique Messonier; an action that not only increased the strikers' determination not to compromise, but caused considerable resentment against the nationalist leaders who, the workers believed, had been involved in the anarchist's deportation. Finally, during January 1890, the manufacturers relented and the workers won a complete victory. For many patriot and labour leaders alike, however, the conflict seemed to suggest that nationalism and a radical labour movement were irreconcilable. The Cuban community was badly divided and many were sceptical that the independence cause could re-establish itself as the primary focus of the émigré colony.[8]

## Martí and the social question

Quietly observing and analysing the complexities in the relationship between the nationalist and radical labour movements in Florida, José Martí was aware of the disruptive potential of these class confrontations on the independence cause. Writing to a friend, Serafín Bello, at the height of the 1889 strike on the Key, Martí revealed a recognition that émigré unity was no longer simply a matter of political compromise between the traditional *independentista* factions, as in the past. 'The social issues have become politicised in our country, as everywhere else,' Martí noted, but 'I am not afraid, because justice and the weight of things are remedies that do not fail.'[9]
In his political programme of 1887, Martí had implicitly warned his compatriots that class and racial conflicts threatened to deepen animosities in the already politically factious émigré centres. This, he knew, had to be avoided.[10] Indeed, since the early 1880s Martí had argued that a successful patriot movement would require the backing of a broad cross-section of Cuban society, and he recognised that the rebel bosses could no longer dismiss labour's grievances by characterising them as divisive and expect to retain their allegiance. Only by confronting the social issues of the day in a more sophisticated manner could Cuban labour be convinced that, in fact, supporting the nationalist cause was in their interest. Once this was accomplished, the rebel organiser had no doubt that the workers' patriotic instincts would re-emerge as their primary focus, and their heightened awareness and militancy would then be of great advantage to a movement in dire need of renewed enthusiasm and commitment.[11]

Martí was perfectly suited to the task of formulating an ideology capable of attracting the radicalised workers. Not only was he an exceptional orator and charismatic figure, but he believed the workers' grievances were legitimate. 'One must pay attention to the social elements and must meet their [the workers'] fair demands if one wishes to study the truth of Cuba's problem and put it into its proper context,' Martí noted.[12] He possessed an instinctive sympathy for labour's struggles that filled his writings and speeches with sincerity and sentiment. 'The worker is not an inferior being, nor should he be corralled and governed with a prod, but in the spirit of brotherhood, he should be extended the considerations and rights which assure peace and happiness among people.'[13] Moreover, Martí defended workers' rights to organise and strike; he condemned unrestrained accumulation of wealth as not only unjust, but immoral; and he declared that the future republic, and thus the nationalist movement, should not serve only the interests of the established classes: 'The republic . . . will not be the unjust predominance of one class of Cubans over the rest, but will be the open and sincere balance of all the country's real forces, and of the thoughts and desires of all Cubans.'[14]

At the same time, these views were in agreement with Martí's attitude regarding class relations in general. He rejected the idea of the inevitability of class struggle, popularised among Cuban workers by the anarchists, and he made clear that he had no quarrel with capitalists who paid fair wages and made an honest profit. A co-operative relationship between workers and capitalists based on a vision of social justice was Martí's concept of how the classes should interact.[15] Martí was never very specific regarding what concrete measures would be taken to ensure social justice in the future republic, but this was apparently of little concern to the workers who were obviously satisfied with Martí's philosophical redefinition of the nationalist movement to include the historically neglected socio-economic dimension. This was an important victory for the Cuban workers, who had no doubt that subsequent to the liberation war Martí intended to define his ideas further and to implement them. Martí also addressed the racial concerns of his black compatriots. His outrage over racism had been publicly expressed during the 1880s and was well known throughout the émigre communities. Martí knew that if the cause were to obtain the support of the Cuban blacks, they would have to be included as equal partners.[16] Symbolic of Martí's commitment to racial harmony and social justice was his co-operation with La Liga, an educational society in New York established by a group of black Cubans and Puerto Ricans for the city's Hispanic working-class community. Martí worked as a teacher and quickly became the society's ideological inspiration. His sincere concern for the rights of his compatriots of colour won him their undying respect and admiration.

Martí's vision of the new revolutionary movement, then, brought together all classes and races behind a movement dedicated to an independent Cuban republic based on principles of social justice for all. This represented a radical change in the émigre nationalist ideology that before the late 1880s had addressed itself simply to the political question and had assumed that traditional nineteenth-century liberalism would form the socio-economic foundation of the future republic.

## Forging social unity in Florida

Although Martí's ideas concerning class relations were well-formed by the late 1880s, it was not until his visit to Tampa in November 1891 that he initiated his public efforts to transform the exclusively political rhetoric of the nationalist ideology into a broader ideal which the socially conscious Cuban workers could embrace as their own. Scholars have assumed that Martí's invitation to be the featured speaker in Tampa was a result of his reputation as a patriot orator. While his well-known nationalist oratory was obviously important, it is likely that his social activism was at least as attractive to the political leaders in Tampa. The presidents of the city's two revolutionary clubs, Néstor Carbonell and Ramón Rivero, had actively backed labour during the late 1880s. In fact, Carbonell openly characterised himself a socialist and Rivero had maintained close relations with the Havana anarchists in 1889.[17] Moreover, prominent black leaders in Tampa, including Cornelio Brito, Manuel and Joaquín Granados, and Bruno Roig, were all aware of Martí's work with La Liga and his aggressive advocacy of racial equality. By extending their support to Martí, Tampa's patriot leaders were seeking to broaden the nationalist movement's exclusively political definition. Indeed, written among the workers, the Tampa Resolutions included the expression of his popular vision. The document declared that the new rebel movement would seek 'a just and open Republic, united in territory, united in law, and united in work and in friendship, raised by all for the good of all'.[18]

Subsequent to his Tampa trip, Martí wrote to Key West's *El Yara* suggesting that he would also like to visit that south Florida town.[19] His letter was published and a group of tobacco workers promptly extended a formal invitation in the community's name. Unlike the Tampa leadership, however, except for *El Yara's* editor, José Dolores Poyo, the traditional political bosses on the Key were not anxious to give Martí an important position within their ranks. Throughout the 1880s, they had considered him a timid revolutionary not at all suited to replace leaders of the calibre of Generals Máximo Gómez and Antonio Maceo.[20] But Martí's message was attractive to the movement's primary constituency, the tobacco workers. During his visit to the Key, Martí was presented with an album by the workers of the Gato factory containing dozens of inscriptions expressing their admiration for the patriot leader and declaring their support for his efforts. One worker succinctly stated what must have been the overwhelming sentiment of the Key's labour force: 'The independence of Cuba will be an indisputable fact when all Cubans think like the eminent Cuban orator José Martí.'[21]

During the 1889 strike, the rebel activists in Key West had established the Convención Cubana in an effort to reinvigorate nationalist sentiment. Although successful in reorganising the patriot movement locally, the Convención failed to attract any of the important labour or black leaders. On 5 January 1892, however, the Partido Revolucionario Cubano (PRC) was founded and among its charter members were Carlos Baliño, Carlos Borrego and Francisco Camellón. Baliño represented labour interests, while the latter two were influential members of the black community on the Key.[22] Clearly, it was not lost on them that Martí's themes of unity and social justice were an integral part of the statutes of the new rebel organisation. Article four noted:

> The Cuban Revolutionary Party intends only . . . to establish within the open and cordial exercise of the legitimate abilities of man, a new and sincerely democratic country, able to overcome through real work and the balance of social forces, the dangers of sudden freedom in a society organized for slavery.[23]

Martí had accomplished in a few days what the local Key West rebel activists had been unable to do since the days of the Gómez and Maceo initiatives of the mid 1880s: to attract a broad cross-section of the émigré community to the new nationalist movement. The traditional political leaders in Key West had little choice but to accept Martí's leadership when they saw his success in mobilising their own community in favour of the separatist cause.

Martí's ideas were developed more concretely in the columns of *Patria* during the next three years, further consolidating the PRC in the Florida émigré centres and obtaining significant worker participation in the organisation. The eight Key West clubs represented at the PRC's founding meeting grew to sixty-two affiliates three years later.[24] Furthermore, many of the popular anarchist leaders of the 1880s eventually found their way into the PRC as office-holders and publicists. The head of the Cuerpo de Consejo in Martí City, and later, West Tampa, for example, was Guillermo Sorondo, a well-known black anarchist organiser who had been deported from Key West in 1889 shortly before Messonier. Other radicals like Messonier, Baliño, Rivero, Enrique Creci, Francisco Segura, Federico Corbett, José de la C. Palomino, and José I. Izaguirre, were also influential in securing worker support for the PRC.[25]

While courting the workers, however, Martí remained true to his vision of social unity by developing a good relationship with the Cuban cigar manufacturers and other entrepreneurs and professionals in the Florida communities. Three of the most influential – Eduardo Hidalgo Gato, Cayetano Soria and Teodoro Pérez – were present at the founding meeting of the PRC and apparently extended immediate support to Martí. Most of the economically prominent Cubans in Key West had staunchly backed the independence cause since the early 1870s and had responded to Martí's nationalist rhetoric with as much enthusiasm as the workers. Furthermore, they did not consider Martí's social ideas a threat to their economic interests. In fact, in a very practical sense, they viewed his call for unity and co-operation between the classes as a moderating influence on the radical labour movement of the 1880s that had incorporated the 'class struggle' as a central tenet of its ideological perspective. Although the political leaders of the PRC defended the workers' right to organise and strike to protect their interests, they also demanded that strike actions be aimed at rectifying specific grievances and that solutions be found through a spirit of compromise. During a strike in Tampa during 1894, for example, the separatist newsweekly, *Cuba*, edited by Ramón Rivero, declared: 'We do not want strikes nor disturbances, but when it is a question of defending the family's bread and overcoming abuses, we place ourselves on the side of justice and this helps the strikers.' On the other hand, after what it considered an ill-advised strike led by anarchists threatening 'dynamite, daggers, bombs, and petroleum', the newspaper sharply criticised the strikers.[26] It is interesting that this same call for co-operation and compromise, made by the nationalist press during the late 1880s, had then been characterised by the labour radicals as demonstrating sympathy for the factory owners, but when seen in the context of Martí's leadership and ideas the same position was understood as the evenhandedness required for the revolution's consolidation.

## A challenge from New York

Despite Martí's successes in Florida, he encountered almost immediate resistance from apprehensive middle-class professionals in New York alienated not only by the PRC's political programme, but by Martí's social rhetoric and the new organisation's openness to Florida's labour radicals.

Opposition to Martí initially focused on political concerns raised by Enrique Trujillo, the editor of the largest circulation émigré newspaper, *El Porvenir*. Trujillo objected to the PRC's revolutionary nature and what he characterised as its dictatorial structure. The editor believed that the émigré communities should not be involved in fomenting rebellion in Cuba, but should simply propagandise in favour of independence. Revolution would come, he argued, when Cubans on the island revolted on their own initiative. Accordingly, he rejected the highly centralised structure of the PRC at the national level, which reflected its revolutionary nature. Furthermore, Trujillo resented Martí's ability to attract uncompromising and virtually uncritical support from his followers. This *personalismo* he deemed dangerous for the future republic.[27]

Soon, however, Trujillo also revealed a deep suspicion of the primarily working-class Florida Cubans. He not only objected to the militaristic traditions of the veteran leaders, but feared the labour radicals' increasing influence in political matters. Trujillo knew that the Cuban tobacco workers were sympathetic to the anarchist movement and that they were predominantly socialist in inclination. Since the early 1890s he had openly expressed opposition to socialism and called on workers to direct their energies exclusively towards the patriot cause.[28] Of special concern was that many of the political leaders in Florida, as we have seen, also considered themselves socialists or co-operated with labour radicals and anarchists. In Tampa, Carbonell and Rivero, among others, defended socialist concepts, while in Key West, Poyo, head of the Cuerpo de Consejo, worked closely with well-known labour radicals such as Messonier and Ramón Rivera Monteresi, secretary of the Consejo. As far as Trujillo was concerned, the revolutionary party had fallen into the hands, or at least under the influence, of the émigré communities' most radical elements.

So concerned was Trujillo that during 1894 *El Porvenir* made an effort to discredit the PRC and Martí by suggesting they were compromised by links with the anarchists. The organ launched a harsh attack on Cuban anarchists and challenged the party's newspapers, *Patria*, *El Yara* and *Cuba*, to take a similar position despite the fact that these organs wre already on record as opposing the anarchists' political propositions.[29] In its second issue, *Patria* had called on the émigré workers to recognise the necessity of political action, arguing that all movements had a political character. Martí further suggested that men interested in improving the condition of humanity should not be tolerant of repressive systems when political action offered a concrete alternative. In addition, like the Florida weeklies, *Patria* made clear that labour radicals were welcome in the PRC and were invited to co-operate in liberating Cuba.[30] *El Porvenir* objected. Trujillo opposed any movement influenced by the labour radicals. 'Every gift creates a commitment,' argued the New York editor. 'If the Revolutionary Party receives, as reportedly it has received, money from the anarchist group, it will feel committed toward this group,' he noted, adding maliciously, 'Not in vain has it caused such surprise that a newspaper, *Patria*, no less than the organ of a party which calls itself serious and one of principles, has not expressed even one word to condemn the assassination of the good and honorable Carnot. This could give way to conclusions about compromises made with the anarchist group.'[31]

Trujillo's view of the PRC as a radical organisation was not an isolated perception. Writing several years later, the annexationist José I. Rodríguez revealed that he too had considered Martí a social radical responsible for introducing class hatreds into the patriot cause. When he labelled Martí's thinking 'eminently socialist and anarchist', Rodríguez was probably reflecting the attitudes of many middle-class Cubans in New York who remained apart from the PRC.[32] Some have argued that the opposition to Martí in New York was limited to Trujillo, but that is not likely. The fact that *El Porvenir* continued to publish as the only economically viable Cuban newspaper in exile and that relatively few clubs were formed in New York in support of the PRC suggests that many in that city, at least passively, agreed with Trujillo.

Martí must have realised early on that the more conservative New York Cubans might react negatively to his ideas, particularly his receptiveness to the labour radicals, but he obviously decided to sacrifice that support to ensure the backing of the more activist Cubans in Florida who became the primary focus of his organising activities. Accordingly, his strategy to defuse social tensions was directed at the Florida centres where unity was maintained despite *El Porvenir's* vigorous attempts to undermine Martí's political credibility and to characterise him as a fellow traveller of the anarchists. Although Trujillo's impact was minimal, during late 1893 economic conditions in Key West did exert divisive pressures on the delicate alliance of Cuban workers, manufacturers, professionals, labour radicals and anarchists, and traditional patriot activists. Had the community not stood together, the PRC might very well have disintegrated, thus leaving the nationalist movement in its traditional state of disarray.

## Solidarity in Florida

The troubles began as the result of the reinitiation of patriot activism. With the establishment of the PRC in Key West, virtually every manufactory with a predominantly Cuban labour force was affected by the activities of the nationalist rebels. Patriot orators and fund raisers went from factory to factory, frequent mass meetings were held, and workers demanded that only supporters of Cuban independence be hired in the cigar establishments. In fact, not only did they ask that loyal Spaniards not be employed, but formed a secret society to discourage Spanish workers from disembarking on the Key at all. The nationalist leaders feared that should peninsular workers be allowed free access to Key West they would not only dilute patriot sentiment and reinforce anarchist influence, but would give Spanish spies the opportunity to infiltrate the *independentista* camp. Besides these political factors, barring the Spanish workers was beneficial to the Cubans whose bargaining position was strengthened by a limited, well-disciplined and organised labour force.

By 1893 the Key's manufacturers were disenchanted with their condition. In addition to having to contend with the general economic downturn of the early 1890s, many believed they had lost control of the factory floors, where, as they saw it, patriot activists disrupted production at will to advance their political cause. More importantly, as Tampa's cigar industry became increasingly competitive, Key West factory owners resented the constraints on their hiring and wage-setting practices. Tampa's more cosmopolitan (large Spanish and Italian presence) and less organised labour force made its industry less susceptible to the pressures exerted by the Cuban community on behalf of their nationalist movement. With this competitive advantage, Tampa managed to attract many factories from Key West and other locations across the United States, and by the early 1890s was challenging the south Florida isle as the primary cigar centre in the state.[33]

This position led to a labour dispute in late 1893 that tested the Cuban manufacturers' solidarity with the PRC. Obviously intending to challenge the Cuban political leaders' influence in the industry, one of the largest cigar establishments, Seidenberg & Co., contracted with thirteen Spanish foremen and workers from Havana to work in Key West. The factory's Cuban workers immediately went out on strike demanding that the Spaniards be removed. When an agreement could not be reached, Seidenberg announced his intention to transfer operations to Tampa, causing consternation among city and county officials who believed that the loss of the factory would initiate a decline of the local cigar industry. The officials decided to challenge the Cubans and assured Seidenberg that workers from Cuba would henceforth be given access to the Key West labour market. Immediately a special commission of city, county and state officers travelled to Havana and contracted 300 workers to replace the strikers.

Co-ordinated by Martí, the PRC leadership came to the support of the Cuban workers and provided an attorney who quickly petitioned the United States Treasury Department to halt the influx of workers from Cuba, arguing that the arrangements made by the Key's officials with labourers in Havana violated the nation's contract labour laws.[34] The Cubans won the case, but not before bitter and sometimes violent confrontations drove a deep wedge between the patriot and Anglo communities, requiring the Cuban cigar entrepreneurs and professionals to choose between defending their economic interests and supporting the PRC. In effect, their commitment to the nationalist cause was put to the test, especially after Martí portrayed the dispute as an effort by North American manufacturers and Spanish authorities to destroy the patriot cause. It is not likely that the factory owners' interest in obtaining labourers from Havana was motivated primarily by a hostility to the Cuban political movement, but Martí skilfully downplayed their economic grievances and appealed to the Cubans' sense of national identity. 'Watch out Cubans,' he noted, 'what they wanted was to disturb the Key, to provoke within it a long and foolish strike, reduce it to misery at the moment when Cuba . . . appears ready for war.' 'Oh, Cubans!' Martí added, 'the foreigner who owes us his bread takes that bread from our mouth . . . Let us rise together before they take away our roof and our work table; and with the last fruits of the city that we gave to the foreigner, let us buy, Cubans, the free fatherland.'[35] In transforming the basically economic dispute into a nationalist crusade, Martí also shrewdly suggested that the Cuban manufacturers not be hampered and that the community redouble its efforts to raise additional funds for the rebellion. In a letter to Serafín Sánchez, Martí declared, 'There, in spite of the local situation, do not let Gato's house fall. Keep encouraging him. I continue with everything.'[36]

Martí's appeal to nationalism was successful and almost to a man Cuban manufacturers remained in solidarity with the PRC.[37] In fact, distressed by the actions of the Anglo community, hundreds of Cubans – workers and manufacturers alike – left Key West for the Tampa Bay area where they reorganised and continued their nationalist activities. Social divisions among Cubans were avoided in a situation that could easily have disrupted the colony. As the conflict subsided, many Cubans were reaffirmed in their belief that whatever their particular political or socio-economic ideals, only as an independent people could they control their destiny. As Martí noted, 'We are stronger for this lesson. There is no help but our own . . . We have, Cubans, no country but the one we must fight for.'[38] Within a year, the revolution was launched; eloquent testimony of Martí's extraordinary success in bringing together the politically and socially divided émigré centres into a revolutionary force that served as a catalyst for a similar process in Cuba that challenged and eventually destroyed Spanish colonial authority.

## Martí's legacy in the émigré communities

While Martí's social rhetoric was deeply felt, it had a specific political purpose: to unite the socially divided émigrés behind the new revolutionary movement. Simple appeals to nationalist sentiment had traditionally been sufficient to mobilise the expatriate colonies in support of the independence cause. In fact, except for abolition of slavery, a social agenda had never been an important feature of any of the rebel programmes since the outbreak of the Revolución de Yara in 1868. No one had ever suggested that the nationalist movement should also serve as a catalyst for significant socio-economic reforms on the island, other than those required to implement standard *laissez-faire* liberalism. During the 1890s, Martí's introduction of a broader ideology directed at addressing the grievances of the highly disillusioned Cuban émigré tobacco workers produced a social coalition in support of the nationalist movement. Indeed, Martí's movement acquired a moral authority that withstood even the continuing socio-economic tensions in the communities subsequent to his death in May 1895. He became the very symbol of insurgent unity in exile; a unity few in the émigré centres violated during the course of the independence struggle.

Nevertheless, Martí represented different things to different sectors of émigré opinion. To the leadership of the PRC, Martí's nationalism was of central importance. Martí's successors as PRC delegate and as editor of *Patria*, Tomás Estrada Palma and José Enrique Varona respectively, focused exclusively on the political question at hand and made few efforts to promote Martí's socio-economic vision.[39] Estrada Palma called on workers to sacrifice and refrain from striking, while *Patria* focused on seeking unity and disseminating insurgent propaganda. *Patria* no longer served as a source of revolutionary doctrine as Martí had no doubt intended it to be. References to Martí's social thought were rare and limited to general allusions to his 'obra moral' or 'república cordial'.[40] While it is clear that the émigré leadership, in Florida as in New York, was consumed with attempting to promote the independence struggle, leaving little time to ponder the social questions of the day, it is also true that the PRC in New York reflected a more conservative social attitude under Estrada Palma; he sought support and advice from many established and influential Cubans who fled the island only after the outbreak of the rebellion.

Others considered Martí's social doctrines an integral part of the nationalist ideology. During mid-1896, a newspaper, *La Doctrina de Martí*, with the subtitle 'The Republic with All for All', appeared in New York to counter Trujillo's *El Porvenir* and the increasingly conservative *Patria*. Edited by Rafael Serra, a black activist of the New York community who had been close to Martí, *La Doctrina* proclaimed: 'We come from the school of Martí. In it our soul was softened and our character was formed . . . He taught us to be intolerant of all forms of tyranny, all arrogance, and to be a friend of honest humility.' The newspaper reiterated Martí's desire for émigré unity. 'The illustrious Martí taught us that a people composed of live and distinct elements and manacled by the same yoke, should be sincerely unified.' But it also noted that the people should be 'equally represented in the creation of the nation: because Cubans who share the sacrifices, should also share in the benefits'.[41] *La Doctrina* expressed a growing concern among many black and working-class émigrés that the insurgency was falling under the influence of conservative and established sectors of Cuban society little concerned with Martí's social vision of the future republic. As such, *La Doctrina* declared that 'from the extreme left of the Separatist Party' it would not only support uncompromisingly the independence war, but work to 'ensure that the rights of the people are real and not fictitious: That Is Our Task.'[42] Throughout its existence *La Doctrina* reminded Cuban émigrés of Martí's broader nationalist vision that included creating a republic based on social justice and racial harmony.

Serra's newspaper gained widespread support, particularly in Florida's black community, where émigrés praised its efforts to sustain Martí's thinking on social issues. A prominent black leader in Tampa, Joaquín Granados, wrote: 'We cordially salute those who are disposed . . . to continue the redeeming work of the sublime master.' 'Do not allow,' he continued, 'false priests to one day profane the majestic temples that he filled with the celestial enthusiasm of his faith, that he consecrated with his exemplary virtues, to which he sacrificed his admirable life and glorious death.'[43]

Florida's labour activists likewise looked to Martí for legitimisation of their continuing concern for socio-economic issues during the course of the independence war. Despite criticism from the PRC's political leadership, labour newspapers agitated for workers to unify and organise, particularly after 1895 when a slowdown in the cigar industry closed numerous factories and left many unemployed. Key West's labour newspapers, *El Vigía* and *El Intransigente*, and Tampa's *El Oriente*, expressed unequivocal support for the independence struggle, but they refused to apologise for encouraging workers to organise and so defend their socio-economic interests. *El Vigía*, a 'Labor and Political Weekly', noted: 'The subtitle of our newspaper indicates that we will not be indifferent to propaganda and defense of the redeeming ideal, for which many men deserving of universal admiration have and will continue to die.'[44] 'We have discharged, and will always discharge our patriotic duty,' it declared. However, the newspaper also stated its intention to combat tyranny, exploitation and immorality in the community through the promotion of labour organisation and unity.[45] The weekly considered this consistent with Martí's basic philosophy. 'Martí, loved by all, the beloved teacher, unified a people and prepared them for a task which others had been unable to accomplish.' This workers should emulate, argued *El Vigía*, to 'gain the respect of exploitive capital and the consideration of the public'.[46] Organised and on an equal footing with capital, labour could protect its interests and thus minimise community conflict. Implicit in this argument was Martí's basic view that organised workers could serve the patriot cause better than an exploited and dissatisfied working class.

Clearly, then, as early as 1896 the images of Martí presented by different sectors of the émigré communities contrasted sharply. Nevertheless all could agree on Martí's fundamental insurgent strategy: independence through political and social unity. The acceptance of unity by the traditional political leaders is easily understood, but its acceptance by Cuban workers and blacks dissatisfied with much of the PRC leadership after 1894 is testimony to Martí's continuing moral authority in the communities subsequent to his death. Dissenting opinions regarding nationalist ideology were frequent, but direct challenges to the legitimacy of the PRC in exile were not. Such a challenge would have called into question Martí's work. Moreover, his fundamental argument to the workers that political independence was a necessary prerequisite to social change was readily accepted by an émigré community that held a deep regard for Martí's humanitarian instincts. Martí's legacy was his enduring symbolic and moral presence in the émigré centres that, despite a great deal of social dissatisfaction, ensured a continued commitment to and enthusiasm for the goal of Cuban independence for which he gave his life.

# 3 Cuban populism and the birth of the myth of Martí

ANTONI KAPCIA

The influence of José Martí on successive generations of Cuban radicals and nationalists and particularly on the revolution of 1959 is by now a commonplace of Cuban historiography:

> José Martí es precisamente la figura cuya eminencia no sólo colma esa etapa propiciatoria del próximo estallido revolucionario sino que la extralimita en proyección histórica que penetra con hondura y largueza en la posterioridad.[1]

> José Martí is, in fact, the figure who not only dominates and bring to fruition that particular period, which was so ready for the impending revolutionary explosion, but who dominates even the period beyond that, with a historical significance that extends far, and deep, into posterity.

Successive observers of Cuban history have written that Martí's 'genius nourished the minds and hearts of succeeding generations of Cuban rebels',[2] that 'Martí and his teachings left a profound mark on the youth of Cuba'[3] inspiring the 1933 rebels and creating the mould that produced the 26 July movements in the 1950s,[4] and that the 1933 rebels 'had been fed on Martí's idealism'.[5]

Certainly many have also seen Martí's influence on Fidel Castro, the rebel movement of 1953–9, and the whole revolution, referring to Martí's 'infinite concern for unity' always being 'Fidel's model',[6] to Martí's 'direct influence',[7] to the 'evident kinship' with 'the spirit of Castroism'.[8] Ample evidence of this link is of course provided by the repeated references to Martí in Castro's Moncada defence speech of 1953 ('La historia me absolverá', 'History will absolve me') and by the references to Martí in the many manifestos of the rebel movement.[9] Beyond this, many of the participants in the revolution ('la revolución martiana de 1959'[10]) have confirmed the movement's *martiano* pedigree by referring to Martí as 'the direct mentor of our revolution'[11] and to the fact that 'each revolutionary event carries the imprint of José Martí'.[12] A study of Martí's influence necessarily

32

concentrates less on Martí's actual ideas or his political categorisation, since the nature of his ideas was almost irrelevant to their usefulness, and more on such questions as what did certain groups believe and maintain were Martí's ideas, what did they seek in Martí, in his ideas and in his image, and why did they turn to him when and as they did.

Within this perspective what emerges is a picture of at least three distinct phases of *martianismo*, considering it at an intellectual level alone since what concerns us here is the political impact of *martianismo* on bourgeois and petit bourgeois groups in the four decades before the revolution and the ways in which these groups used that *martianismo* to legitimise and mobilise support for, their political position.[13]

Broadly the three 'phases' of this 'political' *martianismo* were: first, the 1923–31 period, when Martí's thoughts and writings were revived by the student generation of 1923, of whom Martí was one of several inspirations; secondly, the 1934–52 period, when the image of Martí, rather than his ideas, was deliberately used in the form of myth by certain dominant social groups to legitimise their rule, and by certain political groups in an attempt to create a populist alliance for the purpose of control and distraction; thirdly, the 1952–9 period, when the emergence of a more deeply rooted *martianismo* with more radical, even revolutionary, implications, as a part of a radical political mythology, can be observed.

## The setting for the 'rediscovery' of Martí

Despite the existence of a 'popular' *martianismo*, there is little evidence of any real attention paid, in intellectual circles, to Martí's political ideas (as opposed to the literary Martí) before 1923. Thus the idea of Martí's 'rediscovery' in the 1920s ('Many radical circles began to discover the forgotten writings of José Martí'[14]) seems tenable. But why should this 'rediscovery' have come about at that time?

The economic context was set principally by the 1903 Reciprocity Treaty, which effectively established the pattern of Cuba's external trading relationships and, to a large extent, its domestic economic structure. For the consequences of the treaty were ambiguous, leading to security and prosperity on the one hand, especially for the leading sugar sector, but also, on the other, to restrictions (of possible agrarian diversification and growth in manufacturing), to a further 'Americanization' of the economy[15] (especially of sugar and utilities) and to a further distortion of the economic structure, increasing dependence on the sugar sector and on external (US) capital, which increased the monocultural tendencies within the economy.[16] Events of the 1920s sharpened this profile, with the sudden boom of 1920, the

'Dance of the Millions', being followed immediately, and perhaps predictably, by the precipitous decline of the sector,[17] resulting in the collapse of both Cuban banking and Cuban sugar interests and their replacement by US capital.[18] This, in turn, led to the relative and partial immiseration of the critically important sugar sector (especially of the small planters, the *colonos*, and the wage labour force), the inevitable social dislocation that ensued, and even the temporary bankruptcy of the Cuban government itself which, so dependent on sugar sales for its revenue, briefly failed to meet all its salary and pension obligations.

The result was an equally dislocated social environment. For example, by the 1920s the planter élite had undergone a radical change of composition. The combination of the restrictions of the colonial regime, the crisis of the 1880s, the disruptive effects of the 1895–8 war, the departure of many Spanish landowners, and the steady penetration of US capital, had, even by 1902, seen the disappearance of many 'traditional' small planters and of a 'sugar aristocracy' with a tendency to resident family occupation. In its place had grown up a countervailing tendency to ownership by either an urban (i.e. absentee), 'Americanized', consuming and distributive élite or by corporations, predominantly American, characterised by a much higher degree of integration in the whole refining, distributive structures – indeed an early agro-industrial complex. Such a fundamental social transformation inevitably intensified the degree of alienation of the increasingly proletarianised workforce, of the *colonos* marginalised in the process, of the similarly immiserised tobacco-growers (many of whom by the 1920s had become tenant sharecroppers) and of the seasonal labour force, all further estranged both from the growing urban sector[19] and from the management of their enterprises and the endproduct of their production. In this sense even the extension of the railway network (which doubled from 1902 to 1915, and again by 1931)[20] by facilitating further expansion and corporate capitalisation of the sugar economy further disrupted 'traditional' social patterns.

This class disjuncture inevitably implied a further weakening of the former élite's hegemony which, already limited by the structures of Spanish colonialism, now began to be squeezed out of the little space it occupied in the social and political system by the élite's transformation and steady subordination to external capital – i.e. to become an enclave élite.[21] It also provoked a rise in social tensions, already evident in strike activity between 1899 and 1902. Indeed, in this context it became increasingly possible to see class conflict in purely nationalist terms, especially given the popular base of the former Independence movement which led to an 'identification of the nation of Cuba, such as it was, with the people, the workers, the millworkers, the Negroes, "los humildes" '.[22]

Furthermore, the period witnessed the rise of a large petit bourgeoisie. In part, this was the result of the school and university reforms of 1900–2,[23] but mostly of the new opportunities offered in the sugar-financed service sector and state bureaucracy, and in the managerial and administrative levels of the burgeoning foreign enterprises. But this social group was, in the aftermath of the 1920 crisis, frustrated by the inability of an inherently exclusive system to absorb it sufficiently.

Potentially, therefore, the system contained several disaggregating and conflictive factors. The petit bourgeoisie, given its recent role in the Independence movement, its grounds for nationalism and dissent, and its opportunities for articulation, was ideally placed to express discontent:

> In the absence of any truly national propertied class, this volatile and unpredictable social stratum, squeezed uneasily between the neo-colonial power system and the proletarian masses, was the one element which would provide cohesion and leadership for the belated fulfilment of the frustrated Cuban national revolution.[24]

The political grounds for both nationalism and revolt were, of course, provided by the Platt Amendment and its implications and consequences; for example, a further military occupation in 1906–9. The combination of rapid Americanisation and rapid social change was potentially explosive. There was a degree of consensus over the effects of the American link, with many, even among the élite, questioning 'the wisdom of the relationship', but convinced 'that Cuba had no future outside the sugar economy', feeling trapped by the arrangement that 'left them at the mercy of their capricious neighbour'.[25] There was also even a consensus about the supposed evils of foreign *latifundismo*,[26] a consensus dating from the colonial period and the tensions between Cuban planters and Spanish merchants. But there was no parallel consensus about the 'evils' of the amendment. Indeed, the political cleavage was acute, with many opposed on principle and condemning it in terms of 'betrayal' and 'humiliation'. However, a large section of political opinion either accepted it reluctantly or welcomed it positively, a position based on the long tradition of annexationism (since the 1840s), the survival of a Spanish and pro-Spanish faction, and a conservative element, principally in the Partido Republicano, which argued in 1899 that

Cuba, unprepared for independence and threatened by social revolt, would be better advised to continue as a protectorate and even to accept annexation by the United States. The cleavage was, moreover, exacerbated by the absence of a unifying figure such as Martí and by the dissolution of his Partido Revolucionario Cubano (PRC) and its disintegration into three parties – Nacional, Republicano, and Unión Democrática.[27]

'Plattism' itself had a number of effects. First, through the limitations imposed on Cuban banking and monetary control and through the American right of intervention, it denied any real autonomy to either any Cuban government or, by implication, to the Cuban state itself. This led to a collective, national loss of faith in both the system of governance and the Cubans' ability to govern themselves, and to a growing sense of alienation, humiliation and cynicism. Secondly, it made political labels either irrelevant or patently false, not least the main parties' claim to have inherited the tradition of the Independence movement, and the claim of the system itself to be a competitive democracy. The resulting crisis of legitimacy was deepened by the institutional vacuum created by the absence of a powerful army,[28] and the ideological vacuum left by a Church that, being almost exclusively associated with the colonial Spanish élite, now had few popular roots and little influence. A further result was the development of what has been termed an 'accommodationist nationalism',[29] which capitalised on the undercurrent of resentment and frustration but which intended little more than cosmetic alterations.

But the two most significant effects of Plattism were an intensification of corruption and the lack of a consensus on nationalist mythology. Corruption was, of course, not a new development in Cuba. Its roots were deep in the venality of the old colonial admiration, which with its history of nepotism and personal enrichment was responsible for Martí's ethical emphasis. Now corruption became a logical outgrowth of a system that produced extensive wealth while denying any real moral purpose to political power. In the eyes of the bourgeoisie, an organised graft 'system', offering the prospect of enrichment, access to state contracts, peculation and a free hand in profiteering, at least conferred a degree of legitimacy on the post-colonial state, always provided that it continually expanded to allow access to the graft ladder.

The absence of a nationalist mythology – the consensus on a coherent set of symbols to express a real or imagined collective national identity – was as much attributable to the combination of a lack of a 'heroic' pre-Columbian past to be resurrected (as in Mexico or Peru), the lateness of the liberation struggle, and the possibly dangerous racial overtones of the war of 1868–78, as it was due to the lack of a consensus on the desirability of independence itself. Thus the potential for an integrative role for nationalism was significantly reduced.

This multifaceted and pervasive crisis of confidence, legitimacy and hegemony came to a head in the 1920s when the economic dislocations of 1920 and, after a brief recovery in 1923, of 1926 exacerbated the existing economic imbalance and distortion. The effect was a sudden closing of the graft system, whose acceptability had always depended not only on seniority but also on access – access now critically denied to a whole generation of petit bourgeois youth. This, together with the blow to morale dealt by the economic collapse, which seriously undermined the confidence and faith in modernisation that had, for some, always accompanied the fragmentation and demoralisation of the first two decades, helped generate an atmosphere of critical reappraisal.

## The student rebellion and the 'rediscovery' of Martí

This reappraisal began, predictably, amongst the petit bourgeoisie which now concentrated particularly on the aspects of morality. In the first place, this reflected a recognition of the one issue about which there was at least a degree of national consensus, given the visibility of the corruption system and the ethical stance of at least a part of the Independence tradition. Secondly, it could be interpreted as a 'holier-than-thou' post-hoc rationalisation of the group's new exclusion from the patronage system. Thirdly, it reflected the terms of intellectual analysis which partly influenced the academic circles chiefly responsible for the wave of writings, articles and manifestos which, between 1922 and 1924, highlighted the Cuban 'problem', 'crisis' or 'malaise'. For two significant components of that intellectual framework were the residual influence of *arielista* thought and the dominant influence of the *decadencia* school of analysis.

This latter philosophy extended to historiography, anthropology, sociology and even economics. It viewed the failures of the republic as broadly attributable to the weaknesses inherited from a decadent colonialism, being 'the result of the culture-destroying accommodations made by Cuban politicians, businessmen and landowners to that (US) presence'.[30] Partly influenced by the positivist idea that had so permeated Latin American political thought at the turn of the century, it often implied a need for a cultured, educated, enlightened élite to solve the nation's problems.[31] The principal exponent of the *decadencia* idea was undoubtedly Fernando Ortiz, who, from his position in the Academia de Historia, helped to foment this reappraisal, not least with the publication of 'La decadencia Cubana' in 1924, and the formation of his Junta de Renovación Nacional Cívica in April 1923.[32]

In this context, it was perhaps predictable that Havana's student population should have provided the main thrust of this critical examination. First, as the younger generation, they were both directly affected by the frustration of opportunities and critically aware of their position as the first republican generation, born during or after the Independence struggle and therefore not implicated in the post-1902 'decline'. Moreover, they occupied a unique position in Cuban society – relatively privileged (Havana being, at the time, the island's sole university), but open to the intellectual and political influences of the age – and, in common with their counterparts elsewhere in the continent, they, as a relatively coherent pressure group, had a disproportionate potential for articulating the generalised discontent of a society undergoing rapid transformation.

Although they began their protest by focusing on strictly academic issues – university autonomy, the clearly underfunded and poorly organised administration, the quality of tuition, the lack of student representation, and corruption within the university – almost to the exclusion of political concerns, the protest inevitably took on a wider significance. For, although political issues were initially of secondary importance, the focus on morality clearly gave the protest a broader appeal, since the university could be seen as simply a microcosm of wider social ills.

Thus, given the structural and institutional weakness and fragmentation of the social and political systems, the movement of dissent was able rapidly to aspire to intellectual hegemony over the inchoate opposition or, at least, to determine the language and terms of reference of the 'rebellion', as 'moral indignation, hatred of corruption and compromise, exaltation of the purity of youth, cultural nationalism'.[33]

In one sense, the student 'rebellion' was far from isolated. It came within a context of growing industrial unrest, with the creation of the Federación Obrera de La Habana in 1920, and significant strike activity between 1921 and 1925 over the questions of unemployment and falling living standards,[34] all leading to the foundation, in 1923, of the embryonic Agrupación Comunista de La Habana (out of the Centro Obrero) and, in 1925, of the CNOC trade union organisation.[35] Working-class militancy had several effects, injecting an element of radicalism into the student protest movement and giving it a possible new direction, but also raising the spectre of social revolution to frighten the bourgeoisie.

This latter point already explains in part why the student protest should also have found a response in the ranks of the bourgeoisie. For this group found two reasons for joining the 'reform' constituency at the time. First, it realised that in a context of radicalism and dislocation, reform could help neutralise potential opposition and thus maintain its own position. But secondly, reform could possibly propel it into a position of genuine power, and thus could 'crear nuevos instrumentos'[36] for its aspirations. For the essential problem was that Cuba lacked what could be described as a powerful, hegemonic, national bourgeoisie, that socio-economic class that corresponds to Cardoso and Faletto's depiction.

The industrial group at first appeared in a marginal situation. Nevertheless, it was the only group in the new urban sectors that possessed a real economic base. As the one group that could absorb the urban popular sectors in a productive way, it was strategically situated to establish terms of alliance or compromise with the rest of the social system. This also accounts for its importance in the period following the crisis of the agro-export system.[37]

The particular nature of the US-dominated economic structure and of the lop-sided sugar economy gave that potentially dominated group little opportunity to establish itself and expand. Hence it could be described more as an 'aspiring' national bourgeoisie, aspiring to hegemony and economic power either via a reform of external relationships, to create economic space, or via a reform of the internal structure, to improve its efficiency and thereby its possibilities.

There was also a further generational perspective to the student protest. In 1923 emerged a simultaneous protest by the Movimiento de Veteranos y Patriotas demonstrating against non-payment of pensions and demanding urgent reform and public honesty.[38] This was important to the legitimacy of the students' protest because, while they were separated generationally from those who had 'betrayed' the ideals of independence, their movement coincided with a public protest by that 'betrayed' Independence generation.

Coinciding with Ortiz's Junta de Renovación, the 'rebellion' of 1923 was both opportune and of immediate wider significance. It developed with a remarkable rapidity. In January 1923, the Federación Estudiantil Universitaria (FEU) published its manifesto, calling for reform and modernisation of the university, regular financing and efficient administration, autonomy and the appointment of competent 'responsible' teaching staff. The campaign began with strictly educational concerns. In March came the seminal Protesta de los Trece, with its wider attack on corruption, and by implication, the political system.[39] In October, the FEU established the Primer Congreso Nacional (later Revolucionario) de Estudiantes, dedicated 'al perfeccionamiento de la acción estudiantil en los campos educacional, social e internacional'.[40] The aims of the Congreso represented a considerable step beyond the FEU's limited concerns: for example, educational renewal and democracy, the popularisation of the university, the linking of the university to the wider social and political 'struggle', the creation of a radical mentality amongst the student population. Moreover, the stance of the Congress against 'Plattism', the United States' role and private ownership of the means of production, and in favour of youth, a student-worker alliance and Latin American unity, clearly indicated the velocity of political change.

The Congreso was short-lived, but created in its wake the Confederación de Estudiantes de Cuba, the Declaración de Derechos y Deberes del Estudiante and the Universidad Popular José Martí, in November 1923. The Universidad Popular, with up to 500 students in total,[41] clearly represented the new political emphasis of the student 'rebellion', since not only did it involve the participation of notable radicals,[42] it also set up the Cuban branch of the Liga Antimperialista. There was now no question about the tendency of at least one part, the most activist, of the student body, to adopt a radical political role:

> El estudiante tiene el deber de divulgar sus conocimientos en la sociedad, principalmente entre el proletario manual, hermanándose así a los hombres de trabajo para fomentar una nueva sociedad, libre de parásitos y tiranos, donde nadie viva sino en virtud del propio esfuerzo.[43]

> The student has a duty to disseminate his knowledge of society, espeically among the manual proletariat, linking hands with the working man to promote a new society, free of parasites and tyrants, where nobody lives except by his own efforts.

## The new martianismo: *its nature and its limitations*

Here was the context of the 'rediscovery' of Martí. It seems probable that the same circumstances simultaneously pushed several of the 'rebel' generation towards Martí – notably the Grupo Minorista,[44] which resurrected, discussed and propagated his ideas;[45] but the 'rediscovery' is conventionally attributed to José Antonio Mella. Mostly this arises from the publication of Mella's pamphlet, 'Glosando los pensamientos de José Martí',[46] but an important part may have been played by Mella's political association with Carlos Baliño, the radical Independence leader and former colleague of José Martí; Baliño and Mella formed the Communist Party in 1925. Certainly, Mella was acutely aware of the need to revive the 'essential' Martí:

Martí – su obra – necesita un crítico serio, desvinculado de los intereses de la burguesía cubana, ya retardataria.[47]

Martí's work needs a serious critic, free from the interests of the – already retarded – Cuban bourgeoisie.

Mella's prominence in the new political developments[48] gave the 'rediscovery' a particular prestige.

Until that point the *martianismo* that had existed at an intellectual level (distinct from the already mentioned 'popular' sentiment and the 'official' homage paid) was little different from the standard respect paid to all the 'heroes' of Independence. As the main organiser of the Partido Revolucionario Cubano and the drafter of the programme of the Movement, who had suffered an early death, Martí already occupied a special place. The 'dissident' tradition had long respected his image and his ethics, particularly that strand of romantic, 'utopian'[49] nationalism that sensed and protested against the 'betrayal' and the conflict between American interests and the genuinely popular political movement of 1895–8.

The significance of Mella was that he focused attention on the ideas of Martí. For his picture of the *Apóstol* stressed the element of rebellion, of democracy and of class collaboration in Martí's work, as well as his belief in economic justice, social and racial equality and internationalism. He emphasised too Martí's significance for the 1920s, namely in his recognition of the 'social necessity for transformation at a given moment'.[50] The potential utility of the *ideario*[51] of Martí was, of course, extensive. It was this potential that Mella now tapped.

For Martí clearly struck a chord. Firstly he gave root to a rootless radicalism and offered its followers a means of political identification with his own expressed 'radical' concern, which seemed to transcend his liberal context and have such relevance for the new political generation.[52] Thus, in a context of 'betrayal', 'humiliation', external

domination, corruption, civil unrest and social division, in a Cuba
that had not yet developed the strong institutions necessary in an
independent state and that was undermined by dislocation,
fragmentation and collapse, and in a Cuba that denied respect for
intellectual and educational issues, Martí's ideas offered a perfect
framework for a consensual response.

Since the version of Martí now available was a mixture of image,
symbol, ideas, historical significance and legitimisation, he offered an
ideal basis for a nationalist mythology. The image of 'purity', heroism
and even self-sacrifice, and the tendency, 'in an admiration that
bordered on worship',[53] to idealise Martí as the *Apóstol* and even the
'martyr', enjoyed undoubted popularity and universal identification
within a fragmented Cuba. As one writer expresses it, Martí
symbolised 'Cuban national martyrdom'.[54] As the embodiment of the
subsequently betrayed Independence ideal, the figure of Martí was
placed in a deliberate and stark contrast with most politicians of the
1920s. In this sense, Martí was the ideal basis for the search for a
Cuban identity – for *cubanidad* – which now began to preoccupy
intellectuals and politicians alike. In the fragmentation of the 1920s,
many equated *cubanidad* with a lost unity and 'harmony', and thus
looked back to the embodiment of that idealised state in José Martí;
even the displaced landed and intellectual élites now had a reason to
seek the retrieval of the 'unity' of the past and therefore lent their
support to the search for *cubanidad*. This was particularly true as the
unity posited by Martí was less a social unity and more a 'mystical',
'spiritual' harmony, a 'secularised vision of Christian love',[55] and
safer than any clearly political concept – an important point in a Cuba
where the threat of racial disharmony and even revolt had already
been raised (1912) and where elements of a 'black' consciousness were
certainly beginning to appear.

Furthermore, the figure of Martí legitimised a number of political
positions. In particular, he gave legitimacy to the students'
intellectual and political activism, since he represented the idealised
self-image of the students – rebel, patriot, incorruptible man of letters
and self-sacrificing man of action, and above all the epitome of
intellectual and moral honesty and dedication. He also belonged
outstandingly to that same Independence generation with which the
students already felt a political affinity.

Above all, however, Martí became a symbol to the 'rebellion', with
his image being of greater immediate significance than his ideas. In
particular, he gave historical legitimacy to the 'rebellion':

Al pueblo cubano, y particularmente a su juventud estudiante, corresponde la culminación de la faena inconclusa de José Martí: realizarnos históricamente sin interferencias ajenas.[56]

To the Cuban people and especially to its student youth, corresponds the culmination of the unfinished task of José Martí: to fulfil ourselves historically without outside interference.

As the one Cuban renowned outside the island, Martí became the Cuban symbol for what, to a large extent, was the Cuban version of a wider intellectual, generational, petit bourgeois 'revolt' in Latin America, with its themes of neo-*arielista* 'spirituality' (with which the Martí-oriented *cubanidad* could be identified), 'regeneration',[57] millenarianism, anti-imperialism, nationalism,[58] radicalism and anti-militarism.[59]

It is important to express certain reservations about this rediscovered *martianismo*. The first is that the rediscovery was limited to a small, intellectual grouping (albeit one with a temporarily exaggerated political significance), which tended, despite Mella, to be attracted as much by Martí's image and symbolic value as by his ideas. Thus it differed little in form from either the popular or the official *martianismo*. A second reservation is that the style and tone of this new version often echoed the idealisation of the previous decades, despite the new perspective offered by a group that, as intellectuals and radicals, might have been expected to develop a different style. Yet Roa, for instance, referred to the members of the future Grupo Minorista as 'placing their political hopes under the shadow of the unfulfilled ideas',[60] and to his 'beautiful dream' of Martí,[61] while Ripoll has indicated the use, by the radical-minded *Revista de Avance*, of the image of the 'adored hero'.[62]

The final, and most important, reservation is that *martianismo*, whether 'old' or 'new', represented simply one of several influences which acted on the political consciousness and culture of the 'rebel' generation. For the 1920s was a decade in Cuba, as in all Latin America, of intense politicisation within intellectual and petit bourgeois circles (quite apart from that under way in the *capas populares*), influenced by often contradictory ideas and attitudes combined in different and, at times, complex ways. Thus, at one level, the Cuban 'awakening' was simply part of the wider anti-imperialism that was developing over the continent, partly perhaps explainable by what one observer has called the 'conspiracy theory of neo-colonialism',[63] which attributed Latin America's problems to an unholy alliance between a reactionary élite and predatory foreign interests. It was an anti-imperialism that grew out of a particular conjuncture of forces: the emergence of an aggressively rich, powerful and interventionist United States, the recently proven vulnerability of the region to economic crises and fluctuations,[64] the changes in world economic patterns and political balances (with the decline of the influence of traditional centres and the arrival of the Russian Revolution) and the ferment of new, radical ideas to provide perspective and direction to the new consciousness.

These ideas found an echo in the Cuba of the 1920s. The most fundamental and directly relevant influence on the student 'rebels' was the University Reform Movement of Córdoba in Argentina in 1918, which set in motion a wave of similar reform movements all over Latin America. Indeed, a comparison between the declarations and tone of the FEU and the Congreso of 1923 and of the Córdoba programme reveals the intellectual inheritance of the Argentine movement, with the specific focus on university issues and call for similar reforms and 'popularisation' of a more 'relevant' education, and beyond that student focus the same recognition of a wider political role, all expressed in the same recognition of a wider political role, all expressed in the same *arielista* and generationalist tone – 'The new Hispano-American was the romantic, combative and messianic generation.'[65] In 1921, the International Student Congress in Mexico, held specifically to further the Reform Movement, stressed the need both for a student-worker alliance and for opposition to imperialism. The Reform ideas were certainly well received in Havana, where a student demonstration as early as April 1920, according to Le Riverend, was clearly linked to the Córdoba programme,[66] and where, in the words of Roa, the Córdoba idea 'was the daily discussion inside and outside the lecture-halls'.[67] Thus, when the first rector of the reformed Buenos Aires University, José Arce, visited Havana, he was enthusiastically welcomed; 'he sowed on fertile land'[68] the ideas of the Reform; and his visit was followed briefly by occupations and strikes.

Within the context of the student focus, and specifically Cuban influence of Enrique José Varona was of considerable importance. Once a friend of José Martí and subsequently the reformist Secretary of Education under General Wood's administration, the philosopher and academic Varona remained a harsh critic of the republic's failings and social problems and a firm advocate of *cubanidad*, honesty and education.[69] Given this record and his stance, together with his link with the Independence generation, of which he was one of the most respected survivors, he clearly exercised an influence on the student body as a whole, despite his essential conservatism, and represented integrity and ideals that many felt had been lost since 1898.[70]

Politically and ideologically four influences were outstanding. The first was *aprismo*, the ideology evolved by the Peruvian Haya de la Torre.[71] Although *aprismo* as such was not clearly formulated until 1924, Haya was already renowned as a student leader and, contributing regularly to the FEU magazines *Juventud* and *Alma Mater* between 1920 and 1923, he was clearly already known and appreciated also for his ideas. Although it is probably chronologically inaccurate to speak of Haya's influence on Mella,[72] both almost certainly arrived at parallel anti-imperialist and revolutionary positions simultaneously and from similar backgrounds. Yet the creation of the Universidad Popular José Martí in 1923 was clearly inspired by the Peruvian Universidad Popular González Prada in 1921 (and imitations elsewhere in Chile and Argentina);[73] and after 1924 when Haya visited Havana, with the Cuban 'rebellion' already under way, *aprismo* began to attract those radicals who found its concept of anti-imperialism more comfortable than the increasingly Marxist direction of Mella's Liga Antimperialista. Indeed, the years after 1923 saw an often bitter debate in the Universidad Popular between Mella's followers and the *aprista* faction.[74]

A second ideological influence was that emanating from the Mexican Revolution of 1910, which sent shock waves throughout the continent and played a part in creating the mood of radicalism and anti-imperialism amongst both petit-bourgeois youth and the increasingly active working class. The image of a uniquely 'Latin American' response to imperialism in the form of Mexico's concept of *mestizaje*, the appeal of a peasant-intellectual alliance, which the revolution in part appeared to present, and the whole emphasis on the revolutionary role of education, as advocated by José Vasconcelos, all contributed to the political impact of the process in the continent generally and in the Cuba of the 1920s particularly. Thus, when Vasconcelos visited Havana in 1925 he was welcomed by the Marxist student leader, Marinello, as a 'teacher, revolutionary and precursor'.[75]

A further influence was that of anarchism and anarcho-syndicalism, both of which exercised a powerful attraction and gave a political direction within a part of the Independence movement and later within the early trade unions. Indeed, it was anarchism which provided the ideological impetus for the more revolutionary element of the 1895–8 process, so that 'in its final stage the Independence struggle was also a revolutionary struggle'.[76] In the sharpened class conflict of the post-1902 Cuba, that radicalism carried on in the form of anarcho-syndicalism in the unions, and while such popular radicalism probably only filtered upwards to a very slight degree (as did the popular *martianismo*), the anarchist legacy almost certainly played a part in predisposing the 1920s generation to a 'revolutionary' and anti-imperialist position.

That same legacy in Cuba, as elsewhere in Latin America, contributed to the fourth ideological influence, that of Marxism. The difficulty with identifying any influence lies of course in the distinction between rhetoric and reality, and in unravelling the diverse but often superficially similar threads that make up any individual or collective ideology. This is certainly the case with Marxism in Latin America; it entered the continent, as did every other political idea or ideology, gradually and in an often diluted or hybridised form. For the pattern of ideological adoption has usually been that of post-hoc rationalisation, of particular groups selectively adopting those parts of a political philosophy that suit their environment, their needs and their existing political position. The Marxism that entered Cuba was a mixture of a radical anti-capitalist posture, an explanation of problems that focused on the unpopular élites and foreign interests, an essentially activist prognosis and, in the 1920s, the Marxist–Leninist analysis of imperialism and concept of activism.

In this context, Marxism (as a general attitude) and Marxism–Leninism (as a specific analysis) contributed significantly to the tone, substance and language of revolt and dissent. From 1925, with the founding of the Communist Party and the growing labour unrest to sharpen the political focus, Marxism began to offer a more coherent expression of rebellion and a more effective tool of analysis than either the *decadencia* approach or the *aprista* concept that now underlay much of the 'rebellion'. Given the identification of so many of the intellectual and political leaders of that 'rebellion' with a Marxist perspective, Marxism also began to acquire an intellectual prestige and legitimacy within the dissenting coalition, a prestige which, despite subsequent problems, it continued to enjoy for some time, so that 'Marxism . . . was a part of Cuban nationalist doctrine for bringing about social change'.[77]

In spite of this element of ideological coherence, but perhaps because of the essential selectivity of the absorption of Marxism, even the Marxist Left in Cuba still tended to express their revolt in the triumphalist, moralistic, romantic terms of *martianismo*, and thanks largely to Mella, the early Communist Party displayed a detectable *martiano* flavour in its language. The significance of this is that the relationship between language and ideas can be two-way. The *martiano* tone of the political language of the time was not simply passive, but also reflected back on the content of expression, 'martianising' it in the process. Hence, it seems quite plausible that Mella moved towards a Marxist position partly as a result of his *martianismo* but then proceeded to 'martianise' his Marxism, and that his circle followed his example. Mella's contribution to the political discourse of post-1923 Cuba was considerable, injecting a genuinely new element into Cuban radicalism, giving it intellectual and political respectability and enabling it to adopt a Marxist perspective without 'betraying' the nationalist tradition. This probably helped create the 'spiritual' rather than the 'materialist' tone of much of the anti-imperialism of the period.

None the less, two fundamental traits of this 'rebellion' must be noted, so as to avoid exaggeration of its importance: namely, that it remained mostly socially isolated, with little effect beyond the student population of Havana, and that it was short-lived. By 1927, Mella had been expelled and exiled, many of the hitherto discredited teachers had been reinstated without significant protest from the students, and the ideological and political differences, sharpened perhaps by the 'threat' of labour unrest and the growing importance of the Marxist position, had fragmented the temporary unity of 1923. Hence, after protesting at the extension of Machado's rule in 1927, the FEU was disbanded with relative ease. This fragmentation was aided both by the Communist Party's growing, and possibly deliberate, distance from intellectual politics and by the effectiveness of Machado's rule. The result was the dispersal of the 'rebels' of 1923. The Universidad Popular was closed in 1927, forcing Martínez Villena into the Communist Party;[78] and the unity of the Grupo Minorista split between the reactionary 'nostalgic' element and the more radical, 'popularising' faction. In this context, whatever significance Martí may have had in the limited environment of his 'rediscovery', as a symbol of rebellion he was not immediately popularised.

## The 1933 revolution and its aftermath

By 1933 the situation had altered fundamentally. First, the process of proletarian politicisation and radicalisation had accelerated, with the Communist Party numbering 6000 members by 1933 and dominating the CNOC. This level of politicisation, perhaps proven by the failure of the Communists to halt the 1933 strikes, undoubtedly affected political configurations and perspectives, both among reformers and conservatives. Secondly, frustration had grown and become generalised mostly out of disillusion with Machado's rule. For Machado had been elected in 1924 on a platform of nationalist reform, *cooperativismo* and moral regeneration, but his presidency proved to be a mixed blessing. On the one hand he constructed an efficient patronage system to cater for the interest groups he calculated to be significant: export agricultural interests, domestic manufacturers (with a tariff reform in 1927), and the black population (by protecting the *ñáñigo* cults and offering advancement in both police and army). At the same time he exercised a ruthless authoritarian control through military and police repression. The fact that the established parties either failed to oppose this repression or connived in it, benefiting from the patronage system, undermined their legitimacy and that of the system itself. The 'accommodationist nationalism' that Machado constructed (his Liberal Party had been the recognised inheritor of the residual *independentismo*) came to terms pragmatically with US interests and did much to alter the nature of nationalism, for it created a space and a legitimacy for a more radical nationalist perspective. Discontent was galvanised, as in 1920, by the collapse of sugar and tobacco prices and of the world sugar market in 1929–30, with predictably dislocating consequences.

Since the context of 1933 was different, so too was the nature of radicalism. Student protest was revived in 1930, particularly by a reconstituted and renamed Directorio Estudiantil Universitario (DEU). One characteristic of this new wave of dissent was that its exponents were the younger participants of the 1923 events,[79] often from prominent *independentista* families; and one motive for discontent was the closing of opportunities available to the prospective graduates.[80] Yet the declared position of the DEU of 1930–1 differed little from that of the FEU of 1923–7,[81] despite the change of context. Indeed, the DEU unity was short-lived, and the differences evident in the 1924–7 period now emerged fully. For the ideological split had been compounded by the enactment of a limited number of reforms in the financial, administrative and curricular fields,[82] and by the development of a more coherent and critical perspective, offered not only by the Communist Party but also by the publication of Ramiro Guerra's seminal study of Cuba's history.[83] The consensus about the *programa superficial*[84] of 1923 was not repeated in 1930–1; hence when Machado arrested the entire DEU leadership in 1931, the new student 'rebellion' was thrown into disarray and a clearer Left–Right divide became evident.

The differences within the DEU centred on both the external relationship and internal problems. While the Left saw the complete separation of Cuba from United States' economic and political interests as being essential to any social transformation, the Right tended to pay lip service to 'anti-imperialism' and to conceive of a modified relationship eliminating obvious excesses and limiting its damage. Whereas the Right talked of class collaboration and alliances of 'progressive' national forces, the Left, seeing the way forward lying with the proletariat and perhaps the peasantry, linked the political struggle against the élite, the bourgeoisie and the Machadato to the struggle against the United States:

> Habrá que ir, no sólo contra él, sino también contra la propia raíz del mal o séase, contra las grandes empresas controladoras de nuestra economía, y contra sus aliados y lacayos, los burgueses y latifundistas nativos.[85]

> We must fight not only against it [the USA], but also against the very root of evil, that is, against the large enterprises that control our economy, and against its allies and lackeys, the native bourgeoisie and *latifundistas*.

A debate occurred between an anti-capitalist and a nationalist perspective. The nationalist standpoint was represented chiefly by the 'rump' of the DEU, increasingly influenced by American 'New Deal' ideas, while the anti-capitalist position was represented mostly by the Ala Izquierda Estudiantil. This group, composed in part by former activists of the Liga Antimperialista and the Universidad Popular,[86] incorporated the more orthodox Marxist element as well,[87] leading some observers to see it as a 'front' for the Communists.[88] Furthermore, the views of the Ala Izquierda Estudiantil also reflected its class origins.[89]

It was, perhaps predictably, the DEU element, rather than the Ala, which, from its perspective of an idealist 'mission' to lead a multiclass revolution, saw no contradiction in seizing power in the vacuum following Machado's overthrow in 1933 and leading a 'revolution from above', appointing the five-man government of the Pentarquía and then the Grau San Martín government that succeeded it. Yet, equally predictably, that government had little base beyond the DEU. It was denied the support of crucial factions in the army, of the radicalised sugar-cane workers, and of the small *colonos* and the bourgeoisie which feared the implications of both military and industrial politicisation.

Elements in the bourgeoisie constituted another distinct feature of the new radicalism of 1933. For events since 1927 had, by 1933, made both 'nationalism' and 'reform' acceptable to elements of the bourgeoisie. On the one hand, domestic manufacturers who aspired to the role of 'national bourgeoisie' had been disappointed by Machado's 1927 tariff reform, which protected relatively insignificant areas like textiles and non-sugar agriculture, but conspicuously increased imports of oil, machinery and tools.[90] On the other hand, by 1933 the sugar-linked dependent bourgeoisies had been pushed to a reform position by a belated awareness of the genuine threat of social upheaval and of the need to construct some sort of mechanism to divert or control it, even if by modifiying the existing system:

> Comprendieron que no podían sostener el régimen neocolonial si no realizaban cambios formales, metodológicos, pues las vías que usaron hasta 1924 ya eran anacrónicas y, por tanto, ineficaces.[91]

> They understood that they could not continue to uphold the neo-colonial regime if they did not effect formal, methodological changes, because the paths used prior to 1924 had become anachronistic and, as such, inefficacious.

An ostensibly revolutionary organisation, the ABC, must be considered within this reformist perspective. This body clearly represented, although in exaggerated form at times, the perspective of 'bourgeois radicalism', since the ABC was the most openly class-conscious and class-based of all the 1933–4 rebel groups. Founded in 1931, as a direct result of the failure of a *golpista* uprising in Río Verde,[92] it conceived of itself as a secret, punitive, cellular, terrorist organisation. The ABC was founded by three 'respectable' lawyers[93] and supported by a number of ex-student activists and also by two of the thirteen who had made the Protesta de los Trece in 1923 (Ichaso and Mañach). Thus although it apparently differed little in its aims from the DEU,[94] it laid greater emphasis on small enterprises, reflecting both its class origins and the perceived need to boost artisan production in the opportunity afforded by the 1929–33 slump. The ABC fell short of an out-and-out anti-United States position, recognising the 'realism' of accepting Cuba's position within the inevitable US orbit – a standpoint that led logically to its participation in the Welles 'mediation' in 1933, and also to the secession of a more nationalist element in 1933, ABC Radical. A further distinguishing feature of ABC's approach was its corporatism,[95] which was at one and the same time a traditional position (based upon Hispanic and Cuban experience), a fashionable position (especially in a context of discredited liberal democracy), a 'New Deal' – interventionist position, and even a revolutionary position, offering protection of Cuban national and popular interests against external predations. Yet many have also seen a patent – or a latent – fascism in that corporatism, in ABC's regret at the loss of 'principles of order and social discipline',[96] in its anti-communism and even in its *camisas verdes* organisation.[97]

ABC was revolutionary in two specific ways: in its commitment to violent activism, and in its clear break with conventional economic liberalism. Hence, when ABC publicly adopted Martí as a symbol in 1931, it was the image of a more 'radical', socially aware Martí rather than the traditional 'libertarian' image that it presented.

Located ideologically and socially between the positions of the Ala Izquierda and DEU, on the one hand, and the 'bourgeois radicalism' on the other, was Antonio Guiteras' Joven Cuba organisation founded in 1934. Guiteras in the 1930s played a role as important as that of Mella in the 1920s, but his ideological position is much less easily identifiable, moving as it did from a vague 'romantic' radicalism in the 1920s, finally sharpened by the 1933 experience, to a more activist revolutionary position in 1934–5. His leftist tendency was evident from 1927 onwards, in the commitment to anti-imperialism and the working class and to the ideas of insurrection, but the formulation of his ideas was not as coherent as that of the Ala Izquierda group, and was noticeably more 'romantic' in tone, talking of 'honest men of character and valour', of 'tyranny', and 'martyrs', and phrasing revolt in singularly *culto* terms: 'Sólo vuestra abnegación, vuestro desinterés, vuestro espíritu de sacrificio en la lucha que se avecina . . .'[98]; 'Only your abnegation, your disinterest, your spirit of sacrifice in the struggle that is upon us . . .' Equally, as distinct from the Ala perspective, Guiteras wrote of the need for 'nation-building' as a preparatory stage for socialism; but in 1932–3 his expressed ideas included legalisation of the Communist Party, workers' rights, nationalisation of foreign-owned properties, demilitarisation,[99] and admiration for the Soviet Union[100] and for the idea of collectivisation of agriculture.[101] His participation in the Grau government of 1933 as Minister of the Interior injected an element of 'leftism' into its programme of reforms, not least in social legislation which Guiteras himself described as the immediate priority:

> protección a las clases que sufren, a las explotadas, a las sumidas en la miseria y en la desigualdad. Política a favor de los humildes. En pro de obreros y campesinos contra el latifundismo. Contra el capitalismo acaparador y absorbente. Contra riqueza, fabulosas ganancias que sólo rinden a la nación un fruto exangüe y miserable.[102]

> protection for the suffering and exploited classes immersed in poverty and inequality. Policy in favour of the humble. In favour of

the workers and peasants against *latifundismo*. [Policy] against grasping and absorbent capitalism. Against riches, fabulous profits that give the nation only a wretched and minimal income.

Joven Cuba, founded as a response to the counter-revolution and a successor to the short-lived TNT organisation, built on Guiteras' ideas and the experiences of 1933–4, and called for 'estructuración socialista', with a clearly thought-out programme of anti-imperialism, social and economic change, nationalisation and agrarian reform.[103] But it was as an insurrectionary organisation that Joven Cuba made its mark, for its emphasis was more on action than ideas:

> La obra de la Revolución tiene que ser encabezada por una minoría penetrada de sus principios, con plena conciencia revolucionaria.[104]

The work of the revolution has to be led by a minority imbued by its principles, with a full revolutionary awareness.

It is precisely in this area that an element of élitism, a certain distrust of the 'masses' and their ability to lead the revolution, and a desire to take a short cut through activism rather than mobilisation, can be detected. Despite Guiteras' clear leftist commitment, a parallel with ABC can be observed; and Joven Cuba's image of Martí differed little from ABC's. Yet Guiteras, perhaps because of his ideological heterodoxy and his location within a 'romantic' tradition, remained politically influential long after his assassination in 1935.

This new form of bourgeois or petit-bourgeois radicalism was characterised by three features. First, it had a wider base than in 1933, with the left-wing element of 1923 linking up with popular radicalism, and with the 'moderate' radicalism now tactically supported by the bourgeoisie itself. Secondly, bourgeois radicalism was less united than in 1923, fragmenting both socially and ideologically. Thirdly, it displayed a tendency to adopt almost automatically the talisman of José Martí as a legitimisation of whatever position its component parts assumed. For the 1923–7 'revolt' had established a usable image of a 'radical' Martí that all radical groups, and many not so radical, could legitimately claim as a forebear. Thus the new situation was, in all three respects, both substantially different from, and the logical result of, the post-1923 developments.

These divisions deepened in the aftermath of the 1933 revolution. The character of the 'new economy', established along the lines of the Reciprocity Treaty and the Jones-Costigan Sugar Act of 1934, was characteristically ambiguous. On the one hand, it guaranteed a welcome security for the sugar exporters, and therefore, by extension, for the whole economic complex that depended on sugar production and sales.[105] Also, as the direct US economic hold loosened slightly, some growth and a degree of 'Cubanisation' occurred, particularly in the *colono* sugar sector and even the financial system. At the same time, while new policies lessened dependence, they also paradoxically intensified it, albeit more subtly. For they implied a disincentive to both domestic manufacturing[106] and agricultural and market diversification, by tying Cuba more subtly to its role as primary producer for the preferential American market. The new policies implied too a lack of economic autonomy, given the existence of an unstable quota of sugar exports to be determined annually by the United States. Moreover, what growth there was was strictly limited and the benefits were unevenly distributed; and one by-product of a 'secure' market, determined by the quota, was a tendency towards stagnation.

The partial 'success' of the 1933 revolution was a major cause of deepening divisions among bourgeois radicals. For the post-1933 governments, despite allegations of betrayal and counter-revolution, gained a significant legitimacy from the array of reforms. Many of those reforms enacted by Batista's first government and embodied in the Constitution of 1940,[107] largely Auténtico-inspired (see below, p. 57), improved social and economic conditions for specific groups like organised labour and the *colonos*, and thereby effectively reduced the grievance potential of any opposition from the Left, even though many of the reforms were seen as short-term solutions to immediate political problems and not as the result of a coherent programme, as might have been expected from a genuinely reformist government. But while the governments of 1934–44 enacted these reforms they were not reformist in the sense of seeking a thorough modernisation of the system. Their purpose was adjustment to the modified post-1933 conditions (which made a restoration of the pre-1933 system only a remote possibility), the protection of particular interests and the mainenance of the existing power structure (by reform if necessary) and survival, not least through the patronage possibilities offered by an increased state role. Further legitimacy was conferred by the modifications of the 'neo-colonial' relationship, which made external controls less formal, and therefore less identifiable, and by the development of relative 'Cubanisation'.

In this way, the potential for both nationalist and domestically oriented dissent was diminished. Indeed, the 1933 revolution conferred further legitimacy on those participants who survived as

leading political actors, including Batista, the army and the
Auténticos which provided the governments of the 1934–59 period.
Thus the revolution both as 'success' and 'failure' was incorporated
into the growing, and now potentially integrative, nationalist
mythology.

There were, however, flaws in the picture. First, since the sugar
sector still stagnated, the social mobilisation and patronage that
depended ultimately on its success also tended to stagnate, creating an
obvious potential for later frustration. Secondly, the image of a 'new
bourgeoisie' in a position of political control was misleading. For it
was not fundamentally 'new', in the sense of being a dynamic,
industrially based, national bourgeoisie. Certainly, industrial activity
did increase after 1933,[108] but it was not necessarily indigenously
generated or owned. Furthermore, the class relations and class
composition of Cuba between 1902 and 1959 were complex and
always shifting, and even within the bourgeoisie itself the diverse
groups, relationships and interests were far from simple. In fact, from
1902 there had been no clear, dominant, hegemonic class, partly as a
result of the lateness of abolition and decolonisation, and partly as
a result of steady 'Americanisation', even before Independence.
Therefore, Cuba lacked a dominant, indigenous, landowning class
and a powerful, industrial bourgeoisie – indeed, it lacked a powerful,
coherent oligarchy. Instead, the bourgeoisie was a mix of industrial
(both 'dependent' and 'national'), *rentier*, landowning, managerial
and bureaucratic. Indeed, the 1902–33 period saw considerable flux
in class formation, with new interests emerging to replace those in
decline. The 1934–52 period was still fluid in this respect. On the one
hand, the *colonato* did experience some advancement and the
managerial and industrial bourgeoisies progressed in part, all with
increased access to and even partial control of the State, which, with
power vested in the allocation of resources and quotas, and in the
possibility of protectionism of different kinds, enjoyed some
autonomy. But in the 'new' Cuba of post-1933, no single class
exercised control, and the industrial bourgeoisie scarcely constituted
a recognisable national bourgeoisie, capable of attaining and keeping
economic and political power.

The lack of a strong national bourgeoisie was partly due to the 1934
treaty, which reversed many of the tariffs of 1927 that might
conceivably have initiated a process of class formation. But it was also
attributable to the fact that Cuban manufacturing after 1934 was only
really allowed to develop in sectors that did not threaten US interests.
In this sense, the industrial bourgeoisie, in reality a *seudoburguesía
industrial cubana*,[109] which actually helped integrate Cuba more

subtly into the US economic orbit, was in reality a dependent class. Moreover, linked as it was to the agricultural interests, the lack of a dividing line between components of the bourgeoisie meant that there was no strongly identified class domination. Hence, a 'national bourgeoisie' was still more an aspiration than a reality, which 'was incapable of fighting against the internal and external obstacles that constrained it'.[110] Even the aspiration was often half-hearted, since the readjustments after 1934, domestic and external, clearly met with the approval of many of the bourgeois interest groups.

While the 'old' pre-1933 Cuba had partly disappeared, the 'new' Cuba that replaced it was in reality not so 'new'; and the claim to legitimacy of the 'new' ruling class was patently false, since it did not control either the economy or the State, and its sole claim to authority rested on its privileged access to government. Taken together with the patent impotence of Congress, this false claim and the resulting inability to exercise any real corporate control resulted in a serious crisis of legitimacy.

The potency of nationalism was weakened by the absence of a clearly identifiable US 'enemy', although the quota was a potential replacement for the Platt Amendment in Cuban nationalist demonology. The force of nationalism was further reduced by the fragmentation or moderation of nationalist forces and by the attitude of the Communist Party, which tended to downgrade the US threat. These circumstances increased the possibility of popular dissent being directed against the government or the system itself, undistracted by external factors.

This new, would-be élite was faced with a clear imperative: to fill the void, to disguise its lack of real power and its lack of a real reform programme, and to provide a safe distraction. This it did by the creation of an 'establishment nationalism', which stressed nationalism in one direction while effectively downplaying it by channelling it into 'safer' issues – such as reforming the excesses of the Reciprocity Treaty or the quota, and limited interventionism. In other words, it discovered the value of populism.

## The creation of a Cuban populism

Although interpretation varies widely on the nature, and even the existence, of populism, it is clear that, throughout Latin America, one political response to the crises of the 1930s and 1940s was the idea of tactical or strategic alliance on the basis of certain consensual social and economic policies, which would at least solve immediate problems.[111]

Populism can be seen as a political coalition, formed within a context of dislocation and crisis, of changing social formations and hegemonic vacuum; as a coalition put together on specific issues or on generally perceived or felt grievances; as a coalition between an élite, or an aspiring élite, on the one hand, and an unrepresented and disarticulated popular base, on the other, which was dominated and controlled from above, but whose survival depended on the 'cement' of a semi-'contractual' relationship between the component parts. The purpose of such a coalition was to meet the greatest number of immediate needs of the 'contracting parties', with the object of diverting dissent, incorporating dissenting groups, and modernising the system so as to preserve its basis, or to maintain the existing élite in power or project the aspiring élite into power. Such a coalition depended on certain prerequisites: a disjuncture of hegemony, of political and social stability and of expectations; a disarticulated base, willing to be mobilised, and a 'leading' social group able to affect that mobilisation – typically, a national bourgeoisie – capable of dynamism, able to incorporate, and vitally interested in a readjustment of the economy and a potential set of ideas, policies, myths or symbols to express that mobilisation, to 'explain' the problems being attacked and to legitimise the coalition and the reforms proposed. Where the prerequisites were presented in sufficient strength or viability, then such mobilisation progressed to a successful integrative alliance; but where any were lacking, or weak, the result was a tendency to rising expectations, leading either to coercion and an 'exclusive authoritarianism' or to disintegration. In the latter case, the continued use of the form and language of populism could have the effect either of perpetuating incoherence or of raising expectations further.

In the specific Cuban context, the 'establishment nationalism' created after 1934 clearly raised expectations further. The post-1933 ruling élite was effectively an alliance of Batista, based on the army and the multifarious bourgeoisie, against the 'rebel' alliance that backed the 1925 general strike.[112] It was an alliance made possible by both the greater centralisation of political life and the 'room' offered by the less overt influence of US economic interests. The 'regulatory system' that was created[113] was able to afford some protection to certain interests: to the wide-ranging *colonato*, through the Sugar Stabilisation Institute and the new tenure legislation; to some Cuban banking and manufacturing interests; and to labour, through the sometimes passive, often active, understanding with the Communist Party,[114] which allowed for greater union freedom and an improvement in living standards. Yet such a domination was misleading since, as already indicated, the bourgeoisie lacked real economic, and hence political, power. Therefore, its populism could not be successful integratively, and could not create a corporate structure to maintain it in power. But that populism was successful hegemonically, in using the mechanism of populist mobilisation to divert dissent and to 'de-ideologise' the nationalist radical consensus. In other words, it proved unable to go beyond the mobilisation stage – a critical flaw which contributed both to intensifying the incoherence of politics and, in the long run, to raising expectations. The incoherence was illustrated dramatically by the emergence of the *bonchismo* and *pistolerismo* of the 1934–52 period, in many ways the proof of a degenerated, directionless, de-ideologised activism.[115]

Populism was represented by Batista's political coalition, but mostly by the new Partido Revolucionario Cubano (PRC), better known as the Auténticos. Created by the rump of the DEU and the Grau government of 1933 (specifically the Bloque Septembrista and the Coalición Nacional Revolucionaria, the fourteen organisations of the Revolution), and joined by some of the ABC, the Auténticos deliberately claimed an 'authentic', revolutionary, nationalist heritage, clearly linked to Martí – even using the symbolically important name of Martí's party. Since they were to a large extent the party of the 'heroes' of 1932, the claim – to be faithful to Martí, Mella and Guiteras – had some legitimacy. Hence the Auténticos' attempt at asserting ideological hegemony in the 1940s scored some success. This was due, furthermore, to two factors: first, that in the 1940s the identifiable 'enemy' for a consensus of political opinion was not the United States but Nazi Germany, and secondly, that the potential nationalist or radical alternatives to an external 'enemy' had either disappeared or fragmented still further.

The Communists, for example, were by then becoming increasingly respectable, collaborationist and moderate in their demands, even, for instance, in 1945 calling for increased US investment,[116] and also in some senses increasingly Browderist, or even Stalinist, in outlook – especially with the death of a major national leader, Martínez Villena, in 1934, and the purge of the Trotskyist element in 1938, which then entered the Auténtico party. The conduct of the Communist Party in this way made it lose some of its revolutionary, intellectual and nationalist credentials.

The non-Communist Left fragmented yet further. With Guiteras dead, Joven Cuba stagnated. The dynamic Ala Izquierda was disbanded in 1937 – officially because the unified FEU, created to replace the discredited DEU, made the Ala unnecessary ('when it was confirmed that the right wing had disappeared'[117]) but also probably because of a purge of Trotskyists in 1932 and because of the changes in the Communist Party to which it was closely linked. Some of the Ala group, and others, briefly founded the Partido Izquierdista Revolucionario in 1937,[118] but as that too disappeared many of its adherents gravitated towards the Auténticos. That left the traditional radical Left either with a vaguely expressed view of revolution – 'the protection and stimulus of all those prepared to create wealth for the good of the nation'[119] – or retreating into a moralistic nostalgia that recalled the 'heroic' days of 1933 and spoke of 'the cheated youth'.[120] The traditional Left – Communist and non-Communist – lost its legitimacy as a radical opposition force, and thereby enhanced the claim of the newer populist parties to leadership.

Even the newest party, the Partido del Pueblo Cubano (PPC) – the Ortodoxos – could not effectively challenge the Auténtico hegemony. This was partly because it was simply a generational and even personalist offshoot of the PRC, whose ideas and declared objectives were suitably vague and differed little from those of its parent party – 'nationalism, anti-imperialism, economic independence, political liberty and social justice'[121] – and which stressed such populist concepts as 'el pueblo', class harmony and even leadership, but especially youth and morality (its electoral slogan was 'Vergüenza contra dinero',[122] 'Morality against money!'). The appeal to morality was the PPC's strongest political weapon, since corruption was still a major popular grievance, but the focus was now shifted from peculation towards political 'corruption', the open use of nepotism, patronage and co-option by the same PRC which had promised to rid Cuba of them.

The Auténtico success can also, of course, be attributed to the fact that, as the legitimate heirs of 1933, they had also established, or at least inherited, the language of nationalism and revolution; but, because of their domination, they were now able to sanitise it and render it even vaguer than before:

> 'Revolution' was reduced to the sum total of accumulated reforms, without social upheaval, the use of force, or class conflict.[123]

Thus their concept of nationalism – hostility to *vendepatria* elements, rather than a class-based or anti-imperialist concept – their partial absorption of Keynesian economic ideas, their welfarist strategy and their overall attachment to a corporatist approach could all be presented as 'revolutionary', and with some justification, within the *martiano* tradition. These ideas, appearing in the PRC electoral programme of 1944, were not fulfilled, not least because several of them would have undermined the patronage system on which the

PRC depended.[124] In the ideological vacuum caused by the fragmentation of the 'ideological' Left and the radical-nationalist consensus, the Auténticos were able successfully to manipulate a genuine and popular aspiration for change and to make of it a false, but effective, consensus:

> There is considerable evidence that powerful sectors of Cuban political opinion, very probably the majority of voters, still longed for fundamental reorganization of various institutions and still thought of the 'revolution' as the embodiment of these aspirations.[125]

In this way, the bourgeoisie – which, with such changes as the creation of the first central Cuban bank in 1948, and the steady 'Cubanisation' of sugar production,[126] pretended to play the role of a national bourgeoisie – was able to construct a deliberate mythology out of the nationalist tradition of which it was a part but which it had appropriated. But 'myth' is double-edged. On the one hand, it has a legitimate political function, as a symbol or coherent set of symbols which inspire and direct political actions, programmes, loyalties or groupings, and which, given their nature, inevitably acquire proportions greater thabn 'realism' would attribute to them. None the less, 'myth' retains a 'reality', because it is of critical importance to the cultural, social or political identity of a group, a class or a nation. On the other hand, a myth can be a 'false' consciousness, not only unrelated to contemporary realities or concerns but even invented by the hegemonic groups. In the Cuba of the 1940s it was clearly in the interests of the bourgeoisie to build out of the legitimate nationalist mythology an invented myth, a distant, unreal mythology that focused on the Independence era. This was revived in the scholarly literature of the period that, above all, stressed the figure of Martí as a depoliticised 'hero', presented in a millennarian, almost evangelical and sanctified aura:

> The cult betrayed many of the characteristics of a sect mentality, providing a psychological compensation for a middle class lacking both power and faith in its own ability to change a society corrupted by United States influences. It provided a flight into a world of fantasy, where, in the style of Rodó's 'Ariel', Cuban spirituality was contrasted with United States materialism and greed.[127]

This was *martianismo* devoid of conceptual content, focusing selectively on those ideas that confirmed Martí as a reformist at best (the Auténtico version), a liberal in a moral rather than a political sense, an almost anodyne, mystical patriot (part of the general idealisation of the Independence period).[128] The 1940s was the period of the statuesque Martí, with busts located everywhere, with official tributes on national holidays, with obligatory references at public gatherings – all making Martí into a 'national hero', rather than the radical, anti-imperialist rebel that the 1923 generation had upheld, and that still from time to time emerged as an image.[129] Cuba was now bombarded deliberately by an 'official' *martianismo*; having appropriated the 'popular' Martí and shut away the 'radical' Martí, the bourgeoisie ensured that an acceptable *Apóstol* figure legitimised its rule.

Thus, a clear distinction emerged between the Martí of 1923 and the Auténtico-based Martí of the 1940s. In the 1920s, Martí had been used by the petit bourgeoisie in rebellion as but one among several symbols of rebellion and integrity. Hence, there had been little or no myth-making as, first, legitimacy came from other sources (the consensus for change, and the coherence of the dissenting group), and, secondly, the leading *martianistas* either looked to the example of Martí, or to his ideas (the latter limited almost exclusively to Mella).

In the 1934–52 period, Martí was patently used as myth, to legitimise the illegitimate nationalism of a bourgeoisie no longer in rebellion but, equally, not really in power. He was used by a would-be ruling group that needed a myth to create a false consensus and to keep populism disjointed, directionless and controllable, and as the principal means of political expression.[130] This myth was facilitated by the already ingrained and extensive popular familiarity with the figure of Martí, and the tendency of the fragmented opposition to use the figure of Martí to express a generalised sense of disquiet, moral indignation and even humiliation in front of the United States. All three aspects of *martianismo* – populist, popular and oppositionist – tended towards the 'monumental' image of the *Apóstol*, to see Martí in terms of the 'national hero'. Such a diversely motivated but ultimately similar use of Martí was a reflection of, first, the breadth of his political writings, which enabled all factions to cite them selectively (almost as 'scripture') and, secondly, the accepted equation of *martiano* with Cuban, the universal claim to fulfil the spirit of *martianismo*, either to the letter or simply by definition.

## Martianismo *on the eve of the revolution*

By the 1950s, however, the manipulative capacity of Cuban populism had weakened: for one thing, the economic and social environment had altered. After a steady, albeit partial and superficial, 'Cubanisation' of certain sectors of the economy, the year 1954 saw the renewal of a slight, but perceptible, Americanisation.[131] Moreover, the growth experienced in the late 1930s and renewed in the late 1940s slowed down by 1953. Deceleration of growth influenced the level of social mobilisation, critical to stability and credibilty.[132] The educational reform of 1943 had created a newly educated and expectant generation whose hopes of advancement now lessened considerably. In addition, Cuban society generally was becoming steadily more urban, with all that this implied for social instability and altered perspectives.[133]

Alongside the social and economic changes a steady decline of credibility could be discerned within the political system. For the judiciary and the police were clearly a part of the patronage system, the dual power foci of president and army made Congress increasingly irrelevant, the opposition was in disarray and offered no alternative, and the PRC – the standard-bearer of nationalist legitimacy – had patently failed as a reforming force. But its use of populist rhetoric was dangerous, for the emphasis on morality and 'revolution', contrasting with the reality of a 'corrupt' and conservative party and government, made those issues potentially into weapons to be used against the PRC,[134] as frustration turned inwards on the system itself.

In some senses, the ultimate de-legitimising factor was the survival and success of *pistolerismo*. The degeneration evident in *bonchismo* was explained by the tradition of activism (and the failure to disband the 'action groups' of 1933),[135] the political vacuum, the corruption and patronage that sustained the system, and most importantly, the continued connivance of the Auténticos in *bonchista* domination of the FEU.[136] In 1952, of course, the Batistazo and the collapse or acquiescence of the established nationalist or 'revolutionary' parties, undermined legitimacy still further.[137]

Overall, the Cubans seemed to have little faith in the political system, little faith even in themselves, with the Cuban self-image often reflecting the patronising American image of the Cuban. Cynicism – expressed particularly in the *choteo criollo* (the self-deprecating anti-establishment sentiment[138]) – seriously undermined political activity to such an extent that Batista's attempt at a renewed populism, in his Partido de Acción Progresista, degenerated into a personalist clique and open repression.

In the critical vacuum that characterised Cuban politics of the 1950s, a potential movement of dissent did have an ideology to which it had recourse. This was an ideology of *cubanidad* – a composite of 'revolution', nationalism (albeit, one of unstructured resentment), moralism, generationalism and the role of education represented by the mythology of *martiano* tradition handed down by a succession of 'heroes' who, like Martí, had died 'before their time' – Mella, Martínez Villena, Guiteras and, latterly, Eduardo Chibas – and the tradition of 'youth in rebellion'. It was, of course, a mythology that represented the other side of the nationalist coin offered by the Auténticos, a mythology of revolt rather than accommodation; in which Martí figured prominently – as a sharp contrast to the demoralisation of post-1952 Cuba.

In other words, *martianismo*, after being established and used as the language of politics, could now be used as a legitimation for rebellion. In this sense, *martianismo* was not as safe a myth as it had seemed – a classic case of the danger of an 'unsuccessful' populism. Even emphasising a 'moral' rather than a 'political' Martí had its difficulties, since moralism tends to de-ideologise politics and thereby increase its volatility, and even to lead to a Manichaean view of politics, with revolutionary implications.

This observation was particularly true in 1952–3, since the crisis of legitimacy, now brought to a head, coincided in 1952 with the fiftieth anniversary of the Republic and in 1953 with the centenary of Martí's birth, producing a flood of publications that concentrated particularly on Martí's political thought and his relevance for the Cuba of the 1950s.[139] The memory of Martí began to act as a catalyst for the radicalisation of the new dissenting generation of petit-bourgeois youth, and for the developing nationalist radicalism generally, since a 'radical' *martianismo* had become a part of the ideological framework of a 'rebel' constituency, channelled through the interpretation offered by Mella and the Grupo Minorista, the 1933 revolutionaries, the radical Auténticos and Ortodoxos, and even the Communist Party.

> Los planteamientos de Martí eran de muy hondo calado revolucionario, y su programa venía a ser el del ala radical del movimiento liberador. Exigir igualdad para el negro frente a los esclavistas supervivientes, prometer tierra a los campesinos y emigrantes a expensas de las grandes propriedades inactivas, afirmar el derecho del pueblo a ejercer la dirección revolucionario era acometer a plenitud las tareas de la revolución democrático-burguesa.[140]

The ideology of Martí was deeply revolutionary, and his programme could be perceived to be that of the radical wing of the liberation movement. To demand equality for the black in the face of the surviving slave-owners, to promise land to peasants and immigrants at the expense of large idle properties, to affirm the right of the people to exercise revolutionary leadership, was to tackle in full the tasks of a bourgeois-democratic revolution.

The latest revival stressed the importance of completing the work begun by Martí but as yet unfinished. Such was the traditional popular acquaintance with, and the newly heightened public awareness of, Martí that Castro's repeated acknowledgements of Martí's inspiration not only struck an immediate chord with his followers, most of whom came from the same radical-nationalist tradition,[141] but also with a public to whom even an oblique reference to *El Maestro* made immediate sense. Moreover, the fact that the 26th July Movement came from a generation known collectively as 'la generación del centenario', 'the centenary generation', conferred upon it a particular legitimacy.

## Conclusion

Before 1952 there was little evidence of profound influence exercised by Martí's ideas as opposed to his image. In the 'rebellion' of the 1920s, Martí had been read and appreciated in one important, but restricted, intellectual circle, but not popularised politically. Even within that group, Martí was not a decisive influence, since other influences were more significant. The new radicals used Martí's image and ideas as an instrument of self-legitimacy. The most that can be attributed to Martí in this context is that he acted as a symbol, helping to give a Cuban identity to the generation-class revolt and to create the tone and language of radical nationalism thereafter.

In the 1940s, Martí was clearly used as a myth, intended deliberately to obfuscate and divert. His ideas were used selectively, if at all, to confirm and legitimise, not to influence. An examination of those aspects of his political thought omitted from the establishment version of Martí reveals something of the nature of Cuban populism. For example, Martí's ambiguous attitude to the United States was too complex an issue to make it useful, his agrarian emphasis (basic to his economic ideas) was ignored by a populism that concerned itself with urban groups, and his racial concern hardly surfaced at the level of 'official' mythology.

One of the ironies of the *martianismo* of the 1940s is that it was used to create ideological confusion and an intellectual vacuum, and to perpetuate a superficial but ultimately unsuccessful populism. It is likely that the impact of *martianismo* in the political discourse of Cuba from the 1920s was as much due to the natural genealogy of ideas as to Martí's direct influence. There was clearly a close relationship between successive generations, with a clearly detectable line of political thought transmitted from one to another, developing and being modified to suit each new circumstance or the needs of each group, but fundamentally unchanging. Thus the most important role of *martianismo* in the 1920s was that it set the language of radical politics.

Another corpus of ideas and even specific policies can be traced back to Martí – filtered through Mella, the Ala Izquierda, Guiteras, ABC, the PRC and the Ortodoxos. It can be seen in perceptions of the State's role in economic and social affairs, economic independence, agricultural reactivation and diversification, anti-*latifundismo*, *latinoamericanismo*, education, equality, and even the importance of morality, duty and self-sacrifice, concepts in the 1960s usually attributed in Cuba to Guevara, but in fact having a *martiano* pedigree.

By 1952, *martianismo* was sufficiently ingrained in the language of revolt and of populism, at both a popular and an intellectual level, to make it the obvious mode of expression of the new generation's revolution. *Martianismo* also gave force to the inchoate radicalism of this generation, but did not give it direction. The irony of the near coincidence of the centenary of Martí's birth and Batista's coup presaged a more profound role for *martianismo* and hastened the growing convergence of popular *martianismo* with the more 'political' version among the petit-bourgeois intelligentsia. Only in the late 1950s was this tangible influence unequivocally felt; until then, the accepted idea of Martí's direct influence on Cuban radicalism must be seriously open to question.

# 4 Martí in the United States: The flight from disorder

JACQUELINE KAYE

Martí turned away from the United States and by so doing opened up the space necessary for the creation of the Cuban *patria*. I want to raise the question of what it means to turn away and yet, like Orpheus, be drawn irresistibly to look behind, so that the turning away is both a recognition and a rejection. The concern here is with Martí's published and public writings because it is in the construction of that public gesture that Martí engages most complexly with his response to the northern republic. Writing for an emergent Latin America in the series of newspaper articles over a fifteen-year period, Martí points both to and away from a country which must serve simultaneously as example and warning.

It would be possible to argue that national identity in its very nature is a kind of negative; one can only 'be' a certain nationality by virtue of the mutual existence of those who are not. National identity engages with proximity and distance. Martí is often quoted as saying 'Patria es humanidad', '*Patria* is humanity.' Yet he also wrote:

> Cada cual se ha de poner, en la obra del mundo, a lo que tiene más cerca; no porque lo suya sea, por ser suyo, superior a lo ajeno, y más fino o virtuoso, sino porque el influjo del hombre se ejerce mejor, y más naturalmente, en aquello que conoce, y de donde le viene inmediata pena o gusto: y ese repartimiento de la labor humana, y no más, es el verdadero y inexpugnable concepto de la patria.[1]

> Each person should tackle, within the wider world, that which is closest, not because what is his is superior or finer or more virtuous than that belonging to others, but because man can exercise influence better, and more naturally, upon that which he knows and from which he exacts immediate pleasure and sorrow. This sharing-out of human tasks – and nothing more – is the truthful and impregnable concept of *patria*.

The use of the word 'naturalmente' alerts the reader to the period in which Martí was exiled in the United States; this was a period of large-scale movement of peoples, of emigration, exile and imperial expansion at a time when Darwinian and post-Darwinian speculations about the rootedness of life in particular landscapes, as well as concepts of order, disorder and change, were being fed into political, social and economic thinking. In a novel whose first publication coincided with Martí's arrival in New York, that great explorer of exile, Henry James, attributes to one of his characters, Madame Merle, the following words:

> You must tell me more about America; you never tell me enough. Here I've been since I was brought here as a helpless child, and it's ridiculous, or rather it's scandalous, how little I know about that splendid, dreadful, funny country – surely the greatest and drollest of them all. There are a great many of us like that in these parts, and I must say I think we're a wretched set of people. You should live in your own land; whatever it may be you have your natural place there. If we're not good Americans we're certainly poor Europeans; we've no natural place here. We're mere parasites crawling over the surface; we haven't our feet in the soil.[2]

Madame Merle is reflecting on the exodus of the wealthy from the savagery of America to the more discreetly savage communities of Europe, but behind her words lies the shadow of that massive immigration into the United States which took place with increasing impetus in the 1880s. That large-scale movement of Germans, Poles, Swedes, Slavs, importation of Chinese labourers and, of course, massive immigration of Jews, following on earlier migrations from Europe and Africa, created a crisis of national identity which exactly coincided with Martí's move towards the idea of the Cuban *patria*. Yet where were the nations which in the 1880s could be said to have a secure sense of national cohesiveness? That sense seemed to be located in those European countries which by 1878 dominated and controlled 67 per cent of the land surface of the globe; in particular in a Britain which by the end of the century ruled 105 million square miles and 400 million people.[3] Here, at least, national identity and imperialism went hand in hand. Disraeli, in a speech on 'Imperial Federation' at the Crystal Palace in 1872, had referred to

> the unfailing power of the appeal to national sentiment . . . All other appeals are rooted in interests that must be grasped by reason. This one alone arouses the dark powers of the subconscious, calls into play instincts that carry over from the life habits of the dim past.[4]

Yet if Britain was the world's foremost imperial power, the rise of a phenomenon to be analogically called 'United States Imperialism' seemed to some to arise out of a lack of national identity, and the US colonial problem seemed to lie within the country, not without. For Kipling, that advocate of the civilising mission of the white nations, the Americans presented a comic spectacle of heterogeneous dissent and disorder. In his autobiographical book *From Sea to Sea*, he recounts a voyage in 1888, sailing from Japan on an American vessel, during which he overheard Americans discussing their national problems:

'They call us a Republic with a capital R. We may be, I don't think it. You Britishers have got the only republic worth the name. You choose to run your ship of state with a gilt figurehead; but I know, and so does every man who has thought about it, that your Queen doesn't cost you one-half what our system of pure democracy costs us . . . if I had money enough, I could buy the Senate of the United States, the Eagle, and the Starspangled Banner complete.'
'And the Irish vote included?' said someone – a Britisher I fancy.
'Certainly, if I chose to go yahooing down the street at the tail of the British lion. Anything dirty will buy the Irish vote.' . . .
With one accord the Americans present commenced to abuse Ireland and its people as they had met them, and each man prefaced his commination service with: 'I am an American by birth – an American from way back.'
It must be an awful thing to live in a country where you have to explain that you really belong there.[5]

The conversation then turns to the Chicago anarchist trial following the Haymarket bomb of 1886, an event which one historian has called 'a sort of domestic experiment in colonial administration'.[6] One of the Americans concludes: 'Now a war outside our borders would make us all pull together.'[7] United States' adventures in Cuba, Hawaii, Puerto Rico, Panama and the Philippines were all to show that the lesson of Britain had been learned; the paradox of nationalism was in the assertion of nationality by movement outside national boundaries; the violation of others' territory was a way of safeguarding the limits of one's own; the mapping of others' spaces was preliminary to the intimate assertion of one's own place in an interior space autonomously controlled. To establish his identity Odysseus must return to Ithaca, but to return he must first have departed.
Martí's writings about the United States took place during the period of rapacious plundering of the globe by the European powers

and the US assertion that the United States was itself the lawful heir of that piracy. As a young man in Cuba Martí was organically connected with the nationalist movement against Spanish rule. His double son-hood, fathered by Mendive as well as by his own father, connected him with the double nature of Cuban nationality: Spanish and yet needing to throw off Spain. For Martí, later to be denied his own fatherhood when his wife returned to Cuba with his son, *patria* not family was to become a way of connecting with community: 'Patria es humanidad.' Yet the pain of separation shown in the anguish of the *Ismaelillo* poems is an emotion that cannot be negated. When Martí became leader of the Cuban Revolutionary Party he was once again organically linked to the Cuban independence movement. But during that long period of exile which in fact constitutes most of his adult life Martí wandered like Odysseus, finding at best some temporary refuge which served only to underline that he was not at home.

Martí's early writings, following his arrival in the United States in 1880, show that search for the recognisable that one would expect. He applauds the appearance of a society where everyone works:

> Estoy, al fin, en un país donde cada uno parece ser dueño de sí. Se puede respirar libremente, poseer aquí la libertad, fundamento, escudo y esencia de la vida. Aquí uno puede sentirse orgulloso de su especie. Todos trabajan, todos leen.[8]

> I find myself at last in a country where everybody appears to be master of himself. You can breathe freely, possess freedom, the basis, the emblem and the essence of life. Here you can feel proud of your species. Everyone works, everybody reads.

He contrasts this with 'that idle life and poetic uselessness'[9] of the European societies he has left behind. But coinciding with that early recognition is an ability to note, for it is no more than that at this stage, discrepancies and contradictions in the scene around him. In September 1883 he compares the gaiety of Coney Island with the poverty and squalor of New York slums, where 'infantile cholera sucks life away: a boa would not do so much damage to poor children as the New York summer'.[10]

This noting of discrepancies focuses also on what Martí saw as the grotesqueries of the life around him. Slavery had ended twenty years earlier, yet negro heads furnish targets in the fairground; the United States has capital punishment, yet the man who had assassinated Garfield is allowed to read his poems from the scaffold while his brother gives interviews to the press; the sexual freedom of women alarms Martí as does the apparent lack of concern of young people for the opinions of their elders. Even over a more serious issue, that of the importation of Chinese workers, Martí manifests his bewilderment at the fact that the objections of the American workers are rooted not in the danger ιο national culture but in the fact that the Chinese work for lower wages. Three years later Martí himself seems hostile to the Chinese because they are without women: 'La mujer es la nobleza del hombre',[11] 'The noble side of man is to be found in woman.' He is curiously ambivalent about the role of the Knights of Labour, a union he regarded as pacific and principled but which had been responsible for the massacre of 159 Chinese miners in Wyoming.

Yet Martí did succeed in locating one securely recognisable area – the literature and wide influence of the transcendental movement. In the works of Emerson in particular, but also in Whitman and in the liberal abolitionists and idealist thinkers of the pre-Civil War period, Martí found a way of viewing the world which resembled his own. It is interesting to note that in his piece on the occasion of Emerson's death in May 1882 Martí precisely celebrates Emerson's ability to be at home:

> Vivió faz a faz con la Naturaleza, como si toda la tierra fuese su hogar; y el sol su propio sol, y él patriarca. Fue uno de aquellos a quienes la Naturaleza se revela y se abre, y extiende los múltiples brazos, como para cubrir con ellos el cuerpo todo de su hijo . . . Toda la Naturaleza palpitaba de la tierra. Fue su vida entera el amanecer de una noche de bodas.[12]

> He lived face to face with Nature, as if the whole earth were his home; and the sun his own sun, and he the patriarch. He was one of those to whom Nature reveals and opens herself, and extends her numerous arms, as if to cover with them the whole body of her son . . . All Nature vibrated from the earth. His [Emerson's] life was like a perpetual dawn after a wedding night.

The imagery here is of marriage and at-home-ness, that harmony for which Martí longed but which he could not locate in the life around him. More or less paraphrasing Emerson, Martí embraces his idealistic vision:

> Las contradicciones no están en la Naturaleza sino en que los hombres no saben descubrir sus analogías. No desdeña la ciencia por falsa, sino por lenta. Abrense sus libros, y rebosan verdades científicas.[13]

The contradictions lie not in Nature but in man's incapacity to discover his analogies. [Nature] does not disdain science for being false, but for being slow. Open her books, and they overflow with scientific truths.

If contradictions did not exist in Nature but only in man's false viewing, then even the best of men with the best of intentions could describe, and by describing create, those rifts which once seen were so hard to close. So Karl Marx and Wendell Phillips, both of whom Martí admired, had inadvertently, as it were, by the very strength of their passions pointed to those injustices in society which set men against each other. Phillips' obsession with abolition had led him, according to Martí, to view the whole world in the shape of a negro slave, while the great European revolutionary had manifested a too hasty view of reform. Compare Martí's piece in March 1883 on the meeting commemorating the death of Marx with his piece on the death of Emerson:

Ved esta gran sala. Karl Marx ha muerto. Como se puso del lado de los débiles, merece honor. Pero hace bien el que señala el daño, y arde en ansias generosas de ponerle remedio, sino el que enseña remedio blando al daño. Espanta la tarea de echar a los hombres sobre los hombres. Indigna el forzoso abestiamiento de unos hombres en provecho de otros. Más se ha de hallar salida a la indignación, de modo que la bestia cese, sin que se desborde, y espante. Ved esta sala: la preside, rodeado de hojas verdes, el retrato de aquel reformador ardiente, reunidor de hombres de diversos pueblos, y organizador incansable y pujante. La Internacional fue su obra: vienen a honrarlo hombres de todas las naciones. La multitud, que es de bravos braceros, cuya vista enternece y conforta, enseña más músculos que alhajas, y más caras honradas que paños sedosos. El trabajo embellece. Remoza ver a un labriego, a un herrador, o a un marinero. De manejar las fuerzas de la Naturaleza les viene a ser hermosos como ella.
    New York va siendo a modo de vorágine: cuanto en el mundo hierve, en ella cae. Acá sonrien al que huye; allá, le hacen huir. De esta bondad le ha venido a este pueblo esta fuerza. Karl Marx estudió los modos de asentar el mundo sobre nuevas bases, y despertó a los dormidos, y les enseñó el modo de echar a tierra los puntales rotos. Pero anduvo de prisa, y un tanto en la sombra, sin ver que no nacen viables, ni de seno de pueblo en la historia, ni de seno de mujer en el hogar, los hijos que no han tenido gestación natural y laboriosa. Aquí están buenos amigos de Karl Marx, que

no fue sólo movedor titánico de las cóleras de los trabajadores europeos, sino veedor profundo en la razón de las miserias humanas, y en los destinos de los hombres, y hombre comido del ansia de hacer bien. El veía en todo lo que en sí propio llevaba: rebeldía, camino a lo alto, lucha.[14]

Look at this large hall. Karl Marx is dead. He deserves to be honoured for declaring himself on the side of the weak. The virtuous man is not he who points out the damage and burns with generous anxiety to put it right, but he who teaches a gentle amendment of the injury. The task of setting men in opposition against men is frightening. The compulsory brutalisation of men for the profit of others stirs anger. But an outlet must be found for this anger, so that the brutality might cease before it overflows and terrifies. Look at this hall: dominating the room, surrounded by green leaves, is the picture of that ardent reformer, gatherer of men of diverse peoples, and tireless, powerful organiser. The International was his work: men of all nations come to honour him. The crowd, made up of valiant workers, the sight of whom affects and comforts, shows more muscles than jewels, and more honest faces than luxurious clothing. Labour embellishes. It is renewing to see a farmworker, a blacksmith, or a seaman. By manipulating the forces of Nature, they become as beautiful as she.

New York is a kind of vortex that receives everything that boils up. Here they welcome the man that escapes; there they force him to flee. From this kindness stems the strength of this nation. Karl Marx studied the means of building the world on new foundations, and awakened those that were asleep, showing them how to pull down the broken props. But Marx was in too much of a hurry, and was rather unclear; and he did not see that children who are not the outcome of a natural, slow and laborious gestation, are not born viable, whether they come from the bosom of the people in history, or those of women in the home. Here are the good friends of Karl Marx, who was not only a titanic mover of the wrath of European workers, but also showed great insight into the causes of human misery and the destiny of men. [He was] a man eaten up by a burning desire to do good. He saw in everyone what he carried in himself; rebellion, the highest ideals, struggle.

New York is a Charybdis which might suck down into itself the constantly shifting and changing forms of life. Marx is a reformer and on the side of the poor and needy, but he is precipitate. Martí's feeling about his country of exile is increasingly one of vertigo; a vocabulary of schisms, rifts, struggle, imbalance and discord begins to dominate his prose and this is eventually to be merged with a pathological imagery of disease, poison and decay. Between 1882 and 1886 Martí wrote many articles about the political and economic life of the United States. Those four years were years of depression. At least three million people were unemployed. The surplus goods of this monopoly capitalist economy were too expensive to export. Strikes to secure shorter hours and minimum wages were widespread. In July 1882 Martí had written: 'We are in the midst of the struggle of the capitalists and workers.'[15] He was acquainted with the ideas of reformers like Henry George but also feared, like Herbert Spencer, that proposals for land nationalisation would simply result in even more social divisions by creating a class of bureaucrats. In articles written between 1884 and 1886 Martí showed a strong sympathy for the workers and horror at their appalling living conditions, and underlined the justice of their demands. However, he drew back from the manner in which those demands were made. The workers were ill-educated, *incultos*; and their manner of making their demands altered the response due to them:

La justicia de una causa es deslucida muchas veces por la ignorancia y el exceso en la manera de pedirla . . . el obrero no educado en finezas mentales, ni dispuesto por lo que sufre, y ve, a dulzuras evangélicas cuando tiene que decir o hacer, lo dice o hace a manera de obrero . . . ese es el vicio que daña a casi todas las contiendas do los trabajadores: el pensador lo excusa . . . pero en la acción social es peligroso, y el gobernante tiene que reprimirlo.[16]

The justice of a cause often loses its attraction through the ignorance and exaggeration in the way it is pursued . . . the uneducated worker . . . not ready because of his sufferings and experiences to [adopt] evangelical postures, when he has to speak and act does so as a worker . . . This is the vice that undermines almost all workers' struggles; the thinker excuses it . . . but it is dangerous in its social practice, and the ruler has to repress it.

Martí did not see workers and owners as constituting antagonistic classes. Writing in September 1885 he argues that it was wrong to translate European categories into the United States as 'Acá no hay una casta que vencer',[17] 'This way there is no pure victory.' By March of the following year Martí was describing the United States as a huge battlefield where the growing workers' organisations fight against the employers in a struggle whose first victim is that national good which should transcend sectional interests, 'la vida de la nación',[18] 'the life of the nation'. For Martí national life was harmony and unity; he sought therefore, and found, in those sections which were most recognisably not quite American the source of this disharmony: European immigrants.

Writing in April 1886 Martí identifies, as many others were doing at the time, those Scandinavians, Germans, Scots and Irish as a source of disjuncture:

> Porque esta población revuelta, ya se sabe, sólo tiene de americana la última capa, la última generacion, y en muchas partes ni esa tiene – de modo que sin los frenos del patriotismo . . . esta mezcla de irlandeses, de escoceses, de alemanes, de suecos, de gente que come carne y bebe cerveza y tiene espaldas y manos atlánticas, va rápida y sin bridas, sin más bridas que las del miedo o instinto de conservación a conquistar lo que cree suyo.[19]

> Because in this mixed population, as we know, only the last layer is American, the last generation, and in many parts not even that. Without the restraints of patriotism . . . this mixture of Irish, Scots, Germans, Swedes, of people that eat meat and drink beer and have Atlantic shoulders and hands, goes fast to conquer what it believes theirs. [It acts thus] and without restraints other than fear and the instinct of self-preservation.

These layers cannot cohere, they are intrinsically turbulent. Martí's imagery is of something covering and covered, yet seething and unstable as well as violent. Like horses without a curb, the waves of immigrants are out of control and of course the absent restraint is patriotism. Patriotism is an invisible brake on passions: without it men are rifted from each other but also caught in a motion of increasing momentum. Martí's imagery throughout a whole series of articles reverts again and again to a reliance on geological metaphors of volcanic eruptions and shifting masses of earth's surface. In this turbulence the subjected now assert their will to subject:

> Nadie más que los siervos sienten la necesidad de ser señores; y como la gente trabajadora ha tenido tanto que sufrir del señorío de los que la emplean, le han entrado veleidades de déspota.[20]

> Nobody other than serfs feels the need to be masters. And since the working people have suffered so much as the hands of their employers, they have acquired despotic whims.

Even the most powerful person in the land, the President, had proved to be powerless and in the grip of forces which dominated him. Writing on the presidency of Grant, Martí noted that the man who had been a hero in war had become a kind of victim in peace. For him the paradox of Grant's disastrous presidency was a paradigm of the paradoxical nature of American life. Grant had been brought down from his mountain by the unheroic nature of American politics. Grant had sprung from Nature, yet the venality and corruption amongst which he was forced to move had denatured him.

Aquel abuso de los puestos nacionales en favor de secuaces indignos y de culpables relacionados; aquella inaudita torpeza en la elección de hombres maculados, oscuros y incapaces para los destinos de más momento y representación en la República; aquellas desconcertadas tentativas, acentuadas más que desmentidas en la carta en que se vio obligado a dar cuenta de ellas, hacia el aseguramiento de un poder a cuya permanencia tendían a toda luz los consejos íntimos del deslucido presidente; por más que se excusasen su silencio descortés, su desagrado manifiesto de oir las opiniones propias de sus secretarios oficiales, su determinación de hacer acatar en torno suyo, sin resistencia, su voluntad, inspirada u original en los asuntos públicos, con aquella severa cortesanía que se notaba en sus modales y en sus expresiones; aquella humilde manera suya para con sus subordinados; aquella modestia de su persona exterior que en él, como en tantos otros, parecía en realidad no ser más que hábil cobertor de las inmodestias temibles de adentro, ello fue que, ni todo el brillo de su viaje ostentoso alrededor del mundo, en que la grandeza de su pueblo fue reconocida y festejada en su persona, pudo mover a su pueblo a elegirlo por tercera vez a la presidencia de la Républica. Perdió su majestad, por haber comprometido la de las leyes.[21]

The abuse of public office in the interests of unworthy henchmen and their guilty contacts; that outrageous clumsiness shown in selecting obscure men with shady reputations to fill the most important and representative positions in the Republic; those slovenly attempts of his, more substantiated than contradicted in his letter of explanation, to institute a permanent power which, by all indications, his close advisers had in mind. He [Grant] was forgiven for his discourteous silence, his unconcealed disregard for the opinions of his cabinet, his determination to have everyone around him bow to his wishes in public affairs, whether those wishes were his own or the result of advice. He was excused for the austere politeness in his manner and expression, his humble manner in treating his subordinates, the superficial modesty which in him, as in so many others, appeared to be but a cover for the fearful lack of modesty within. Yet in spite of this, not even all the splendour of his ostentatious trip around the world, in which the greatness of his nation was fêted in his person, could move his people to elect him president of the Republic for a third term. He lost his own majesty for having jeopardised the majesty of the law.

Yet even the arch-conspirator President Arthur, upon whose death Martí wrote in December 1886, had shown himself incapable of rising above the corruption he himself had fostered. Here was an apparently appropriate president, the very product of the system; in him was also concentrated one aspect of the character of the nation. His attempt to reform and his failure to achieve that reform was a sign of the terminal decay of American life. 'Once the rot sets in, the social body can never recover.'[22] This corruption in the cause of personal power was a record of the decay of the spirit in America. In writing of the body of the States Martí embellishes pathological metaphors of poison and venom seeping across the continent. What we see in these articles, like those on the schism in the Catholic Church in New York, those on the South, on the lives of black people, on Indians and moves for female suffrage, is Martí's construction of the United States as a society built on difference and it is from this that he is eventually to turn away.

For Engels the tremendous industrial unrest in the 1880s was a sign of the awakening of the American working class to the idea that they too lived in a class society. In a letter of 3 June 1886, Engels wrote:

What the breakdown of Russian Czarism would be for the great military monarchies of Europe – the snapping of their mainstay – that is for the bourgeois of the whole world the breaking out of class war in America. For America after all is the ideal of all bourgeois: a country rich, vast, expanding with purely bourgeois institutions.[23]

In September of the same year he argued that American workers should and would make their own mistakes in discovering for themselves the nature of American capitalism:

Hence the American masses had to seek out their own path and seems to have found it for the time being in the K[nights] of L[abor] whose confused principles and ludicrous organisation seem to correspond to their own confusion.[24]

Engels is referring to the bomb which had exploded in Chicago's Haymarket on 4 May 1886, and which effectively put an end to the labour agitation for an eight-hour day. For Martí that bomb, following a meeting to protest at police brutality against workers the day before, is not a sign of the confusion of the American working-class movement but another example of that volcanic eruptiveness which always threatened as a result of the shifting instability of American life. In his first piece on the case, which was to become one of the most important cases in the history of the American working class, Martí wrote of the German anarchists who had been rounded up and held responsible:

En otros lugares, lo traído de Europa, violento y criminal, predomina en el movimiento obrero y lo mancha y afea . . . los que con la pujanza de la ira acumulada siglo sobre siglo en las tierras despóticas de Europa, se han venido de allá con un taller de odio en cada pecho y quieren llegar a la reorganización social por el crimen, por el incendio, por el robo, por el fraude, por el asesinato.[25]

In other places, the violent and criminal [element], brought from Europe, rules over the working-class movement, stains it and spoils it . . . those whose powerful anger accumulated over the centuries in the despotic lands of Europe have arrived from them with a store of hatred in their breast. [They] want to reorganise society through crime, arson, robbery, fraud, murder.

These men were not 'the true American workers'; Martí refers to them as 'all that foam'.[26] With metaphors of inundation, Martí creates a scenario in which the true Americans are drowned by immigrants who alternately swamp and contaminate the body of America:

Esos trabajadores, en su mayor parte alemanes, se trajeron esa turquedad rabia, esa cabeza cuadrada, esa barba hirsuta y revuelta que no orea el aire y en que las ideas se impastan. Se trajeron a sus anarquistas que . . . ní hacen más que propalar el incendio y muerte de cuanto vive y está en pie con un desorden de medios y una confusión tal de fines que los priva de aquella consideración y respeto que son de justicia para toda especie de doctrinas de buena fe encaminadas al mejor servicio del hombre.[27]

Those workers, mostly Germans, brought with them their rage, their square heads, their hairy and unkempt beards, which neither air nor ideas can percolate. They brought with them their anarchists that . . . do nothing but attempt to propagate arson and death to everything that is alive, with such disorganised means and such a confusion of aims that they forfeit that consideration and respect that are due to every doctrine that in good faith sets out to serve man.

The very nature of the Germans has put them outside human respect, they arouse disgust and fear. What is notable here is not Martí's analysis or even his description of events, for he does not describe them to any notable extent, but his struggle to find a language in which to express feelings of rejection and revulsion. This is not a prose of narrative or political argument but of emotions aroused and unleashed finally to seek a verbal form in a language which pushes into areas where logic cannot go. Martí is seeking a verbal container to structure his feelings about the United States.

On 2 September 1886, a few days after the 'guilty' verdicts, the same violence of expression is manifest:

Aquellos siete alemanes, meras bocas por donde ha venido a vaciarse sobre América el odio febril acumulado durante siglos europeos en la gente obrera; aquellos míseros incapaces de llevar sobre su razón floja el peso peligroso y enorme de la justicia.[28]

Those seven Germans, mere outlets from whom all the hatred accumulated over centuries by European workers has spewed out on America, those wretches incapable of sustaining in their feeble minds the dangerous and enormous weight of justice.

Again Martí talks of men in terms of forces of Nature and of the simultaneity of destructive and creative forces in life. The nature of society in the United States has unleashed the destructive forces of Nature itself:

Todas las grandes ideas de reforma se condensan en apóstolas y se petrifican en crímenes, según en su llameante curso prendan en almas de amor o en almas destructivas. Andan por la vida dos fuerzas, lo mismo en el seno de los hombres que en el de la atmósfera en el de la tierra. Unos están empeñados en edificar y levantar: otros nacen para abatir y destruir. Las corrientes de los tiempos dan a la vez sobre unos y otros: y así sucede que las mismas ideas que en lo que tiene de razón se llevan toda la voluntad para su justicia, engendran en las almas dañinas o confusas, con lo que tienen de pasión estados de odio que se enajenan la voluntad por su violencia.[29]

All the great ideas of reform can become apostolic in loving souls, but in destructive souls can be petrified into crime. Within man as within life, two forces live together. Some are intent on building and raising upwards; others are born to demolish and destroy. The currents of the times flow at once to one group and the other, and thus it happens that the same ideas that in rationality promote an impulse towards justice, engender through passion in confused and evil souls states of hatred that through violence alienate the power of will.

Martí describes the Chicago anarchists as

> condensados en crimen, por la herencia acumulada del trabajo servil y la cólera sorda de las generaciones esclavadas.[30]

> having become intent on crime, through the accumulated heritage of servile labour, and the silent wrath of generations of slaves.

Martí is here moving towards the position he was to take in November 1887 when he wrote after the hanging of four of the accused that it was

> un crimen nacido de sus propios delitos tanto como del fanaticismo de los criminales, para aterrar con el ejemplo de ellos, no a la chusma adolorida que jamás podrá triunfar en un país de razón, sino a las tremendas capas nacientes. El horror natural del hombre libre al crimen, junto con el acerbo encono del irlandés despótico que mira a este país como suyo y al alemán y eslavo como su invasor pusieron de parte de los privilegios en este proceso que ha sido una batalla, una batalla mal ganada e hipócrita, las simpatías y casi inhumana ayuda de los que padecen de los mismos males, el mismo desamparo el mismo bestial trabajo, la misma desgarradora miseria cuyo espectáculo constante encendió en los anarquistas de Chicago tal ansia de remediarlos que les embotó el juicio.[31]

> a crime born from their own offences as much as from the fanaticism of the criminals, to terrorise by example not the suffering rabble that could never triumph in a rational country, but the fearful emerging strata. The natural horror felt by the freeman towards crime, together with the bitter hatred of the despotic Irishman, who views this country as his own and [who sees] the Germans and Slavs as invaders, placed them [the freeman and Irish] on the side of the privileged in the trial. [The trial] has been a battle, a false and hypocritical victory, because those that suffered the

same evils [as the tried], the same helplessness, the same exploitation, the same wretched work, the same soul-destroying misery [sided with the privileged rather than supporting the] Chicago anarchists who had tried to remedy [social evils] without stopping to think.

Now it is clear where responsibility for this 'crime' lies: it is intrinsic to the United States which is so imbalanced that this 'chusma adolorida', this 'suffering rabble', can cause such a cataclysmic upheaval. And this imbalance is intrinsic because it arises out of the very history of the country: a nation made up of a series of immigrations which never cohere and a political system which cannot rectify manifest injustices.

Martí's claim that 'this Republic, through the unbridled cult of wealth, has fallen, without any of the traditional restraints, into the same inequality, injustice and violence as the monarchies' [32] is a facile dismissal of the real anger of American workers at the unequal distribution of wealth. Nor can it in any way be argued that the vast continent–country was like a despotic European kingdom. However, he was to write more certainly, and at a time [March 1894] when he could at last grasp the prospect of homecoming, in the journal which he himself had named *Patria*, a statement which can serve not as an analysis of the United States, but as a plotted map of his views of a society which existed for him as a negation of *patria*:

Lo que ha de observar el hombre honrado es precisamente que no sólo no han podido fundirse, en tres siglos de vida común, o uno de ocupación política, los elementos de origen y tendencia diversos con que se crearon los Estados Unidos, sino que la comunidad forzosa exacerba y acentúa sus diferencias primarias, y convierte la federación innatural en un estado, áspero, de violenta conquista. Es de gente menor, y de la envidia incapaz y roedora, el picar puntos a la grandeza patente, y negarla en redondo, por uno u otro lugar, o epinársele de agorero, como quien quita una mota al sol. Pero no augura, sino certifica, el que observa cómo en los Estados Unidos, en vez de apretarse las causas de unión, se aflojan; en vez de revolverse los problemas de la humanidad, se reproducen; en vez de amalgamarse en la política nacional las localidades, la dividen y la enconan; en de vez robustecerse la democracia y salvarse del odio y miseria de las monarquías, se corrumpe y aminora la democracia. [33]

What an honest man must observe is that in three centuries of common life, and one of political engagement, the different elements and tendencies of which the United States is composed did not melt. On the contrary, the forced coexistence of those [diverse elements] exaggerates their basic differences, and converts an unnatural federation into a different state of violent conquests. Only small people, capable of the worst envy, will attempt to score points off patent greatness, or even deny it altogether . . . But he that observes how in the United States a weakening occurs, instead of the causes of union getting stronger, does not predict, but confirms; the problems of humanity are not resolved, they are reproduced. Instead of unifying the regions into national politics, they are divided, and those divisions are deepened. Instead of strengthening democracy and avoiding the hatred of monarchy, democracy is corrupted and diminished.

'La federación innatural', that 'unnatural' union based on difference, is Martí's most appropriate summary of the United States In the *Odyssey*,[34] looking at the land of the Cyclops Odysseus noted to himself the potential abundance not exploited by its inhabitants:

> And they could have made this island a
> strong settlement for them.
> For it is not a bad place at all, it could
> bear all the crops
> in season, and there are meadow lands near
> the shores of the grey sea,
> well watered and soft; there could be
> grapes grown there endlessly.

This potential was not realised because of the anomic nature of the Cyclops' social structure. The society of monsters where each lived only for himself and where Odysseus was destined to encounter 'a man who was endowed with great strength, / and wild, with no true knowledge of laws or any good customs' is a land where 'each one is the law / for his own wives and children, and cares nothing about others'. In order to survive in this lawless and disordered place, Odysseus becomes Nobody; only as he sails away after maiming the monster Polyphemos does he name himself as 'Odysseus, sacker of cities'. Certainly we know, from what must be the most quoted of all Martí's remarks about the United States, in which he conflates Goliath and Leviathan, and portrays himself simultaneously as Davis and Jonah, that he saw the United States as a monster and himself, like Odysseus, who was to Polyphemos only 'a little man, niddering, feeble', as the small man who would bring that monster down. As he sailed away, Martí too turned away from the monster and named himself.

Exiled from Cuba and displaced within the United States, Martí's working out of what constituted for him culture and *patria* was a reversing out of the emotions aroused in him by that displacement and exile: anger and rejection. Restraint, moderation, harmony and unity come into being for Martí in so far as they do not exist in the United States. That society of rifts, collisions, contradictions and imbalances posits a society based on reconciliation and equilibrium. Culture and *patria* are controlling and cohering forces. Even Martí's class displacement in the United States, where he was neither one of the middle class for which his training had fitted him nor one of the émigré workers whose leader he was to become, resolved itself with the foundation of the Cuban Revolutionary Party when he took on an authentic role as agitator and organiser; when, to use Gramsci's terms, his theoretic and practical consciousnesses became one.

Martí was undoubtedly, in philosophical terms, an idealist. His love of polarities and dualities, however, is not only a result of neo-Kantian influence but was also verified by that feeling of vertigo he experienced as someone forced to live where he had 'no natural place'. From his earliest writings we can see in Martí the power of negative feelings. In 1869, in his play *Abdala*, he defined love of country as a duality between male and female, as a negation of the Other and as an act of memory:

> El amor, madre, a la patria
> No es el amor ridículo a la tierra,
> Ni a la hierba que pisan nuestras plantas;
> Es el odio invencible a quien oprime,
> Es el rencor eterno a quien la ataca;
> Y tal amor despierta en nuestro pecho
> El mundo de recuerdos que nos llama
> A la vida otra vez, cuando la sangre,
> Herida brota con angustia al alma;
> La imagen del amor que nos consuela
> Y las memorias plácidas que guarda[35]

Love, mother, for the *patria*, is not like the ridiculous love for the land, nor for the grass upon which our feet have trodden. It is the boundless hatred of its oppressors, it is the eternal rancour against the attacker. And such love awakens in our breast the world of memories that calls us to live again, when wounded the soul erupts; the image of love brings us consolation and quiet memories.

Martí was, to use Retamar's words, 'voluntarily marginalised'[36] in the United States. He lived on the periphery in a constant tension of resistance to what he felt as the massive centrifugal force of that country and drew strength, energy and purpose from his having survived that vortex. Cuba remained his centre, homecoming his destiny.

# 5 Martí and socialism

## JORGE IBARRA

Certain of the scholars that have investigated Martí's thought have sought to define him as a socialist. This fallacy arises from extreme Marxist scholars looking at the nineteenth century through the eyes of the present. The eminent British historian G. D. H. Cole argued in his *History of Socialist Thought* that Martí merits inclusion in his book. According to Cole, Martí was a revolutionary nationalist, not a socialist, whose perceptions of racial equality linked him with later developments in socialist and communist thinking in Latin America. Martí was also deeply opposed to colonialism and, according to Cole, he vigorously condemned US capitalism, especially in its imperialist dimensions. Cole concluded that Martí believed in an alliance of the working class and the nationalist middle class against the landed aristocracy. These attitudes were sufficient for Cole to consider Martí a direct predecessor of socialism in Latin America. The case for including Martí as one of the precursors of Latin American socialism is strengthened by the influence that he has exercised in the social and liberation struggles of *nuestra América* and in the manner in which his ideas were taken up by the Cuban Marxist–Leninist vanguard led by Fidel Castro.[1]

Some of Martí's contemporaries among the Cuban dependent bourgeoisie identified him as a dangerous enemy, namely a socialist. Thus, according to the annexationist José Ignacio Rodríguez, Martí was a 'victim of mental illness', a condition manifest in his vibrant oratory and fervent imagination. Rodríguez accused Martí of having been the first to introduce 'hatred for the rich, cultivated and conservative man' to the Cuban struggles, and, worse still, a hatred of the United States. This odium was evident in the 'socialist and anarchic sentiment that later dominated the revolution that owed so much to his efforts'.[2] Rodríguez left no doubt that Martí was a dangerous enemy of the interests of his class.

In this chapter, three distinguishing characteristics of Martí's ideological universe and its relationship with socialist thought are tackled: his attitude towards the working class; his critique of the competitive impulses of the bourgeoisie, i.e. the profit motive; and his relationship with current socialist Utopias and with Marxism.

## Martí and the working class

An understanding of Martí's attitudes towards the working class in the 1860s should begin from an examination of his social origins. Martí came from an artisan family who did not share the socialist and anarchist ideas that were taking root among Cuban workers. His father, mother and sisters worked at home on a putting-out basis for a small tailor's business producing military uniforms for the Casa Borrel. Hence the words of Professor Herrera Franyutti:

> It is possible that the origins of Martí's interest in the working-class question lay in his private reactions towards the daily conditions of work in his own home that he was not subsequently to develop. In his own words, in *Versos sencillos*: 'I think of my father, the soldier: / I think of my father, the worker.' The working-class question has not been forgotten by Martí but it is a problem that resides in himself, not a political one.[3]

Although their living conditions did not differ significantly from those prevailing among the proletariat of Havana, Martí's family was not subject to the same exploitation as factory workers, nor did it show solidarity with their plight. Martí's sensitivity to his environment was not translated into a theoretical formulation of the class struggle and of the role of the proletariat. His innate sympathy for the suffering of the working class is clear, but he was precluded by his ideological horizon from fully grasping the problems of the working class. By birth Martí belonged to the humblest sectors of the Cuban colony, but he shared the intellectual formation of the enlightened sectors of the *independentista* middle class exiled in the USA. The memories, the nostalgia and the patriotic yearning of this charmed circle incited Martí continuously to action. Martí's radical opposition to the anti-national attitudes of the Cuban bourgeoisie – annexationism and autonomism – was shaped largely by his membership of the uprooted émigré community that obstinately rejected both absorption by the *entrañas convulsas* of US society and reintegration with the decadent world of the Colony. The émigré community had become the repository of patriotic ideas, beliefs and traditions that came to constitute the national consciousness.

Paul Estrade has usefully re-evaluated Martí's ideas on the working class around 1875–6. At that time Martí had neither come into contact with the Cuban émigré workers nor become aware of the exploitation borne by the proletariat in the United States. He could be said to have a liberal position permeated by reformist ideas present among Mexican workers. Paul Estrade put it as follows:

> His social ideas while in Mexico do not stand out for their originality or their radicalism, but they are coherent and healthy, moulded by a certain social praxis. They place Martí among the most advanced of his contemporaries and even make of him the most open of Latin American political thinkers to the working-class movement.[4]

Martí's connections with the US working class in 1883 enabled him to understand its fundamental role in social production:

> El hombre crece con el trabajo que sale de sus manos. Es fácil ver cómo se depaupera, y envilece a las pocas generaciones, la gente ociosa, hasta que son meras vejiguillas de barro, con extremidades finas, que cubren de perfumes suaves y de botines de charol; mientras que el que debe su bienestar a su trabajo, o ha ocupado su vida en crear y transformar fuerzas, y en emplear las propias, tiene el ojo alegre, la palabra pintoresca y profunda las espaldas anchas, y la mano segura. Se ve que son ésos los que hacen el mundo; y engrandecidos, sin saberlo acaso, por el ejercicio de su poder de creación, tienen cierto aire de gigantes dichosos, e inspiran ternura y respeto.[5]

Man grows with the work that comes from his hands. It is easy to see how the idle are impoverished and degraded in a few generations, until they are but fragile vessels of clay, with feeble legs which they cover with sweet-smelling perfumes and patent boots. He that owes his well-being to his work or has spent his life creating and transforming forces using his own strength, has a happy eye, a colourful and profound word, broad shoulders and a sure hand. These are the people that make the world; and maybe unknowingly, through the exercise of their creative powers, they acquire a certain air of happy giants, and inspire tenderness and respect.

The more that Martí got to know US society the more he came to grasp the bitter realities that lay behind the façade of general prosperity. He delivered an increasingly vigorous onslaught against the living and working conditions of the lower strata of society, especially the urban workers.

Se oyen de estos estados pompas y maravillas. Se dice que un albañil gana tres pesos al día, sin contar con que apenas trabaja seis meses al año, lo cual lo deja en peso y medio diario, que es lo que necesita para no caerse al suelo. Se dice por los filósofos amables, y por los caballeros que saben griego y latin, que no hay obrero mejor vestido y calzado que el americano, y que ésta es Jauja, y que hacen muy mal en enojarse, en vez de estar agradecidos a su eximia fortuna.

¡Ah! Así como los jueces debieran vivir un mes como penados en los presidios y cárceles para conocer las causas reales y hondas del crimen, y dictar sentencias justas, así los que deseen hablar con juicio sobre la condición de los obreros, deben apearse a ellos y conocer de cerca su miseria.[6]

Much is heard of the glories of the States. It is said that a bricklayer earns three pesos a day. But this does not take into account that he hardly works six months a year, which leaves him with one and a half pesos a day, just enough to keep him alive. It is said by amiable philosophers and gentlemen who know Greek and Latin that no worker is better clothed and shod than there in the United States, and that the United States is Eldorado and the workers should be grateful for their good fortune.

Just as, in order to be able to pass just sentence, a judge should spend a month as a prisoner to understand the profound causes of crime, so those that want to pronounce on the condition of the workers must know their misery closely.

On another occasion Martí described the conflicts between workers and capitalists as follows:

Estamos en plena lucha entre capitalistas y obreros. Para los primeros son el crédito en los bancos, las esperas de los acreedores, los plazos de los vendedores, las cuentas de fin de año. Para el obrero es la cuenta diaria, la necesidad urgente e inaplazable, la mujer y el hijo que comen por la tarde lo que el pobre trabajó para ellos por la mañana. Y el capitalista holgado constriñe al pobre obrero a trabajar a precio ruín.[7]

We are in the midst of a struggle between capitalists and workers. For the capitalist the problem is credit from the banks, expectations from the creditors, loans to salesmen, and the end-of-the-year accounts. For the worker the problem is the daily expenses, the day-to-day need for the wife and child to consume in the evening what the poor worker earned for them during the day. And the well-to-do capitalist compels the poor worker to toil for a song.

The years 1885–7 are decisive in the ideological evolution of Martí. In 1885, Martí had complete trust in the popular vote, which he considered suitable for the United States but not for Europe; he had faith too in the representatives elected by the people and he believed that the democratic system ruling in the United States was the solution to all problems. But by 1887, he understood that such a system was a fraud. It has been rightly said that these years marked Martí's transition from liberal thought permeated by the reformist ideology of the Mexican workers to the most advanced democratic-revolutionary thought of his era, a transition in which he was influenced decisively by the Cuban émigré workers and his adoption of an anti-imperialist ideology.

Between 1885 and 1887 Martí wrote his seminal essay, 'Nuestra América', in which he set out the basis of an alliance between the enlightened middle classes, the peasantry and the working class against the landowning oligarchy and US imperialist penetration. In this period, Martí became convinced that the US Congress and US executive represented the interests of large landowners, railway magnates, mining bosses and industrial tycoons rather than those of the people.

When the trial of the Chicago workers began in 1886, Martí admitted that the accused 'incited butchery'. For him, the accused were 'mere mouths which emptied on America the feverish hatred stored for centuries by the working class in Europe'.[8] While in 1886 Martí accepted the guilty verdict, in November 1887 he castigated those that applied the law rigidly. He wrote that it was unforgivable to 'pass judgement on social offences without knowing and weighing up the causes that gave rise to them and the generous impulses that produce them'.

In the same years, Martí's critique of the US monopolies began to take shape. He argued that the small industrialists with few resources beyond their own energy and scant capital could not expect to resist vast corporations formed by the concentration of unemployed capital. Martí concluded this discussion as follows:

La tiranía acorralada en lo político, reaparece en lo comercial. Este país industrial tiene un tirano industrial. Este problema apuntado aquí de pasada, es uno de aquellos graves y sombríos que acaso en paz no puedan decidirse, y ha de ser decidido aquí donde se plantea, antes tal vez de que termine el siglo.[9]

Tyranny, defeated in politics, has reappeared in commerce. This industrial country has an industrial tyrant. The problem noted here in passing is so grave and sombre that it may not have a peaceful solution. This must be found here, where the problem is posed, perhaps, before the century ends.

Far from being solved the problem was to become more complex, profound and dangerous.

Finally, 1885–7 were the years when Martí became interested in the social programme of Henry George and the socialist Utopias of Edward Bellamy.

## Martí's response to competition

Martí's stand against the mercantile spirit that underpinned the capitalist system of production amounted to an attack against its very foundations. According to Marx, merchandise and, by extension, trading relationships constitute the nucleus of capitalism. In this sense, Martí's critique of the profit motive which he saw as the moving force of capitalist society, is a first step towards a socialist awareness. For the young Marx and many of his disciples, the critique of the profit motive preceded an adoption of a socialist consciousness based on scientific premisses. The 'moral republic' of which Martí spoke in the Manifiesto de Montecristi, must be the antithesis of the 'imperial republic'. In all his subsequent writings, Martí developed the proposition that a *pueblo* should be founded on the basis of ethical, not mercantile, principles:

El pueblo más grande no es aquel en que una riqueza desigual y desenfrenada produce hombres crudos y sórdidos, y mujeres venales y egoístas: pueblo grande, cualquiera que sea su tamaño, es aquel que da hombres generosos y mujeres puras. La prueba de cada civilización humana está en la especie de hombre y de mujer que en ella se produce.[10]

The greatest people is not one in which an unequal and boundless wealth produces crude and sordid men and venal and egoistic women: a great pueblo, regardless, of its size, is one of generous men and pure women. The yardstick of any human civilisation is the kind of men and women it produces.

Education is the most appropriate means by which to create, from the nursery, men and women of this new type, who are not guided by monetary considerations.

Y otros padres fomentan en el hijo la pasión de la riqueza, sin ver que sólo dura aquella que se cría sudor a sudor; y le espolean la ansiedad de acaudalar, sin ver que las agonías de la fortuna intrigante son de más naúseas, y de fin más cruento, que el de la riqueza natural o la plaza decorosa. ¡A qué vencer a los viles en la pelea falsa del mundo, si para vencerlos es preciso ser más vil que ellos? En ser vencidos es en lo que está el honor: en verlos pálidos de miedo, colorados de champaña, espantosos de odio, muertos de frenesí. El rincón de la casa es lo mejor, con la majestad del pensar libre, y el tesoro moderado de la honradez astuta y un coro amigo junto a la taza de café.[11]

And some parents instil in the child a passion for wealth, oblivious to the fact that the only durable wealth results from the sweat of the brow. They spur their children into accumulation without seeing that the agonies of cunning fortune are more loathsome and have a more deadly end than natural riches or a decent profession. Why win over the evil men, in the false quarrels of the world, if to defeat them it is necessary to be more evil than they? Honour is to be found in defeat, in seeing them pallid with fear, red with champagne, trembling with hatred, shaking with frenzy. The hearth of the home is the best place, with the kingdom of free thought, the small treasure of clever honesty, and a group of friends to drink coffee.

A boundless desire for riches leads to the extinction of society and of the individual:

Así mueren los pueblos, como los hombres, cuando por bajeza o brutalidad prefieren los goces violentos del dinero a los objetos más fáciles y nobles de la vida: el lujo pudre.[12]

Thus die peoples, like men, when through brutality and abjectness they prefer the violent pleasures of money to the easier and more noble object of life: luxury rots the soul.

On the question of evolving an alternative to the US model of society Martí wrote:

En este pueblo revuelto, suntuoso y enorme, la vida no es más que la conquista de la fortuna: esta es la enfermedad de su grandeza. La lleva sobre el hígado: se le ha entrado por todas las entrañas: lo esta trastornando, afeando y deformando todo. Los que imiten a este pueblo grandioso, cuiden de no caer en ella.[13]

In this mixed, luxurious and vast people, life is but the conquest of fortune: this is the infirmity of its greatness. It is consuming its liver, gnawing its entrails: changing, deforming and corroding everything. Those that imitate this great people should take care not to fall for its illness.

And to crown the idea that moral and not mercantile values must govern the society that he yearned for, Martí wrote:

La prosperidad que no está subordinada a la virtud avillana y degrada a los pueblos; los endurece, corrompe y descompone.[14]

Prosperity that is not subordinate to virtue vilifies and degrades peoples; it hardens them, corrupts them and is reasonable for their decomposition.

Many analogous thoughts can be cited in the writing of Martí. These are sufficient to demonstrate that Martí was radically opposed to the corrupting power of money.

## Martí, Marxism and social Utopianism

The relationship of Martí with the social Utopianism of his time and with Marxism has now to be established. His singular position in the history of socialist thought does not allow a precise placing of Martí among the ideological currents of the nineteenth century. For this reason attempts to classify him in the same terms as European and Asian revolutionary democrats of the past century have encountered difficulties. Paul Estrade has drawn out with prudence and clarity the points of difference between Martí and his contemporaries. Only a study of the social and historical context in which he formulated his view of the world can help in a theoretical approach to his thought. To fail in making such a study would result in the writing of a history of ideas that went no further than a Hegelian scheme of history.

Hans Otto Dill, a prominent philologist, in his analysis of other facets of Martí's thought has reached the conclusion that Martí was a convinced anti-capitalist who aspired to a non-capitalist path of development for Latin American countries.[15] There are insuperable difficulties in this argument. Martí's point of departure in his project of national liberation was a society based on small producers. He did not envisage a way to socialism in which the evils of a highly developed capitalist society would be wiped out. Hans Otto Dill does not go so far as to make Martí into a socialist, but when writing that Martí sought non-capitalist forms of organisation, Dill omits to mention that Martí championed the small trader and farmer. Doubtless, Martí did not realise that the society that he visualised would be equally antagonistic to the ethical principles that would govern social relations in his theoretical scheme. He saw a total hostility between the excesses of industrial capitalism and the moral values that he preached.

A society organised on the basis of the individual producer must, in the long run, be opposed to the moral postulates of Martí. This contradiction stemmed from the total incompatibility of the values of Martí with those of capitalism. Martí could not accept that man was reduced to a dehumanised instrument of an economic system, or was obliged to sell his labour in the market place. In order to establish how far his ideology was open to radicalisation it is necessary to compare it with related ideological systems, namely with the social programme of Henry George, and with Marxist theory. It is important to establish how much further Martí went than George in his critique of profit-motivation as the mentor of capitalism and in his indictment of the political and economic power of monopolies. It is also important to point out where Martí was as advanced in his critique of US capitalism as those German socialists who had embraced Marxism, and where he stopped short.

This is the appropriate moment to elucidate the ideological framework behind Martí's critique, written in 1884, of the article by Herbert Spencer, 'The Future of Slavery'. As is well known, Martí openly admired the logic of Spencer's discourse and the clarity of his style. In the introduction to his critique the *martiano* purpose of drawing out, amplifying and debating the ideas he was reviewing can already be seen. Martí's first objections to the Spencerian idea that socialism was the future slavery, were expressed as marginal comments on the personality and style of the British sociologist. According to Martí, Spencer's study was written 'in the manner of a Greek citizen for whom the lower orders do not count'. This attitude of Spencer was connected, in Martí's eyes, to his perception of English literature as aristocratic and snobbish ('como en ropas de lord'). For Martí English literature does not achieve that desirable universal influence which its profound thought and melodious form merit, because of its disdainful and haughty manner, which at the same time constitutes its originality.

Martí continues by outlining the fundamental ideas of Spencer. The poor laws encourage idleness; the construction of workers' housing and the nationalisation of the railways give rise to a caste of employees and bureaucrats that lives off the workers. Martí begins by objecting that the nationalisation of the railways, though having some disadvantages, fulfils 'high moral aims', like terminating 'the corrupting games of the stock exchange'. Martí goes on to agree with Spencer that the increasingly active and dominant intervention of the capitalist state would impose a very heavy burden upon the population at work so as to benefit the poor. 'The poor', according to Spencer, consisted of the unemployed and lumpen proletariat of the English cities of the nineteenth century.

Martí claimed that the poor laws in a capitalist state 'do not cure the evil' but merely attack its symptoms. Martí favoured the building of workers' housing because it contributed to the relief of urban poverty, and rejected the notion of Spencer that such construction would inhibit the market in 'housing of a richer style'.

In his review Martí referred to Spencer's anxiety that George's proposal to nationalise railways and the project of the Democratic Federation to create 'industrial and agrarian armies' 'would increase terribly the already inordinate number of public sector workers' that formed 'a new caste of functionaries'. Since 1884 Martí had been broadly sympathetic to the ideas espoused by George.

Martí reviewed with precision the argument of Spencer that man would cease to be 'his own servant and become that of the state. From being a slave of capitalists man would become a slave of functionaries. A slave is a person who works for another who has total control over him; and under the socialist system the country exerts control over the individual.' It is interesting to stress that Cuban exile historians have attributed to Martí the views of Spencer which he merely describes. This crude falsification of Martí's thought is used by dissident Cubans to justify their opposition to socialism.

Martí's review finishes by opposing Spencer's condemnation of

los modos naturales de equilibrar la riqueza pública dividida con tal inhumanidad en Inglaterra, que ha de mantener naturalmente en ira, desconsuelo y desesperación a seres humanos que se roen los puños de hambre en las mismas calles por donde pasean hoscos y erguidos otros seres humanos que con las rentas de un año de sus propiedades pueden cubrir a toda Inglaterra de guineas. Nosotros diríamos a la política: ¡Yerra, pero consuela! Que el que consuela, nunca yerra.[16]

the natural modes of balancing public wealth which in England is so inhumanly divided that it must provoke the wrath, sorrow and despair of these human beings suffering a desperate hunger. [These people share] the same streets with other human beings that walk with a haughty and hostile air. [They are] property-owners whose annual incomes could cover all England in guineas. We make mistakes, [Martí] would say to politicians – but we bring consolation! Those who bring comfort, can never be mistaken.

## *Martí and Henry George*

Martí's adherence to the nationalisation programme of Henry George can be seen in his 'Escenas norteamericanas' which he wrote for the Buenos Aires newspaper, *La Nación*. Referring to George and other social reformers who advocated some form of land nationalisation, Martí wrote:

> Estos son santos nuevos, que van por el mundo cerrando puertas al odio. Ven venir al huracán y lo van guiando. Como método usan la paz. Como fin, ven que la tierra se administre de modo que su producto sea repartido equitativamente entre todos los hombres. Creen estos apóstoles que, puesto que el suelo público ha de llegar a ser del pueblo que en él vive, mientras menos se vaya dando de él, menos costará luego sacarlo de las manos de los que por cohecho o astucia se fueron alzando con los dominios públicos.[17]

> These are new saints that walk the world closing doors on hatred. They see the hurricane coming and they channel it using peace as their instrument. Observing that the land has never denied man his needs, they [the reformers] want the land to be administered in such a way that its products are shared equitably among all men . . . These apostles believe that since lands must eventually belong to those that live upon them, the less often they are sold the fewer problems there will be in recovering them from those that acquired them through corruption and trickery.

In another passage in which he refers to the movement created around the social ideas and political personality of George, Martí shows his close allegiance to the programme of nationalisation:

> Pero lo que en realidad tiene el himno es el empuje, el cariño, la fe contagiosa y simpática con que los trabajadores de Nueva York unidos por primera vez en un serio esfuerzo político, intentan elegir corregidor de esta ciudad del trabajo a uno de los pensadores más sanos, atrevidos y limpios que ponen hoy les ojos sobre las entrañas del nuevo universo, a Henry George. El, con su frente socrática, parece irradiar luz sobre esta apostólica campaña.

Sacerdotes lo ayudan, y reformadores que parecen sacerdotes. Lo auxilian con su palabra y su influjo muchos latinoamericanos.[18]

The strength of the hymn lies in the thrust, the tenderness, the contagious and sympathetic faith with which the workers of New York united for the first time in a serious political endeavour, try to elect as mayor for this labouring city, Henry George, one of the cleanest and most daring thinkers that cast their eyes on the confused entrails of the new universe.

He, of the socratic head, seems to radiate light on this apostolic campaign. Priests help him and priest-like reformers assist him with their words and their influence over many Latin Americans.

In another commentary upon the new political party, Martí advocated a break with its German socialist members:

El partido que asomó hace ocho meses con la candidatura de Henry George en Nueva York, ya se insinúa en el campo, arrebata falanges enteras a los partidos antiguos decrépitos, y en su segundo esfuerzo reaparece organizado y triunfante en las capitales de más riqueza e influjo. Sucede lo que en estas cartas se ha previsto: Los trabajadores, los reformadores vehementes que los dirigen o combaten a su lado, están decididos a luchar juntos por las vías de la ley para obtener el gobierno del país, y cambiar desde él, en lo que tienen de injusto, las relaciones de los elementos sociales. Lo que les falta para el triunfo, o para estar en disposición de aspirar con probabilidades favorables a él, es su constitución definitiva como partido americano libre de ligas con los revolucionarios europeos.[19]

The party that came into existence eight months ago with the candidacy of Henry George in New York, is already making inroads in the countryside, and is tearing away entire phalanxes from the decrepit old parties. In its second drive the party reappears organized and triumphant in the richest and most influential cities. What is happening is what has been foreseen in these letters. The workers, the vehement reformers that lead them or fight by their side, have decided to struggle together through legal channels to gain the government of the country and to bring justice to all. What is needed to triumph or to be ready for it is for the party to become an American party free of all ties with European revolutionaries.

The support that Martí gave George on his decision to expel the German socialists from the movement is, in a certain sense, explicable. As Engels pointed out, the German socialists had divorced themselves from the US masses by adopting dogmatic procedures and methods and by opposing integration into the nation. Thus in a letter to Florence Kelly, dated 28 December 1886, Engels pointed out one serious error of the German socialists. They tried both to impose on a US movement with its own traditions European theories that they did not understand and to convert these theories into exclusive dogmas. In his rejoinder Engels claimed that the theories that he had elaborated with Marx were not dogmas but expositions of an evolutionary process. 'To expect that the [North] Americans began from a fully fledged awareness of a theory elaborated in the old industrial countries is to expect the impossible . . .'[20] In a letter to F. A. Sorge, dated 29 November 1886, Engels criticised the German socialists further:

> The Germans have not learnt to use their theories as a springboard to mobilise the [North] American masses. The majority does not understand the theory, and treat it in an abstract and dogmatic manner, as something to be learnt by heart, which without further ado will cover all needs. For them it is a creed, and not a guide for action. To this must be added that in principle they refuse to learn English.[21]

Engels had rejected the pretensions of one of the German socialist leaders, John Most, to be a disciple of Marx. Martí had referred to Most as 'a persistent boaster and firebrand, that did not carry in his right hand the balm for the wounds which his left hand had opened'. In a letter to Philip Van Patten on 18 April 1883, Engels wrote that Marx and he despised Most's anarchist ideas and tactics.[22] Marx, who had been acquainted with Most in England, called him a man of the most puerile vanity without intellectual stability. Writing about the newspaper directed by Most, Marx wrote that it lacked revolutionary content and was outstanding only for its revolutionary phraseology.[23] It is evident that the presence of people like Most in the United States confused Martí's perception of Marx.

The features of George's theories that most attracted Martí were described by him in several articles. He wrote, for example, the following enthusiastic description of a public event at which George spoke:

> 'La pobreza es injusta', decía Henry George, en su discurso salpicado de sabia ironía, de patéticos recuerdos, de familiares abandonados, de aquellas sentidas y profundas palabras en que se

revela su ardiente concurso con los dolores humanos. 'No queremos quitar a nadie su riqueza, sino crear más riqueza de la que hay. Cada vivo, el negro más infeliz, el niño mísero que nace sin pañales en una casa de vecindad, tiene derecho a la extensión de tierra necesaria para nutrir su vida, puesto que nace.' [24]

'Poverty is unjust', Henry George would say in a speech flavoured with shrewd irony, sad memories, full of images of abandoned families, of heartfelt and profound words in which is revealed his burning empathy with human pain. 'We do not want to take wealth from anybody but to create more wealth than there is. Every human being, the unhappiest black, the wretched child born to misery in a slum, has a right to a plot of land sufficient to feed him. This is his birthright.'

Martí wrote on George's *Progress and Poverty* as follows:

En la obra, destinada a incurrir las causas de la pobreza creciente a pesar de los adelantos humanos, predomina como idea esencial la de que la tierra debe pertenecer a la Nación. De allí deriva el libro todas las reformas necesarias. Posea tierra el que la trabaje y la mejore. Pague por ella al Estado mientras la use. Nadie posea tierra sin pagar al Estado por usarla. No se pague al Estado más contribución que la renta de la tierra. Así el peso de los tributos a la Nación caerá sobre los que reciban de ella manera de pagarlos, la vida sin tributos será barata y fácil, y el pobre tendrá casa y espacio para cultivar su mente, entender sus deberes públicos, y amar a sus hijos. [25]

In this work, which examines the causes of growing poverty in spite of human progress, the essential idea is that the land must belong to the nation. From here, the book derives all the essential reforms. He who works and improves the land should own it. He should pay the state for it while he uses it. Nobody should possess the land without paying the state for using it. Nobody should pay the state a tax beyond the land rental. Thus the weight of national taxes will fall upon those that have received [from the nation] the means of paying them . . . Life without taxes will be cheap and easy and the poor will have a home and time to cultivate their minds, understand their civic duties and love their children.

George has been extensively quoted in order to demonstrate beyond all doubt the extent to which Martí identified with him. It remains necessary to explain the principal tenets of George's theory and their special appeal for Martí. The US preacher sought to preserve the capitalist system in the United States by diverting the floating population of the cities and the mass immigration of the North American ports towards farming. This device was his principal means of mitigating class confrontation in the great cities. The condition of the working class should, he argued, be improved with the abolition of all taxes. Any worker that felt exploited by the demoralising conditions of the factories could emigrate to the countryside where he would be guaranteed a plot of land. Consequently, industrial wages must be equal to the income of farmers.

George's theory set out to achieve a relative stability in social conflict. The properties of the industrial and commercial bourgeoisie of the large cities and also of the urban middle class were considered intangible. The rural proprietors would become tenants of the state, the sole rural landlord. The aim of the fiscal system was to reallocate to the state through taxation the incomes previously due to the large landowners, in order to level down their incomes to those of the small producers who would rent their land from the state. The originality of George lay in his use of socialist methods and procedures, like land nationalisation, in order to preserve the capitalist system. The facilities offered by the state to any worker to establish himself as a tenant farmer were intended to have the same effects upon the consciousness of the working class as the abundance of free land for the dispossessed had in the eighteenth century and the first half of the nineteenth. George's theories could not find a sustained backing among the exploited classes in US society. They attracted neither the small proprietors who, in George's scheme, would be dispossessed of their land in order to become tenants of a bourgeois state, nor the urban workers who were denied genuine support in their daily struggles in the factories.

Nevertheless, Martí felt attracted to George's project because it offered an egalitarian ideology for small producers as an alternative to the path of industrial capitalism, with its gross inequalities and contradictions. George's model proposed a utopian solution to the inevitable crisis of industrial capitalism. Martí wanted to shield the Cuban republic from the inhuman relationships of industrial capitalism experienced in the United States. His ideal of social harmony must be realised in a model of bourgeois society that was opposed to all contemporary models. Such an ideal did not imply a return to a society of natural economy or to pre-capitalist forms. Believing in the harmonic development of all productive forces, Martí was neither a populist nor a romantic apologist for the past, like some of the critics of Lenin in Russia.

The political movement led by George soon demonstrated its utopian character. As a consequence of the expulsion of the German socialists, the movement lost its fighting edge and dissolved. It is difficult to establish what lessons Martí learnt from the dissolution of George's movement, but in 1893 his call to the Cuban émigré workers to embrace the independence cause was still linked to his *idée fixe* that Cuba should found a new society based on specific humanistic principles of the middle class. The political failure of George did not dissuade Martí, who wrote, in 1893, of the necessity of making land available to those that worked it and taking it away from those that did not.

## The social criticism of Martí

Although the programme that Martí espoused could not resolve all social ills his critique of US capitalist society was one of the most thorough of the period. His social criticism, which had as its point of departure a revolutionary ethic, could, therefore, act as a weapon against capitalist societies. Martí's critique of US society coincided with its Marxist counterpart and in certain respects preceded and enriched it. His analysis of the arbitrary and irrational nature of monopolies and of industrial capitalism extended to include the political power that results from such a social formation. Martí described with unusual precision the relationship of the industrial and monopolist bourgeoisie with US politics. In this light he said that Congress must be an expression of the popular will, not of the monopolies. US democracy could be nothing but fraudulent while the large monopolies ruled the country. Martí harboured no illusion about US democracy and its institutions:

¿Qué ha hecho para atajar esos males el Senado, donde los millonarios, los grandes terratenientes, los grandes ferrocarrileros, los grandes mineros componen mayoría, aunque los senadores son electos por las legislaturas, elegidas directamente por el pueblo, que no tiene las minas, ni la tierra, ni los ferrocarriles? ¿Por qué mágico tamiz sale filtrada la representación popular, de modo que al perfeccionarse en el senador, que es su entidad más alta fuera de la Presidencia, resulta ser el Senado la contradicción viva de las opiniones o intereses de los que, por medio de la legislatura, los elige? ¡Los senadores compran las legislaturas! ¿Qué ha hecho la Casa de los Representantes, electos ya por tan viciados métodos que, aunque el país vote por ellos directamente, no hay elección que no resulte forzada por el uso de recias sumas de dinero? ¿Ni se ha alzado en la Casa una voz sola que denuncie el peligro y clamo por los necesitados?[26]

What has the Senate done to stop these evils, the Senate where the millionaires, the large landowners, the railway magnates, the mining tycoons, form the majority, despite the fact that the senators are chosen by the legislatures elected directly by the people that do not own the mines, the land or the railways? Through what magic sieve has popular representation been filtered . . . that the Senate, the highest entity outside the Presidency, turns out to be the living contradiction of opinions and interests of those that through the legislature elect the senators? The senators buy the legislatures! Although the country votes for it directly, the House of Representatives is chosen by such corrupt methods that every election is falsified by the use of vast sums of money. Has a single voice been raised in the House to denounce the danger and to speak for the needy?

The moral sensitivity of Martí points continuously at the inhumanity of capitalist relationships. When he spoke of Chauncey Depew, the great shareholder in the Vanderbilt railway monopoly, who became a presidential hopeful, Martí described him in the following terms: 'The man matters little, what matters more is the railway.' In a similar way he wrote of the social relationships to which Cuban workers were subjected in the United States. The language of Martí always found the most acid vocabulary to describe such relationships. Cuban workers were exposed to the 'sharpened jaws' of capital and to the 'oven of wrath' of US society. Of US congressmen he said during a vote on popular reforms: 'If they voted for the Motherland, they would be going against their own interest. They are serfs ruled by a whip of gold. The vote was shameful and sordid, and they came out with their heads bowed in shame like beaten dogs.'[27]

The moral indignation pervading Martí's critique of the de-humanising power of monopoly capital is comparable only with that felt by Marx and Engels against the abuses of bourgeois society. This attitude goes hand in hand with Martí's repudiation of the tendency within industrial capitalism to reduce all values to the commercial. Martí's language is more harsh and violent than that of George and other contemporary US critics – both socialist and reformist. In order to evaluate the theories of Martí in terms of those of George, a comparison of both figures is inescapable. The subjective reasons that led George to elaborate his social theory were different from those that converted Martí into one of its most vehement defenders. The main difference was that George conceived his theory as an instrument for preserving industrial capitalism, while Martí perceived George's theory as an alternative to industrial capitalism, since that could be used to overcome the vast inequalities of landownership. For George the problem was to rescue the industrial monopolist bourgeoisie from social revolution, while for Martí the most important priority was to alleviate the conditions of the middle and working classes. While in *Progress and Poverty* George abstained from criticising monopolistic practices, Martí in 'Escenas norteamericanas' delivered one of the most severe attacks of the nineteenth century against monopoly power. A genuine difference in their theoretical positions is evident. George did not censure the profit motive as the driving force behind capitalism. Martí, on the contrary, focused his attacks against industrial capitalism on the drive for profits and on the commercialisation of all human relationships. In a letter to F. A. Sorge, dated 30 July 1881, Marx defined the objectives of George as 'an attempt, thinly disguised as socialism, to save capitalist domination, and, what is more, to re-establish it on a wider basis than at present'.[28] However, Marx in the same letter said that the measures on rural rents recommended by George as a panacea constituted one of the transitional measures included in *The Communist Manifesto*.

The liquidation of the movement led by George forced Martí to find other channels for his social conscience. As early as 1889 he had referred in *La Opinión Pública* of Montevideo to the progressive character of certain intellectual circles sponsored by the industrial bourgeoisie of Boston. In his first comment he confined himself to acknowledging the liberal spirit prevailing there: Paris apart, Boston was 'the city, where new opinions were treated with most respect'. While in New York 'they hunt socialists through the streets', in Boston 'the thinkers get together to discuss public ills'.

## Martí and Bellamy

The climate was now propitious for the diffusion of the ideas of the Utopian socialist Edward Bellamy in the so-called socialist clubs which started in Boston and covered the whole country. The movement published a paper, *The Nationalist*, which propagated its vision of a future Communist society. It had its origins in the novel by Bellamy, *Looking Backward*, which foresaw the shape of US society in the year 2000. The novel's protagonist explains that all US citizens, regardless of their class origins, had reached the conclusion that the solution of all contradictions lay in the establishment of a communist society. Martí assessed the book in the following way: 'And all Texas goes around with Bellamy's book under their arms, reading the chapter where he tells how railways will be managed in a hundred years' time . . . and they use the railways without paying just as now, they use the streets.'[29]

Martí refers twice to the communist society foreseen in Bellamy's newspaper in terms that suggest that he approved of its last projected stages. After referring to the 'farsighted thinkers of the country' who wrote for *The Nationalist* as those that neither 'trample on people's backs', nor address the people 'with voices that come from Europe', Martí cites textually a paragraph taken from one of the articles of the newspaper, which sums up the socialist ideas of Bellamy and his colleagues. They wanted the inhuman order of proud castes and the new feudalism of the landowners to be changed, without violent methods, into a new, less vain and more serene order where industries and natural resources were not concentrated in the hands of private monopolists for their exclusive benefit, but in the hands of the nation for the benefit of all.[30]

This sympathy for the Utopia of Bellamy will be considered with more depth in a final note on the socialist projects of the Bostonians. According to Martí, they had gone as far as seeking.

> que este orden inhumano de castas soberbias, este feudalismo nuevo de los terratenientes, se cambie, sin métodos rudos, en otro orden menos vano y más sereno, donde las industrias, y los bienes perennes y comunes de la naturaleza, no están concentrados en manos de monopolios privados, para el beneficio de los monopolios, sino en manos de la nación, para el beneficio nacional.[31]

> that industries be nationalised, to eradicate the tempter magnate and these venal politicians, and not to work in order to have more than the neighbours. [They sought] not to cultivate what is base and vile in man but to live frugally, within individual freedom and with time and leisure to enjoy the things of the heart and of the mind.

Martí continues by citing a commentator – evidently himself or a critic with many of the same ideas – in order to elaborate his view on the future communist society outlined in these Utopias: 'The day will come', says the commentator, 'in which a manner will be found – because it is only a question of manner – of overthrowing this immoral order, without violence, and without taking any action contrary to individual nature or even the inevitable but necessary defects of men.'[32] Doubtless this is a decisive moment in the ideological evolution of Martí, as he comes to accept the necessity for the pillars of capitalism to collapse in the future and for a new society to be built according to the outlines of current socialist Utopias. It is necessary to analyse these marginal comments within context.

In the first place, the relationship that Martí establishes with this project is purely intellectual. Martí assumes a distance from the space and social time of the utopias he describes. The imaginary programme that Bellamy envisages would be a reality only towards the year 2000. Because the project was so distant, it did not constitute for Martí a moral imperative that compelled him to act immediately to realise it. Furthermore, the nature of the transition to the new society of Bellamy, the instruments for building it and the composition of its leadership are not spelt out. When Martí writes that in the future 'a manner will be found', he wants the reader to understand that he does not contemplate these Utopias as a basis for political practice, nor as within the scope of his revolutionary project of national liberation.

Secondly, there are conceptual differences between Martí's ideas and the ideal future society of Bellamy. Martí believes that the new society should not 'be contrary to individual nature and even those inevitable but necessary flaws in men's character'. He raises a similar objection to the ideas of German socialists who have generously offered the United States their idiosyncratic brand of socialism without taking into account the distinct nature of the US individual. Apparently, for Martí, the individual nature came to be the antithesis of the social nature of man. Yet Martí has explained on earlier occasions the relationship between the individual and society, underlining that there is not an unbridgeable gap between collective forms of life and his idea of the individual nature of man. For Martí, the values of the individual are not immanent or previous to social and historical existence, as postulated by natural law, as codified, but are the result of social relations. At no moment does Martí give overall priority to the individual over society; on the contrary he recognises man's eminently social nature:

Nada es el hombre en sí, y lo que es, lo pone en él su pueblo. En vano conceda la naturaleza a algunos de sus hijos cualidades privilegiadas; porque serán polvo y azote si no hacen carne de su pueblo, mientras que si van con él, y le sirven de brazo y de voz, por él se verán encumbrados, como las flores que lleva en su cima una montaña.[33]

Man is nothing in himself and what he is; his pueblo makes him. In vain does nature grant some of its children exceptional qualities, for they will be nothing unless they are part of their pueblo. If they are [part of their pueblo] and act as its mouthpiece and its strength, they will achieve great heights, like the flowers that embellish the peaks of mountains.

## Martí and social conflict

On the question of the role of personality in history, Martí asserted in his writings on Bolívar and San Martín that they shaped events because they were faithful to the mandates of their pueblos. This observation, mentioned elsewhere by Martí writing on the limits of the individual in society and his intensely social conditioning, leads the reader to the conclusion that, when referring to the individual nature of man in opposition to the preaching of the German socialists, Martí does not uphold the absolute values of the individual in the face of a possible evolution towards a classless society but opposes certain extremist attitudes in the political discourse of these social reformers. Extreme egalitarianism, or the subordination of man to the omnipotent will of the state or of a collectivity which refuses to acknowledge individual characteristics transmitted from the past in order to make possible his integration into the proposed new society, seems to have been the dominant feature of the pronouncements of the German socialists criticised by Marx and Engels. In his review of the thinking of the Utopians, Martí recognised the justice inherent in the abolition of bourgeois ownership of the means of production.

Martí was not hostile to the blueprint of a communist society in the remote future. But Martí's main concern was the project of national liberation in the immediate future. He did not visualise the realisation of great theories and social Utopias as a task for his own generation, however much he admired them.

Martí had made many of these ideas his own without having actively participated in the class struggle in the United States. These ideas, indeed, left their mark on his political project. As Marx pointed out, social Utopias, at a certain moment, perform a positive role because they bring to the attention of contemporaries the possibility of alternative social models. Many of Martí's reflections on the immediate future of the Cuban republic were illuminated by his belief in the inherent justice of current social theories. Martí's appraisal of the distance between the realisation of socialist Utopias and his short-term project of national liberation, did not bring him to consider that the republic would usher in a period of absolute peace. He wrote in 1891:

> Con los oprimidos habrá que hacer causa común, para afianzar el sistema opuesto a los intereses y hábitos de mando de los opresores.[34]

> Common cause will have to be made with the oppressed in order to strengthen their cause against that of the oppressors.

In 1893, foreseeing the conflicts that would take place between the Cuban landowning oligarchy and the people, once the republic had been installed, Martí wrote:

> Moriremos por la libertad verdadera; no por la libertad que sirve de pretexto para mantener a unos hombres en el goce excesivo y a otros en el dolor innecesario. Se morirá en la república después si es preciso, como se morirá por la independencia primero.[35]

> We should die for true liberty; not for that liberty that serves as a pretext for some men to enjoy an excess of pleasure while others suffer unnecessary misery. If necessary we will fight to the death in the republic, but first we must die for independence.

On 24 February 1894, speaking in honour of Fermín Valdés Domínguez, whose socialist ideas were well known, Martí referred again to his willingness to die in the battle for liberty 'or in the struggle that the just and the wretched of the world wage against the proud to insure liberty'.[36]

Martí was not unaware of the class character of his confrontation. In his last will and testament, written to Mercado and dated 18 May 1895, he made explicit his position, denouncing annexationism:

> La actividad anexionista; menos temible por la poca realidad de los aspirantes, de la especie curial, sin cintura ni fuerza que por disfraz cómodo de su complacencía o sumisión a España pide sin fe la autonomía de Cuba, contenta sólo de que haya un amo yanky o español que les mantenga o les cree, en premio de oficios de celestinos, la posición de prohombres, desdeñosos de la masa pujante – la masa mestiza, hábil y conmovedora del país, – la masa inteligente y creadora de blancos y de negros.[37]

> Annexationism is less frightening because of the feebleness and

spinelessness of its advocates, who only appear to work for Cuban autonomy the better to disguise their complacency, or even their outright submission to Spain. They are happy to exist under a Spanish or a yankee master who keeps them and gives them important exalted positions as a reward for acting as procurers. In exchange for acting as procurers they are given exalted jobs. They despise the mighty masses – the *mestizos*, skilful, vital; the blacks and whites, intelligent and creative.

In a letter to the *New York Herald* on 2 May 1895, Martí again displayed his anxiety that the dependent Cuban bourgeoisie would resort to the United States to assure its ascendancy over the Cuban people. He called that class

la oligarquía pretenciosa y nula, que sólo buscase en ellos el modo de afincar el poder local de la clase, en verdad ínfima de la Isla, sobre la clase superior, las de sus conciudadanos productores.[38]

the pretentious and ineffectual oligarchy that looked to the United States only as a means of strengthening the power of their own small class against the superior class [that consists of] their superior co-citizens.

Martí foresaw too that conflict between the oligarchy and the people could not be simply a national confrontation but would assume broader dimensions. On comparing the struggles for independence with the social struggles of the future, he called the former 'the simple battles of independence' and did not vacillate in pointing out that after the coming of the republic, the definitive liberation of the nation would still have to be won in another, more profound and universal struggle 'between selflessness and selfishness, between liberty and pride'. This observation appeared in his article, 'The Wretched of the Earth', whom, with Ruskin, he called 'the most sacred among us'. Here Martí pointed out:

En un día no se hacen repúblicas, ni ha de lograr Cuba con las simples batallas de independencia, la victoria a que, en sus continuas renovaciones, y lucha perpetua entre el disinterés y la codicia y entre la libertad y la soberbia, no ha llegado aún en toda la faz del mundo, el género humano.[39]

Republics are not made in a day. Cuba with the simple battles for independence will not achieve that victory which is to be seen nowhere in the world: a victory that comes from constant renewal and perpetual struggle between selflessness and selfishness, and between liberty and pride.

The conjunction of Martí's identification with the labouring classes in both the United States and Cuba, and his connections with Utopian thinking, enabled him to look into the immediate future of the Cuban republic. He judged Utopian and Marxist thinking not from the perspective of the US proletariat but from that of the vanguard of the Cuban liberation movement.

Martí made fundamental criticisms of those aspects of advanced industrial capitalism whose replication in Cuba could present a menace or a real obstacle to the ideal of a harmonious and moderate republic, free of the crises and excesses of the world capitalist system. Martí was more sensitive to the absorbent character of the imperialist policies of monopoly capital than to the role of the proletariat as the gravedigger of capitalism. The relationship of the thought of Martí and Marxism, requires prudence and rigorous definition. Martí's critique of social reality stems from theoretical presuppositions quite distinct from those of Marxism. In line with the views elaborated by the Hungarian philosopher Andras Gëdo upon the relationship between Marxism and other modern systems of theory, the ideology of Martí is located near Marxism and even precedes it in the objective evaluation of some features of historical development. On a subjective plane, it can be proposed that leanings towards Marxism are not always directly connected to the development of the working-class movement or Marxist theory. Philosophical questions and ideas that stand in objective harmony with the content of Marxism can arise without its exerting an immediate influence.

The evolution of Martí's thinking took place in the context of the early stages of development of both a Cuban émigré worker identity and the US working-class movement. The level of ideological maturity of these groups and the isolation imposed by numerous constraints – political, ideological and moral – became an obstacle to Martí in seeking a comprehension of Marxism. Another obstacle was that for Martí Marxism was filtered through the distorting lens of German socialists resident in the United States. In spite of the theoretical and social limitations of his time, Martí was able to outline the principal mechanisms lying behind the social relationships of capitalism and to evolve a critique of the profit motive.

Without setting as an objective either a synthesis or a coherent social theory, Martí predicted the future development of monopoly capital in the United States, its propensity to dominate the continent and its inevitable confrontation with the countries of *nuestra América*. His critique of bourgeois values and of monopoly power, from the perspective of the vanguard of the Cuban national liberation movement and its ethics, was one of the most advanced and profound in its period. Martí's complex relations with Marxism confirm the Marxist tenet that reality can be understood from different theoretical positions, so long as they converge in general terms in the way that they view historical development. The thought of Martí preceded and notably enriched Marxism in its understanding of imperialism and the forces that animated it. An image that could sum up the relationship between the two sets of ideas is that of two rivers that flow towards each other, but before they can meet they flow into the sea, from which emerges the classless society. Before Martí could conceive of such an end, which he never formulated in those terms, he had defined his position in life in another respect: 'I want to share my fate with the poor of the land: I prefer the mountain spring to the sea.'

# 6 José Martí and his concept of the *intelectual comprometido*

JOHN M. KIRK

> Acercarse a la vida – he aquí el objeto de la literatura – ya para inspirarse en ella; ya para reformarla conociéndola.
>
> Martí, 1881

> To get closer to life in order to be inspired by it, and to reform it, having lived it – here I have the aim of literature.

José Martí was a very popular writer, whose poetry was especially respected among a Spanish-speaking readership. His profound newspaper chronicles – and in particular the incisive 'Escenas norteamericanas' (syndicated in most of Latin America's major newspapers) – assured him of a a further mass following. In addition to being the most widely read chronicler of his time in the Spanish language and clearly the most respected contemporary Latin American literary figure, Martí also played a political role, both as a diplomat representing Argentina, Uruguay and Paraguay, and as prime mover behind the Cuban movement for independence, the Partido Revolucionario Cubano. Martí was not tempted by his widespread fame but preferred instead to remain an intellectual, a true radical, for as he noted in August 1893:

> A la raíz va el hombre verdadero. Radical no es más que eso: el que va a las raíces. No se llame radical quien no vea las cosas en su fondo. Ni hombre, quien no ayude a la seguridad y dicha de los demás hombres.[1]

> The genuine man always goes to the roots. That is what it means to be a radical. Let no man call himself a radical that does not go to the bottom of things, and that does not strive for the happiness and safety of all other men.

This moving and eloquent auto-definition of Martí begs several questions, which this chapter attempts to study. Of key importance is an analysis of the nature of Martí's *compromiso*, and more specifically an investigation of the main elements which compose this commitment. Similarly it is necessary to pose the question of how Martí viewed his literature, and what he conceived the function of the intellectual to be. Finally the question of the relationship between Martí's intellectual career and his crucial political role in the revolutionary war for Cuban independence should be analysed. When these questions are answered, a basic understanding of Martí and his concept of the intellectual's role can be obtained. Before dealing with any of these problems, however, it is helpful to reflect on a few disparate notions, arising from various stages in Martí's career, on the value of literature, and on its basic functions. An analysis of the literary vocation, as defined by Martí, is clearly of major assistance in assessing his views on the role of the intellectual and, a vital word in Martí's work, his duties.

It can perhaps be stated from the outset that, for the Cuban writer, literature was a means of developing *alma*, a profound spiritual awareness of man's nature and aspirations, obligations and potential. Much has been written about Martí's earliest views, published in English, on life in the United States. In his famous chronicle 'Impressions of America (By a very fresh Spaniard)', for example, Martí emphasised (10 July 1880) the need for spiritual development as well as commercial activity. His views can be cited as supporting evidence in showing the fundamental importance of intellectual pursuits in any society:

> When the days of poverty may arrive – what richness, if not that of spiritual strength and intellectual comfort, will help this people in its colossal misfortune? Material power, as that of Carthage, if it rapidly increases, rapidly falls down. If this love of richness is not tempered and dignified by the ardent love of intellectual pleasures . . . where shall they go? . . . Life is unpleasant without the comforts of intelligence, the pleasures of art and the internal gratification that the goodness of the soul and the exquisiteness of taste produce to us.[2]

Later, he spoke bluntly about the North American nation: 'This splendid sick people, in one side wonderfully extended, in another side – that of intellectual pleasures – childish and poor.'[3] The pursuit of intellectual pleasures was a fundamental privilege and duty (*deber*) of the human race, since it developed the ability to analyse more objectively, while fortifying 'the well-being of the soul, which makes life's sorrows lighter and men ready for exertion and work. To enrich life is to give it an aim,' he noted approvingly after introducing his Latin American readers to the work of Oscar Wilde.[4]

This socialising tendency of literature, of using his writing as a means of fomenting *sociabilidad* among his fellow Latin Americans, is to be the focus of this sketch of Martí's work. It can of course be argued – as Fernández Retamar has indicated in masterful fashion in a recent article, 'Cuál es la literatura que inicia José Martí' – that the reader can find abundant references to 'pure', literary questions, self-contained and possessing their own specific value. He can look, for example, at Martí's feelings on Heredia, where he noted 'that real poetry has to have the resistance of bronze and the vibrant qualities of china. It is no use to try to disguise its shortcomings as patriotism and philosophy.' Two years later, in 1890, Martí went on to insist that 'a man is no poet . . . who puts politics and sociology into verse'.[5] This chapter does not seek to negate what, at the risk of confusion, may be termed the 'literary' qualities of Martí's work, which would be ludicrous, but it does attempt to cast light on an aspect of *la obra martiana* not widely studied, namely its socio-political function, since this is a useful gauge for assessing the parallel problem of the role of the intellectual. The analysis is based on an essential premise that the concern of Martí with aesthetic values and his obsession with the inherent political value of literary work, are facets of his consistent determination to follow an original, radical and revolutionary credo. Commending in 1919 on the relationship between Martí's poetry and revolutionary activities, Miguel de Unamuno underlined the closely intertwined nature of these aspects of Martí's legacy, noting:

> I am deeply interested in Martí . . . as a writer and a man of feeling – more as a man of feeling than as a thinker . . . and on calling him a poet, I want to stress that he was a man of action, not merely a pure writer, a 'man of truth and simplicity and not an ambitious and passive page-filler', to use his own words.[6]

## Literature as a means of 'concientización'

Turning now to his work proper, it may seem to many a self-evident truth to claim that, from all his literary experiences in various genres, Martí was first and foremost a poet. Many others might argue – convincingly – that equally important were his masterful chronicles and essays on life in the United States. For his part, Martí paid comparatively little attention to analysing the importance of these journalistic pieces (possibly because many were written fundamentally as a means of putting bread on the table), while conversely he went to great pains to explain the lyrical tone and content, as well as his intent, in his poetry. Writing in 1887, on Whitman for example, Martí claimed categorically that poetry 'is more necessary to peoples than industry itself, because while industry gives them the means of subsistence, poetry gives them the desire and the strength of life'.[7] In a moving and spirited piece, 'Mi poesía', Martí summarised succinctly the nature of his work:

> No la pinto de gualda y amaranto. Como aquesos
>   poetas; no le estrujo
> En un talle de hierro el franco seno;
> Y el cabello dorado, suelto al aire,
> Ni con cintas retóricas le cojo;
> No: No la pongo en lindas vasijas
> Que morirían; sino la vierto al mundo
> A que cree y fecunde, y ruede y crezca
> Libre cual las semillas por el viento.[8]

I do not paint [my poetry] with gold and amaranth, like some poets. I do not attempt to restrict its freedom with an iron corset. And I let the golden horse run free without trying to confine it with rhetorical bridles. No, I do not put her [poetry] in beautiful vessels that will perish; but I pour her over the world so that she grows and bears fruit, and rolls and flows free like the seeds scattered by the wind.

Given the evident importance of cultural pursuits for Martí, and his passion to harness his talents for educational purposes, it comes as no surprise to see the missionary zeal held by the Cuban writer-revolutionary in the noble pursuit of *concientizar* citizens of less education. This was particularly necessary, he noted in 1884, given the atrocious level of reporting employed by most newspapers: 'It pains me to see how these newspapers woo the masses: how they flatter their tastes; how they sacrifice their own culture; how they feign in order to ingratiate them, vulgar and brutal.'[9] In this disturbing state of affairs it fell to the intellectual to educate the population at large. Martí went further, condemning openly 'he who does not see in his intellectual capacities a mission of unselfish tutorship of those of lesser talents, but an efficacious tool to disturb and direct them to his own benefit'.[10] Quite simply, then, Martí viewed the intellectual's *true* role as a teacher and as a seeker of the truth who foments the 'creación de conciencia', 'creation of consciousness', as Julio Le Riverend has indicated:

Objetivamente la revolución necesita no solamente un hacer para
destruir el viejo régimen, sino también y sobre todo una nueva vida.
Lo que se necesita, en suma, es una creación de conciencia que
produzca cambios sustanciales en la conducta del hombre . . .
Martí intenta, y lo logra en su nivel histórico, educar a unos,
convencer a otros, de que la Revolución no es cambio de nombre
sino del hombre.[11]

Objectively revolution needs more than the mere destruction of the
*ancien régime*, it needs above all a new life. What it requires, to sum
up, is a creation of consciousness which results in substantial
changes in human conduct . . . Martí attempts to educate some and
to convince others that revolution is not just a change of names but
of man's nature; and he achieves it.

As has been ably illustrated by Philip Foner, the field of education
was treated by Martí as the keystone on which all social reforms were
based. Indeed, in talking about the need for sweeping educational
reform Martí often seems to regard teachers with some reverential
awe, as if they were mystics with unlimited supernatural powers.
Martí was astute enough to realise that a lack of awareness in cultural,
social and political matters would prolong injustices in these areas,
and that conversely 'personal morality and pride in independence,
guarantee the good exercise of liberty'.[12] The role of the intellectual
was seen by Martí is essentially moral terms. He went to great pains to
point out that a process of *concientización* was to be undertaken by
intellectuals, who were not to be 'vessel(s) in which pupils place their
intelligence and their personality . . . but a guide that teaches with
good faith what they must see'.[13] Moreover, for Martí, the intellectual
– like any other human being – was the recipient of talents which
brought along with them social obligations:

El talento es el deber de emplearlo en beneficio de los
desamparados. Por ahí se mide a los hombres . . . El talento viene
hecho, y trae consigo la obligación de servir con él al mundo, y no a
nosotros, que no nos lo dimos. De modo que emplear en nuestro
beneficio exclusivo lo que no es nuestro, es un robo . . . Es un
ladrón el hombre egoísta.[14]

Talent carries the duty of assisting the helpless. This is the
yardstick by which man is measured . . . Talent is a gift, which
implies the obligation of serving the world, and not ourselves, who
did not create it. To use for our exclusive benefit what does not
belong to us is theft . . . The egoist is a thief.

Put simply, the intellectual and the skilled worker had the same essential moral obligations and duties towards their fellow man: the possession of talents, in whatever capacity, implied a series of inescapable debts towards mankind.

Having outlined briefly Martí's general views on the function of culture as a means of avoiding what he termed 'pigmeísmo moral', 'moral dwarfism'[15] and too the role of the intellectual in the task of raising consciousness, it is worth pausing to examine some specific comments on how he viewed his own mission and work. This will provide a theoretical basis for comparison with his actual deeds. An understanding of how he viewed his own literary and intellectual functions will assist the reader to assess whether Martí's practice followed his teachings.

## Martí on Martí

On at least four occasions in his *Obras completas* (XXII, p. 129; VII, p. 112; XX, p. 518; XIII, p. 333), Martí reveals clearly his views that his intellectual mission and his literature were of far less importance than his actions. The first, chronologically, dates from November 1877. In a letter to Valero Pujol, editor of *El Progreso*, Martí thanks the editor for his praise, but requests a significant favour: 'You have already done much for me. Please do one further favour. Do not say of me, because it is worth little: "He wrote well, he spoke well." Say instead, "He has a sincere heart, an ardent temperament, he is an honourable man." '[16] This deliberate downplaying of his intellectual talents in favour of his actions is found constantly in his work. In his sharp note of probably a decade later Martí says: 'Before collecting my poems, I should like to collect my actions.'[17] And in his terse advice in *La Nación* (29 April 1888) he writes: 'One should not write with letters, but with acts.'[18] Finally, Martí wrote in his dedication to Alfonso Mercado, son of his life-long friend Manuel Mercado, in 1894: 'Loyal Alfonso: You want my autograph at all costs. The only autograph, my son, worthy of man, is that which is written in his works.'[19] These annotations show clearly Martí's concern with living out his ideals and with subordinating purely intellectual or aesthetic pursuits to practical goals. The subsequent repetition of this theme shows the importance he attached to it. Some twenty-seven years after outlining his views Martí still held them with equal fervour.[20]

When analysing Martí's clear and rather strict interpretation of his intellectual role, it is important to bear in mind his rigorous moralistic approach both to his work and to his life. As a sympathetic, sensitive and highly concerned intellectual, Martí proclaimed an inherently serious intent for much of his work. By contrast, his prologue to the novel *Amistad funesta* allowed Martí the opportunity to criticise the frivolous tone of an entire genre that he disliked:

> El género no le place, sin embargo, porque hay mucho que fingir en él, y los goces de la creación artística no compensan el dolor de moverse en una ficción prolongada; con diálogos que nunca se han oído, entre personas que no han vivido jamás. Menos que todas, tienen derecho a la atención novelas como ésta, de puro cuento en las que no es dado tender a nada serio, porque esto, a juicio de editores, aburre a la gente lectora . . . Lean, pues, si quieren, los que lo culpan, este libro; que el autor ha procurado hacerse perdonar, con algunos detalles, pero sepan que el autor piensa muy mal de él. Lo cree inútil; y lo lleva sobre sí como una grandísima culpa.[21]

> The genre does not please the author, because there is too much pretence in it, and the joys of artistic creation do not compensate for the pain of moving in such a prolonged fiction, with dialogues that have never been heard, among people that have never lived. Even less claim to our attention have novels like the present one which are pure fiction without any serious objectives, because this seriousness, according to the publishers, bores the reading public . . . Let those who think the author frivolous read this book, if they want, [in the knowledge] that the author has tried to exonerate himself [by including] some serious details; but let them be reminded too that the author thinks ill of it. He believes it to be useless, and he carries it on his shoulders, like a great burden.

Martí believed that the novel was *inútil* because it was not serious, because it had little transcendental moral content, and finally because it had reduced social relevance. For Martí literature or cultural expression without far-reaching social impact was rather meaningless – since the basic function of literature, as he noted in 1881, was to 'come close to life . . . either to take inspiration from it, or to reform it after a proper knowledge of it'.[22] Commenting on the close relationship between literature and his work, Ivan Schulman emphasises eloquently this parallel: 'His harmonic vision comprises life and art, so that Martí, great integrator, admits no schism between them. According to Cintio Vitier, [Martí] saw art arising passionately from life, and life as the supreme art.'[23]

A highly moralising tone, and an interpretation of the intellectual's mission of *deber* and *servicio*, is seen most clearly in a section of Martí's work, 'Libros que proyectaba escribir'. In this list of intended works there are several noteworthy 'literary' topics, including a study of Latin America's young poets like Mirón, Gutiérrez Nájera, Darío and Palma, another on 'Los poetas rebeldes' (Wilde, Guiseppe Carducci, Guerra Junqueiro and Whitman), an epic poem on the Americas, a book on popular music and poetry in South America, a study of European and North American drama, and finally, a 'Libro sobre Plácido, como el q. proyecto sobre Horacio: "Horacio, poeta revolucionario".' Further evidence of Martí's moralistic intent can be observed, not only in anthologies and readers of scientific material for *nuestra América*, but also in projected studies of contemporary social conditions of the native peoples, the condition of blacks in Cuba, the theme of revolution, a dictionary of the 'Juicios de los grandes hombres', a study of educational reform, biographical accounts of Bolívar and Juárez, and a three-volume philosophical study entitled 'El concepto de la vida'.[24] Only one concession towards the novel is found in Martí's extensive list of literary projects, where he writes in an aside, 'Equally necessary are novels that depict ideals higher than themselves and paint life, with the intention of bettering it.'[25] But this was secondary for Martí, since the function of the intellectual was, as he noted in 1884, 'to raise the spirit of the enormous ignorant mass'.[26]

## 'La Edad de Oro': an example of Martí's literary 'compromiso'

> No son hombres distintos en América el anciano de Mount Vernon, el sacerdote de Dolores, y el héroe que en las llanuras del mediodía fatigaba con la carrera su caballo . . .
> No son hombres distintos en América, Washington, Bolívar e Hidalgo . . . Un hombre es el instrumento del deber; así se es hombre.[27]

> The old man from Mount Vernon, the priest from Dolores and the hero that tired his horse out on the plains at noon are not different men in America . . . Washington, Bolívar and Hidalgo are not different men in America . . .
> A man is the instrument of duty; this is how you become a man.

After examining the concepts of *deber* and *abnegación* alluded to by Martí as the essential obligations of the intellectual, it is necessary to

identify the lowest common denominator of the *compromiso* found in
his work. At the risk of appearing over-schematic, I conclude that
there are four areas in which this commitment can be most clearly
seen: in instilling pride among Latin Americans, which can perhaps
be best summed up by his famous comment, 'El vino, de plátano; y si
sale agrio, es nuestro vino!' ('The wine I like is from banana; and if it
is sour I do not care, because it is our wine!');[28] his nation-building
and revolutionary activity for the Cuban cause; his astute, and
increasingly disturbed, warnings concerning the selfish nature of US
goals; and finally, a general plea for all to pursue – and to be allowed to
pursue – goals of freedom and dignity.

From Martí's copious writings, numerous examples could be
provided to sustain this thesis. His 'Escenas norteamericanas', for
example, clearly show his dread of the increasingly avaricious North;
his letters, perhaps more clearly than anything, constitute a
compendium of these *compromisos*: the journal *Patria* alone provides
an eloquent summary of his clearly formulated goals for a free Cuba –
to say little of his impressive *Versos sencillos*, complete with their
introduction,[29] his other poetry, or his journalistic writing in general.
As a means of clarifying Martí's views on the role and *obligations* of the
intellectual – an inseparable combination for Martí – a different
yardstick, the magazine *La Edad de Oro*, published between July and
October, 1889, and written expressly for 'los niños de América', 'the
children of America', is adopted here.[30]

The very history of this journal, or more specifically its short-lived
nature, reveals Martí's determination not to compromise his ideals in
the face of editorial pressure. As is well documented, only four
numbers of the journal appeared, after which there was a serious
difference of opinion between Martí and the publisher (a wealthy
Brazilian, A. d'Acosta Gómez), apparently over the religious content
which the publisher wanted in the journal and which Martí refused to
include. Writing to Manuel Mercado in November 1889, Martí
explained the reasons for the death of the journal:

Le quiero escribir con sosiego, sobre mí, y sobre *La Edad de Oro*,
que ha salido de mis manos – a pesar del amor con que la comencé,
porque, por creencia o por miedo de comercio, quería el editor que
yo hablase del 'temor de Dios', y que el nombre de Dios, y no la
tolerancia y el espíritu divino, estuvieran en todos los artículos e
historias. ¿Qué se ha de fundar así en tierras tan trabajadas por la
intransigencia religiosa como las nuestras?[31]

I want to write serenely about myself and about *La Edad de Oro*. [It] has escaped from my hands, despite the great love with which I began it, because, be it from conviction or commercial anxieties, the publisher wanted me to write of 'the fear of God', and [wanted too] that the name of God, and that of tolerance and the divine spirit, appeared in all the articles and tales. What new start can be made in lands like ours so ploughed by religious intransigence?

Martí's break with General Máximo Gómez in 1884 provides clear and eloquent testimony of his uncompromising conviction that an individual must remain true to his ideals, even when such a stand proves a major blow to the revolutionary cause.

In *La Edad de Oro*, the reader can find a brilliant mixture of historical and political commentaries, insightful summaries of major currents of literature, music and philosophy, and a basic introduction to the grandeurs of Hispanic civilisation, all presented in an intimate, personal and moving fashion.[32] The historical context of this work should be borne in mind: Martí wrote the four issues shortly after his fierce denunciations of US designs on Cuba, 'Vindicación de Cuba', and prior to his illuminating and effective reports on the Pan-American Conference held in the United States. There is a criticism of North American life-styles implicit in the abundant praise bestowed on *nuestra América*; but in general Martí carefully refrained from explicit criticism of the United States. He adopted a strongly anti-monarchist position, condemning both the oppressive Spanish control of Hispanic America and pre-revolutionary France, and even dreaming up kingdoms employing Greek mythology to show the anachronistic nature of the institution of monarchy.[33] His sharp condemnation of the *conquista*, and of the actions of colonial powers in Africa and Asia, in addition to his cajoling the ancient Greeks who 'believed like the Hebrews, and like so many other peoples, that they were the nation favoured by the creator of the world',[34] reveal even more clearly Martí's dedication to freedom and his conviction that every nation should be allowed to forge its own path and destiny.

Martí's plea for national self-determination, and his political foresight, are seen nowhere more clearly than in the fascinating article 'Un paseo por la tierra de los anamitas', where he illustrates various cycles of invasion, and documents attempts by the Chinese, Siamese and French to dominate and exploit Vietnam. Praising the centuries-old Vietnamese resistance to colonial designs, Martí stresses the need to fight against all external aggression, claiming that otherwise man becomes reduced to the level of unthinking animals: 'Those peoples that tire of defending themselves can be compared to donkeys pulling their fat and contented masters in their carts.'[35] Martí therefore encourages all exploited peoples to cast off the colonialist yoke and follow the moral example of the Vietnamese, who continued to struggle tirelessly against the incursions of their enemies:

> Usamos moño, y sombrero de pico, y calzones anchos, y blusón de color, y somos amarillos, chatos, canijos y feos: pero trabajamos a la vez el bronce y la seda: y cuando los franceses nos han venido a quitar nuestro Hanoi, nuestro Hué, nuestras ciudades de palacios de madera, nuestros puertos llenos de casas de bambú y de barcos de junco, nuestros almacenes de pescado y de arroz, todavía, con estos ojos de almendra, ¡hemos sabido morir, miles sobre miles, para cerrarles el camino! Ahora son nuestros amos, pero mañana ¡Quién sabe![36]

> We wear a pigtail, a pointed hat and white leggings, and also a coloured blouse. We are yellow, flat-nosed, puny and ugly. But we work both the bronze and the silk. When the French came to take away from us our Hanoi, our Hué, our cities of wooden palaces, our ports full of junks and bamboo homes, our stores full of fish and rice, we, with our almond-like eyes, have known how to die in our thousands in order to close their way! Now they are our masters, but tomorrow? Who knows?

The struggle for freedom and dignity remained an essential component of Martí's *compromiso*; for as he noted in 1883, 'What is done outside this struggle is imperfect, while what is done inside it is fruitful. This is the ineludible condition of all useful work.'[37]

A major component of Martí's *compromiso* was his determination to inculcate into his readers throughout all Latin America, a pride in their Latin American origins: 'Our *patria* is one. It begins at the Río Grande, and it ends in the muddy hills of Patagonia.'[38] In each of the issues of *La Edad de Oro* references to *nuestra América* abound, as Martí continues with his plan to raise the consciousness of his young readers, instilling in them a profound respect for their Latin roots, an objective explained in a letter to Mercado:

> Llenar nuestras tierras de hombres originales, criados para ser felices en la tierra en que viven, y vivir conforme a ella, sin divorciarse de ella, ni vivir infecundamente en ella, como ciudadanos retóricos, o extranjeros desdeñosos nacidos por castigo en esta otra parte del mundo. El abono se puede traer de otras partes; pero el cultivo se ha de hacer conforme al suelo. A nuestros niños los hemos de criar para hombres de su tiempo, y hombres de América.[39]

To fill our lands with original men, educated to be happy on the land where they live, and to live according to its [authenticity], without divorcing themselves from it, or living fruitlessly as rhetorical citizens or disdainful foreigners born as a punishment in this other part of the world. Fertilizer can be brought from elsewhere, but the culture has to correspond to the soil. We have to educate our children to be men of their time, and men of America.

The extent of Martí's programme of developing in his readers an awareness of their *americanismo* can best be appreciated by studying his articles: 'Tres héroes' (Bolívar, San Martín, and Hidalgo), 'Las ruinas indias', in which he compares the grandeur of pre-Colombian America with its tragic post-Conquest remnants, and 'El Padre Las Casas', a brilliant denunciation of the Conquest and of the unjust social and political structures which it created. In all three articles Martí embarks unashamedly on a path of nation-building, attempting to instil ethnic pride in his followers. Furthermore, as a *modernista*, Martí seeks a new Latin-American way of expression, affirming that 'to be eloquent and original in Spanish it is not necessary to drink the malpractices of the *siglo de oro* in the twisted vase of the *neocastizos castellanos*, neither to suckle . . . from the dry udder of Paris the last drop of blood'.[40] Martí also outlines his own immediate political aspirations, the political independence of Cuba, as the logical development of the central thesis found in these articles, for in all of them the primary issue is the right to freedom.[41] These observations in 1889 were not an ephemeral interest of Martí's, but were expressions of a concept treated by him throughout his work, from his teenage journalism to his last moving letter to Mercado shortly before his death.

## Martí and the struggle for Cuban independence

> Sé desaparecer. Pero no desaparecería mi pensamiento ni me agriaría mi oscuridad. Y en cuanto tengamos forma, obraremos, cúmplame esto a mí o a otros.[42]

> I know how to vanish. Being out of the limelight will not embitter me, because my thoughts will not disappear. When we have formed an organisation we shall act. This goes for me and for others.

Martí performed a twin role as an *intelectual comprometido* and as the driving force behind the movement to bring political independence to Cuba. The second facet of Martí's role was the logical result of his first, since from his earliest literary work, Martí had shown that literature was for him a vehicle to develop support and understanding for the cause of the *patria*. It is necessary to look at his drama *Abdala*, published in the journal *La Patria Libre* in early 1869, to establish this point:

ABDALA　Morir sabremos: hijos de la patria
　　　　Por ella moriremos, y el suspiro
　　　　Que de mis labios postrímeros salga
　　　　Para Nubia será, que para Nubia
　　　　Nuestra fuerza y valor fueron creados.[43]

ABDALA　We shall know how to die. We children of the *patria* shall die for her. The last sigh from my lips will be for Nubia, because for Nubia were our strength and courage created.

The arrest and deportation of Martí's *padre espiritual*, Mendive, increased repression by the Spanish forces in Cuba, and then his own arrest, imprisonment, and subsequent deportation to Spain, combined to strengthen Martí's resolve to dedicate his life to the liberation of Cuba.[44] Following his enforced exile in Spain, Martí collected his thoughts on the condition of Cuba, in two denunciations of colonial domination, *El presidio político en Cuba* (1871), and *La República Española ante la Revolución Cubana* (1873). What is abundantly clear from an analysis of these two works is Martí's firm conviction that the primary role of the intellectual was to condemn injustice, and to seek to enlist the support of all to right the obvious wrongs being committed. In other words, the function of literature was seen by him, even as a youth, as being a vehicle for the denunciation of wrongs, and for the organisation of like-minded followers with a similar cause. This was as true of Martí's work in 1869, as of his writings in the 1890s in the journal *Patria*.

These two pamphlets from the early 1870s illustrate both the righteous indignation of Martí, and the fiery tone of denunciation found in much of his work. *El presidio político en Cuba*, in particular, is notable for its highly personal interpretation of prison life, a life so brutal that Martí claims: 'If there existed a providential God, and if he had seen it, with one hand he would have covered his face, and with the other he would have thrust that denial of God into the abyss.'[45] Martí was not content, however, with merely presenting an emotionally charged criticism of life in a political prison; he went one step further, challenging Spanish readers to explain their continued selfish interest in Cuba:

¿Por qué firmáis con vuestro asentimiento el exterminio de la raza que más os ha sufrido, que más se os ha humillado, que más os ha esperado, que más sumisa ha sido hasta que la desesperación o la desconfianza en las promesas ha hecho que sacuda la cerviz? ¿Por qué sois injustos y tan crueles?[46]

Why do you acquiesce in the signing of the death-warrant of the race that has been your greatest victim, that has humiliated itself most before you, that has expected so much of you, that has been submissive until despair or distrust in your promises has pushed it into shaking its yoke? Why are you so unjust and so cruel?

A useful comparison can be made between this work and Martí's writing in *Patria*, in which he skilfully outlined the programmes of the Partido Revolucionario Cubano (PRC) – particularly in light of Martí's position as editor of the journal, and leader or *Delegado* of the PRC.[47] While in *Patria* the literary style is predictably more developed and mature, and the political concepts dealt with are more clear and more radical, there are important similarities in style and content between the two works, despite the twenty-year hiatus in their publication. Julio Le Riverend, echoing the opinion of Manuel Isidro Méndez, accurately notes that 'the Maestro's formation is complete by the year 1870'.[48] While the consistency of these ideas after such a long interval is itself significant, also of crucial importance is Martí's interpretation of the intellectual's role. Common to both periods is his determination to denounce an immoral political system; but, in *Patria*, there is a distinctly constructive tone to his work, since he is planning for the establishment of a radically new society in Cuba after Spanish colonial rule is overthrown, 'a just and open Republic, united in territory, in law, in work and in friendliness, created by all for the benefit of all'.[49] Once again, then, the mission of the intellectual is seen by Martí as the use of literary expression as a means of criticising injustice, of offering suggestions for improvement, of raising the collective consciousness, and of organising people to fight for justice. As Luis Toledo Sande has recently shown: 'He applauded the work of thought, because "after action, it is the best and cleanest work that can be done in this world"; but he preferred the union of thought and action, because action is "the arm of thought".'[50] Writing in *The Sun* of New York in 1880, on Pushkin, Martí noted succinctly the intellectual's obligations: 'The hand must follow the inspiration of the intellect. It is not enough to write a patriotic strophe; you must live it.'[51] Writing about José de la Luz, he developed the theme of the moral obligation of intellectuals both to inspire others to participate in the revolutionary struggle, and to fight directly themselves:

¿Qué es . . . pensar sin obrar, decir sin hacer, desear sin querer? . . . ¿Qué es aborrecer al tirano, y vivir a su sombra y a su mesa?

¿Qué es predicar, en voz alta o baja, la revolución, y no componer el país desgobernado para la revolución que se predica?[52]

What is . . . thinking without acting, saying without doing, desiring without loving . . . What is the value of abhorring the tyrant, while living in his shadow and eating at his table?

What is the value of preaching revolution, loudly or softly, without preparing the ill-ruled country for the revolution that is preached?

Martí's entire literary life and revolutionary career confirm that he followed these maxims to the letter, and his untimely death at Dos Ríos in 1895 reveals his faithfulness to his creed.

## Concluding remarks

A picture emerges of a revolutionary who not only frowned upon the armchair politics so often played by liberal intellectuals, but also made use of his literary work for both enjoyment and the task of *concientizar*.[53] Martí felt no need to hide behind empty philosophical concepts or contrived expressions, for as he noted in his *Versos sencillos*:

> Callo, y entiendo, y me quito
> La pompa del rimador:
> Cuelgo de un árbol marchito
> Mi muceta de doctor.[54]

I keep silent, understand; and I cast off the versifier's pomp, and hang my doctoral robes upon a withered tree.

Toledo Sande has indicated too that Martí's aversion to the concept of 'form for form's sake' – 'la forma por la forma' – is also important. This 'concept as well as being an expression of lack of content and of evasion, conceals or hurts what is substantial in the work: "The pearl is lost under so much shell".'[55] The nub of Martí's theory of literature was that it should be aesthetically pleasing and original, possess educational or moral content, and be relevant and understandable to the masses. On a political level, driven by a fierce and unrelenting patriotism, both for Cuba and for the broader *patria* of *nuestra América*, Martí struggled throughout his life to win a true and meaningful freedom. As a writer he expected no privileges, and would surely have criticised intellectuals who claim special status for their profession. He wrote in 1885: 'The human race has but a cheek: wherever a man received a blow in his face, all men receive it!'[56] Filled with a sense of continent-wide mission, Martí subordinated everything and gave his life to meet the demands of this self-imposed crusade. When viewed in this light, his use of artistic expression was but another, albeit extremely important, facet of his *deber*.[57] Writing in the children's magazine *La Edad de Oro* in 1889, Martí summarised eloquently his interpretation of the intellectual's *compromiso*:

Lo que ha de hacer el poeta es *aconsejar a los hombres que se quieran bien, y pintar todo lo hermoso del mundo* . . . *y castigar con la poesía,* como un látigo, a los que quieran quitar a los hombres su libertad, o roben con leyes pícaras el dinero de los pueblos, o quieran que los hombres de su país les obedezcan como ovejas y les laman la mano como perros. Los versos no se han de hacer para decir que se está contento o se está triste, sino *para ser útil al mundo*, enseñándole que la naturaleza es hermosa, que la vida es un deber, que la muerte no es fea, que nadie debe estar triste mientras haya libros en las librerías, y luz en el cielo, y amigos y madres.[58] [Emphasis added]

What the poet's duty is is *to advise men to love each other and to paint the beauties of the world* . . . and *to punish with his poems*, as if they were a whip, those who want to take liberty from man or to steal with crooked laws the wealth of the people, or want the men of the nations to follow them like sheep and lick their hands like dogs. Poetry should not be written to express one's sadness or happiness, but *to be useful to the world*, teaching it that nature is beautiful, that life is duty, that death is not ugly, and that nobody should be sad so long as bookshops are full of books, the sky is full of light, and the world is full of good friends and mothers. [Emphasis added]

# 7 Martí, Latin America and Spain

## CHRISTOPHER ABEL

América se llamó Bolívar
Cuba se llamó José Martí . . .
sin esos hombres, la Historia carecería de sus más
bellas páginas:
y los pueblos habrían perdido sus mas bellos
destinos:
ningun pueblo ha hecho nunca cambiar de rumbo
la Humanidad, han sido los grandes hombres,
los que han producido los más grandes cambios
de Ideas, en el corazón del Mundo;
la Renovación . . .
Napoleón . . .
la Constitución . . .
Bolívar . . .
la Emancipación . . .
Martí . . .
la Multitud es incapaz de Ideas; no es capaz sino
de sentimientos;
los pueblos sufren la magia de los Genios;
los Genios, se apartan de los pueblos . . .
hay una valorización, entre el Genio y el Pueblo;
el Pueblo sufre al Genio . . .
el Genio salva al Pueblo . . .
y el Pueblo devora al Genio, si la Muerte no se
encarga de devorarlo . . .
Roma, sacrificó los Gracos.
Colombia, devoró a Bolívar;
la Argentina, expulsó a San Martín;
¿que habría hecho Cuba de Martí?;
¿no hay derecho, a exterminar aquello que no
ha nacido?;
respetemos la virginidad de lo que es.

America was called Bolívar, and Cuba was called Martí . . . Without them
History would be denied its most beautiful pages; and the people would not
have reached its beautiful destinies. The people has never changed the destiny
of Humanity; great men have done so, changing Ideas, in the heart of the
World. Renovation . . . Napoleon . . . the Constitution . . . Bolívar . . .
Emancipation . . . Martí . . . the Crowd is incapable of Ideas; it is incapable
of feelings. The people is bewitched by the magic of Genius; but the Genius
distances himself from the people . . . There is a difference of value between

124

the Genius and the People. The People suffers the Genius. . . . the Genius saves the People . . . and the People devours Genius, if Death has not already done so . . . Rome sacrificed the Gracchi. Colombia devoured Bolívar; Argentina expelled San Martín. What could Cuba have done with Martí? Do we have a right to exterminate the unborn? Let us honour the virginity of the living.

> J. M. Vargas Vila, *Obras póstumas de J. M. Vargas Vila. José Martí, Apostól-Libertador*, Paris, 1938; 2nd edn Santo Domingo, 1975, pp. 96–7.

Recent writing on José Martí has endeavoured to restore his humanity. No longer is he always to be seen smiling as inscrutably as the Mona Lisa. Prominent Cuban scholars have sought to dispel the 'extra-historical' writing and much of the confessional vocabulary – dreamer, apostle and martyr, prophet of universal love, man of concord and comprehension, *martiano* Gospel – that especially in the 1920s and 1930s, surrounded his name and obscured his significance.[1] Literary scholarship has, without falling into the trap of dwelling pruriently upon his personal problems, accomplished the task of de-beatification, of removing Martí from a pedestal of superhuman perfection.[2] Recent historiography has reappraised Martí's career, looking closely at changes in his attitudes and revising schemes of periodisation. Historians now emphasise the years 1886–7 as a transitional phase in his life when his views were radicalised.[3] This chapter sets out to take these trends a stage further by reconsidering Martí in the light of the changing international order of the last decades of the nineteenth century of which he was so astute and perceptive an observer. I write from two assumptions: that there remains a risk of abstracting Martí from the world; and that historians cannot explain his attitudes and actions without exploring the historical matrix on which they were imprinted and the nature of the resistance of the socio-economic and political fabric at which they were directed and which therefore co-determined their outcome.

## Martí and Bolívar

The link between Bolívar and Martí is clearly vital to an understanding of Martí. Yet the continuities and the differences between them and the circumstances in which they worked have not been established with sufficient sharpness.

Martí and Bolívar worked in and were constrained by distinct international environments. On the one hand, Bolívar confronted a

Spain that remained a major European power, whose absolute monarchs still had some confidence in their divine right to rule and could draw succour from the recent reinvigoration of the imperial economy by Charles III. By contrast, Martí faced a shabby, decadent and anachronistic Spanish monarchy that enjoyed a seat at international European conventions only because it possessed, by the grace of the great powers, scattered colonies in the Caribbean, the Far East and Africa. Whereas fierce debate occurred in the 1820s over whether the successor states of the Spanish American mainland should be monarchies or republics, protagonists of independence in Cuba were irrevocably republican.

Martí and Bolívar saw the United States differently. For Bolívar the nascent United States posed no immediate threat to Spanish America, both because the possibility of a British reconquest remained, at least until the Anglo-American War of 1812, and because expansionist energies could be concentrated upon frontier settlement. Yet Bolívar was wary about the United States, and, indeed, about monarchical Brazil, both of which he wished to exclude from discussions of Spanish American federal arrangements.[4]

By the 1880s the international context had changed decisively. An earlier emphasis upon a weakly linked North Atlantic commercial nexus, into which western Cuba and other sugar-cane and coffee producers of the Caribbean were partly integrated, was overtaken by more dynamic international economic relationships and the emergence of an incipient international, and perhaps world, economy, with which western Cuba had close bonds, and with which eastern Cuba and Puerto Rico enjoyed ties of a less intimate character. A restructuring of capitalism at the centre was complemented by the consolidation of frontier settlement in the United States, and the emergence in the 1880s and 1890s of the United States as an expansionist force characterised by a dynamic corporate capitalism, whose dominant groups were committed to the assertion of the United States as a continental and then a world power co-equal in status with Britain, Germany, France and Russia. Opposition minorities, meanwhile, sustained inconsistent campaigns of anti-imperialism, contending that overseas expansion was contrary to the spirit of the republic. They argued that aggressive expansion made the United States indistinguishable from the European monarchies, involved incalculable political risks and excessive military spending, and was incompatible with the economic interests of the majority of the US citizens.[5] Martí's views of the United States, shaped during long periods of exile, were influenced both by personal observation and experience and by a thorough reading of contemporary US social critics whom he reinterpreted through the lens of a Latin American refugee.

Changes in the ideological context were equally evident. Whereas the ideal of nationhood spread in the Andes as the struggle for independence unfolded, in Cuba the ideal antedated and animated the first, abortive war of independence of 1868–78, and was thoroughly absorbed before the war of 1895–8 began.[6] Whereas Bolívar evolved a theory of national self-determination in response to immediate exigencies, no such theory required elaboration in the 1880s and 1890s. Martí shared with Bolívar a view of revolution as a social movement and not only a political struggle;[7] but their perceptions of nationalism were different, if not antagonistic. For Martí, nationalism was inextricably bound up with multiracialism, the imperative of a revival of writing in the Spanish language and, to some degree, with anticlericalism – factors to which Bolívar gave less emphasis.

⌈In certain respects Martí and Bolívar were similar. Like Bolívar, Martí wanted Spanish America to occupy a world stage. Martí celebrated the recognition of Mexico at an international exhibition at Philadelphia; and later that of Venezuela and Peru. He also recorded the presence of Guatemala at an exposition in Paris.[8] As Bolívar had envisaged Colombia as a world power competing on equal terms with France or Britain, Martí, perhaps in exile losing a sense of the finite nature of Cuban interests and possibilities, entertained exaggerated notions that the Hispanic Caribbean was the balancing-point of the world.⌉

In other ways the two leaders were sharply different. They shared the view that class conflict should be postponed until the national struggle was completed. But they differed in class origins. Bolívar, a member of a wealthy cacao-producing family, had more in common with Madero than with Martí, and placed a higher emphasis upon property, stability and security. Martí and Bolivar differed too in life-span. Martí did not live to take part in the independence settlement; and thus was neither compelled to detail his notions of popular representation and accountability in a *Cuba libre,* nor to undergo such criticisms as were made sometimes of Bolívar by critics arguing that the unitary theme of his career was a Napoleonic vanity and unscrupulousness.[9]

Bolívar was an effective civilian leader and a soldier committed to military professionalism. Martí, by contrast, was not a soldier but a civilian leader. He acknowledged the degree of professionalism and of military experience that General Máximo Gómez and other insurgent military leaders contributed to the independence cause, and preferred to leave the conduct of warfare to specialists while retaining in civilian hands decisions about co-ordination and allocation of resources.

Martí's praise for Bolívar was qualified. He lauded Bolívar's military exploits. He also sympathised with Bolívar's early constitutionalist commitments, his campaigns against personalism, his confrontation with *caudillismo* in Venezuela and some of his measures to subordinate the Church to broader national interests. But on social issues Martí was severely critical of Bolívar. Perhaps underestimating the extent to which Bolívar sought the abolition of slavery, Martí held Bolívar responsible for a failure to complete the process of liberation in the Andean countries. Characteristically, Martí did not attribute this alleged failing to Bolívar's class origins, but to an inability to observe the dehumanising impact of the caste system that arose from a lack of confidence in the populace, not knowing the 'fuerza moderadora del alma popular' – 'the moderating force of the popular soul'.[10] Here Martí felt more kinship with Rivadavia: 'Rivadavia, el argentino, tenía razón: "Estos pueblos se salvarán." ' 'Rivadavia the Argentine was right: "These peoples will save themselves." '[11] Of Cuba itself Martí was unequivocal:

> creo a mi pueblo capaz de construir sobre los restos de una mala colonia una buena república.[12]

> I believe my people capable of constructing a good republic on the remains of a bad colony.

## Martí, political structures and ideology

Martí's attitudes towards democracy and dictatorship were shaped first by childhood and adolescence under the colonial regime and then by youth and early manhood in Spain. Martí identified with the Federal Republic, most strongly with Pi i Maragall, the Spanish Prime Minister who was also the translator into Spanish of Proudhon.[13] Martí shared a widespread disenchantment at the aftermath of the Federal Republic, seeing the Republic of 1874 as little more than a camouflaged monarchy: and he regretted that the *sano y pujante* elements in a generous and honourable bourgeoisie had little influence in the Cortes.

Martí's principal concerns in Spain were liberal – day-to-day political events and constitutional issues: Cortes debates, ministerial changes, press freedom, electoral practices, the impact of personalism, university autonomy, diplomatic relations and power politics. Martí used liberal categories like 'public opinion', and displayed an admiration for clear-cut republican leadership, like that of Gambetta and Sagasta, observing unremarkably, by liberal criteria:

> Las naciones en sus períodos críticos, producen hombres con quienes se encarnan: hombres nacionales.

> Nations, in their critical periods, produce men with whom they are one: national men.[14]

Martí's concerns in Church-state relations were conventional: lay versus confessional university, freedom of conscience and civil marriage. He reported conscientiously on threats by Pope Leo XIII to abandon Rome for Malta, and expressed hopes for a transition to constitutional monarchy at the Vatican. Martí's political journalism was complemented by reportage on the arts which stressed such features of a bourgeois, if republican, culture as elections to the Acadèmie Française.[15]

For Martí the foundation of republics was ethical, not structural. He looked to a fundamental change in human behaviour and a selfless civic conduct as its basis. Thus his explanation of the fall of the Spanish Republic was couched in terms of personal qualities – a lack of profundity, purity, energy and vision of its political leadership, with the honourable exception of Pi i Maragall.[16] Martí's analysis was expressed in terms of personal qualities, not political structures. The quality of his description was evident in his ironic depiction of Sagasta in the Cortes:

> Satisfecho de su triunfo, Sagasta se sienta a reposar, y deja vagar sobre sus labios, como una mariposa harta de miel de flores, su sonrisa volteriana. Cree a despecho suyo, en la libertad. Rompe en cada combate todas sus lanzas en provecho de si mismo, – menos una, – que rompe siempre en beneficio de la libertad.[17]

> Satisfied by his victory, Sagasta lets a Voltairean smile settle on his lips like a butterfly with a surfeit of honey. He believes, despite himself, in liberty. He breaks his armour in each combat for his own benefit, except one sword which he reserves for freedom.

Making passing reference to 'the Spain that works, suffers and lives, but does not vote', Martí observed but did not analyse the problems of putting into practice the moral and political imperatives that he preached. He made no analysis of how liberal values – of tolerance, restraint, etc. – might be superimposed upon political structures where entrenched regional and local interests paid lip-service to liberalism, while shifting blocs of votes in line with private priorities and perpetuating habits of *caciquismo* that belied a liberal vocabulary. To say this is not an *ex post facto* criticism of Martí. For Spanish contemporaries were already making structural observations and discriminations that were fine, sharp and appropriate, if not systematic. Such critiques of Spanish politics and society reached their apogee in the voluminous writing of the Aragonese polymath, Joaquín Costa, who gave them formal expression, after Martí's death, in 1901.

Llegó septiembre de 1868; ocurrió el alzamiento del día 29, tan soñado; surgieron por todas partes Juntas revolucionarias; vibraron los himnos patrióticos; proclamóse la soberanía nacional; y en medio del mayor entusiasmo una Constitución democrática fue promulgada. Pues lo mismo que si no hubiéseis promulgado nada. Se habló de obstáculos tradicionales, y el trono del monarca fue derribado; pero el verdadero obstáculo tradicional, el trono del cacique, quedó incólume, y todo aquel aparato teatral, manifiesto de Cádiz, juntas revolucionarias, destronamiento de la reina, Constitución democrática, soberanía nacional, no pasó de la categoría de pirotecnia: la graduamos de revolución, y no fue más sino un simulacro de revolución . . . Es como la superposición de dos Estados, uno legal, otro consuetudinario: máquina perfecta el primero, regimentada por leyes admirables, pero que no funciona; dinamismo anárquico el segundo, en que libertad y justicia son privilegio de los malos, donde el hombre recto, como no claudique y se manche, sucumbe.[18]

September 1868 arrived: the famous uprising of the 29th [September] took place; revolutionary juntas sprang up everywhere; patriotic hymns rang through the land; national sovereignty was proclaimed; in the midst of the greatest enthusiasm a democratic Constitution was promulgated. It was as if nothing had happened. The traditional obstacles were invoked. The throne of the monarch was overturned, but the true traditional obstacle, the throne of the *cacique*, remained intact, and all the theatrical apparatus – the manifesto of Cadiz, revolutionary juntas, the removal of the queen, democratic Constitution, national sovereignty – did not go beyond verbal fireworks: we gave it the title of revolution, and it was but a parody . . . It is like the superimposition of two states: the one existing by law, the other by custom. The first has a perfect machine, ruled by admirable laws, but does not function. The second is powered by anarchic dynamism, where liberty and justice are the privileges of evil men, and where the upright man, if he does not surrender and become corrupt, succumbs.

The same absence of structural analysis is evident in Martí's portrayal of the Spanish connection with Cuba. He reported the energetic repudiation by Sagasta of violations in Cuban elections and his protests at the disdain for Cuba exhibited by Cánovas. Martí protested at the adverse impact upon Cuba of timid tariff reforms, and censured the incomprehension of Cubans shown by a reformist Canary Islander Minister of Ultramar, León y Castillo, who branded as ungrateful those Cubans who rejected his proposals of assimilation as an alternative to colonial or autonomous status.[19] Linking Spain's determined refusal to relinquish control of Cuba with other unhealthy features of Spanish nationalism, Martí censured attempts to inflate national pride by exaggerating minor humiliations in Morocco and alleged offences committed against Spaniards by the French in Tunis.[20]

Who were the principal intellectual influences upon Martí? His debt to Lamartine has been a subject of much conjecture.[21] Estrade has cautiously attributed Martí's emphasis on regeneration to freemasons and his stress to the need of fallen man for personal redemption to Victor Hugo.[22] A minority view sees Martí as a pupil of the idealist materialist, Luis Büchner.[23] Conventionally, Martí is associated with the diffusion of the ideas of Karl Krause in Spain in the years 1868–74. *Krausismo* has been variously seen as a premature synthesis and as an ill-defined eclecticism that contains a restatement of Kant. Some scholars argue that *Krausismo*, if intellectually of little weight, was nevertheless a valuable and timely tool for Spaniards who had been isolated from the mainstream of European thought and subject to periods of religious intolerance. According to this view *Krausismo* provided an appropriate ethical orientation for youth – a religion of reasoned virtue – that rested upon categories comprehensible to a generation steeped in Catholic orthodoxies. Such a view identifies *Krausismo* with liberalism, educational and penal reform, decentralisation, and educational change, especially in philosophical studies. A relationship between the main tenets of *Krausismo* and Martí's evolving ideas can be observed: a mystical belief in natural harmony, a subjective mysticism with possibly pantheistic overtones and a philosophical radicalism that elevated moral purpose rather than utility as a criterion for institutions.[24]

Perhaps, however, it would be more appropriate not to try to fit

Martí into a category of direct discipleship, partly because the breadth of his reading suggests a willingness to absorb diverse ideas, and partly because *Krausismo* itself was heterogeneous in content and subject to numerous influences. Instead, Martí is better seen as a product of the intellectual climate shaped by *Krausismo* – characterised by openness and concern for moral, educational and cultural regeneration – than as a pupil of any single tradition.

The breadth of Martí's interests is evident in his debt to romanticism. It is anachronistic to consider the politics of Martí without taking into account the romantic context of his political attitudes. Far from being a literary romantic in the sense of writing egocentrically, he was a modernist in his use of metaphor and symbolism and the intimacy of his subject-matter. Equally, he was hardly a romantic, either in rejecting the tyrannically rigid rules of classicism, since these were never applied in Cuba and barely influenced Spain, or in reacting against scientific method. Perhaps romanticism can be seen in Martí's interest in deism; but it is clearly not observed in commitment to a personal version of a reinvigorated Roman Catholicism.

But, in a broader political sense, a delayed romanticism transferred to a non-European environment can be observed. The epic connotations of Martí were in his politics, not in his poetry, especially in his crusade to break Cuba away from the monolithic view of reality imposed by an authoritarian colonial state, which denied a relationship between thinking and feeling that Martí sought to illuminate. Martí rejected exponents of an authentic experimentation without social and political content, seeing journalism as a patriotic service and poetry as an accessory necessity that was sometimes unjustifiable.[25] A poetic insistence upon self-comprehension was translated into a political notion of Latin America moving from defeat to self-comprehension and then to a full emancipation.

Like the romantics, Martí had no belief in absolute values, and sought a liberation from a political and ecclesiastical absolutism and a hierarchical social system rationalised only in terms of obsolete cosmologies that failed in the late nineteenth century even to provide reassurance for their own advocates. He looked to a revolution that made possible the recovery of the authentic self. His quest for self-identification became more acute in long periods of exile. In his private correspondence in 1886 Martí admitted frustration at not being in control of his own fate; and expressed anguish at exile in countries where he had no right to try to improve conditions, impotence at his inability to change Cuba and distress at being unable to fulfil family obligations.[26] Without rejecting individual rights,

Martí emphasised individuality; without rejecting reason, he stressed intuition.[27] Both individuality and intuition are visible in Martí's repeated stress upon selfless civic conduct, simplicity and austerity – and also in his periodic returns to the theme of martyrdom. This was evident as early as 1871:

> El martirio por la Patria es Dios mismo, como el bien, como las ideas de espontánea generosidad universales.[28]

> Martyrdom for the *Patria* is God itself, it is goodness, like the universal ideas of spontaneous generosity.

The theme of martyrdom recurs emphatically and explicitly in 1889: 'Yo creo en el culto de los martires.'[29] 'I believe in the cult of martyrs.'

The political romantic in Martí admired heroism rather than genius, most strikingly in Garibaldi:

> La libertad, patria humana, tuvo un hijo, y fue Garibaldi: – fue él. Su inteligencia, no hecha al yunque ni al esmero, vaga y yerra: mas su magnánimo corazón que no conoce cansancio ni vejez, recaba prestamente para el héroe la admiración que un extravío intelectual o un exceso irreflexivo de bondad momentáneamente le enajenan. Se le conoce como a salvador y como un padre.[30]

> Liberty, human *patria'*, had a son: Garibaldi. His intelligence, neither pliable nor 'refined', ambles and is not a stranger to mistakes. While his magnanimous heart which knows neither tiredness nor old age demands admiration of the hero, it is an admiration sometimes extenuated by his impetuousness and intellectual errors and excesses. He is known as a saviour and a father.

Martí was selective. The translator of Victor Hugo's *Mes Fils*, he shared Hugo's prophetic force and intensity and perhaps his tendency towards the grandiose gesture; but there is no evidence of Martí adopting a stress on the grotesque and evil, although an emphasis upon the harmony of the universe perhaps owed more to Hugo than Krause. Martí repudiated romantic views that restraint, decorum and order should be thrown to the wind, since for him the colonial regime represented disorder, lack of restraint and lack of decorum; and he repudiated totally the view that the average man was a philistine. In these circumstances his concern with infusing political activism with literary commitments is explicable, especially his interest in a

Sociedad literaria hispanoamericana in the United States and his welcome to a Hispanic American publishing house in New York in 1894.[31]

For Martí a revolution in sensibility was wedded to a revolution in politics and society; the emancipation of society was linked irrevocably to an emancipation of the imagination. This fusion should be placed at the service of the Caribbean and Hispanic American cause.

A political romanticism in Martí was linked with anticlericalism. His writing was infused throughout his life with a standard anticlericalism and a broad deism.[32] In Cuba itself the Church played no significant part in the authoritarian colonial order. Liberal, anticlerical government in Madrid, in alliance with the propertied Creoles, had early in the century assaulted the privileged status and wealth of the Cuban Church; and it had never recovered. The official Church, itself a slave-owner, had little influence among the black and mulatto elements in Cuban society which found more solace among Afro-cults and popular syncretisms. The quality and commitment of the clergy in Cuba (mainly Spanish, because few Cubans were ordained) was reputedly low. According to one jaundiced British Protestant traveller, Cuba was an unpopular assignment for Spanish priests, because they enjoyed more power and income in metropolitan Spain as well as better health; Cuba was the 'Botany Bay of the Romish clergy'.[33]

Probably both a freethinker and a freemason, Martí was not hostile to private religious belief but was deeply opposed to Church interference in politics. Martí attributed to Christ human qualities only.[34] In Spain he wrote ironically of religion as a political instrument of the privileged classes when the monarchy fell.[35] In Mexico Martí assumed a conventional, anticlerical line, speaking disparagingly of the Catholic press as 'vestirse con el manto de piedad', 'dressed with the mantle of piety'. But he observed approvingly that US Protestant missionaries in Mexico confronted not only rural clericalism and urban ultramontanism but also

el pueblo de las ciudades . . . si no religioso, ha ido demasiado adelante en su fe en la libre razón para volver a las negaciones tímidas y concepciones incompletas del protestanismo.[36]

city dwellers . . . who if not religious, have gone too far in their faith in reason to return to the timid negations and incomplete concepts of Protestantism.

In Guatemala Martí exhibited a chic anticlericalism, underestimating the underlying seriousness of purpose and resilience of the clergy, and displaying a dry amusement at the voluptuousness of virgins depicted in the churches: 'Afortunadamente hay vivas vírgines.'[37] 'Fortunately there are living virgins.'

In one sense Martí's religious attitudes had no need to develop, since the Church was not an issue in the independence struggle and put up only a token opposition to the introduction of an explicitly atheistic constitution after independence. Martí's attitudes were in Cuban terms unexceptional: 'Hay un Dios: el hombre . . .', 'There is one God: man . . .'

El ser religioso esta entrañado en el ser humano. Un pueblo irreligioso morirá, porque nada en el alimenta la virtud.[38]

The religious being lies within the human being. An irreligious people will perish because there is nothing in it to nourish virtue.

The lack of clarity surrounding Martí's position towards socialism and anarchism can be explained largely by their own imprecision. The predominance of Marxism within international socialism was, contrary to the assertions of some later Marxists, far from assured, while followers of Marx and Lassalle still vied for influence, and other variants upon socialism had continuous appeal.[39] Martí was endeavouring to evolve an ideology appropriate to the requirements of Hispanic America, and acknowledged that the main European socialist ideas were evolved in an environment of rapid urbanisation and industrialisation. In 1883 Martí saw Marx as an ardent reformer and internationalist:

Karl Marx estudió los modos de asentar al mundo sobre nuevas bases, y despertó a los dormidos, y les enseñó el modo de echar a tierra los puntales rotos. Pero anduvo de prisa, y un tanto en la sombra, sin ver que no nacen viables, ni de seno de mujer en el hogar, los hijos que no han tenido gestación natural y laboriosa. Aquí [New York] están buenos amigos de Karl Marx, que no fué sólo movedor titánico de las cóleras de los trabajadores europeos, sino veedor profundo en la razón de las miserias humanas, y en los destinos de los hombres, y hombre comido del ansia de hacer bien. El veía en todo lo que en si propio llevaba: rebeldía, camino a lo alto, lucha.[40]

Karl Mark studied the ways of placing the world on new bases. He awakened the sleeping, and taught them how to rid themselves of broken supports. But he went too fast and did not understand that children that have not had a natural and laborious gestation are neither born of woman nor are viable in their context. Here [New York] there are good friends of Karl Marx who was not only a titanic force behind the anger of European workers but also a profound interpreter of the causes of human misery and of men's fate. He was a man eaten up by the anxiety of doing good. He saw in the outside world that which he held within himself: rebelliousness, lofty objectives, struggle.

While pursuing radical alternatives to the egoism of Adam Smith, Martí remained distant from socialism. Retamar cites Martí in 1894:

Dos peligros tiene la idea socialista, como tantas otras; – el de las lecturas extranjerizas, confusas o incompletas, – y el de la soberbia y rabia disimulada de los ambiciosos.[41]

Like so many others, the socialist idea carries two dangers – that of imported, confused and incomplete readings – and that of arrogance and the undisguised rage of the ambitious.

Martí, in the words of Portuondo, did not accept the class struggle, but came to recognise class differences and the necessity of social justice.[42] Only in 1899, after Martí's death, was a socialist party founded in Cuba. Its ideological origins were heterogeneous: it counted both the work of Martí and the social thinking of Pope Leo XIII among its antecedents.[43]

Similar problems applied to anarchism. While in Spain, Martí showed slender interest in anarchism, despite the gradual diffusion from 1870–1 by the Spanish section of the International of a knowledge of the Marx–Bakunin debate and also, in 1873, a wave of spontaneous strikes and factory burnings.[44] Doubtless, Martí's lack of interest in anarchism is explained principally by his priorities, especially his concern for the precariousness of a nascent bourgeoisie. It may also be explained by the peripheral location of anarchism in Spain and by the fact that anarchism had none of the broader significance that it acquired in the 1930s.[45] However, it is curious that he failed to observe that anarchism might acquire an earlier significance in Cuba than in Spain, if only because many anarchist immigrant workers of dispersed Spanish origins were strategically located in Havana. Indeed, European immigrants frequently envisaged New World countries as a *tabula rasa*, free from the encrusted structures of their lands of origin, where their visions might be put readily into practice.

Martí displayed much in common with anarchism. He shared a sense of the present as a climacteric; he sought to elaborate an ideology for countries of lesser or no industrialisation where socialism was not influential. He had similar notions to anarchists of embracing the entire community of the poor; and he shared a perception of common cultural institutions and incipient unions as structural bases for radical political activity.[46] Other features of anarchism were clearly out of keeping with *martiano* thinking, especially an outright hostility to all notions of *patria* as inconsistent with internationalism and the anarchist resort to individual acts of terrorism and symbolic vengeance. Furthermore, pragmatic observation of US expansion rendered Martí insusceptible to anarchist ideals of a federal society based on self-contained, self-regulating communities that would be ill-prepared to confront a belligerent corporate capitalism.[47]

A gradually radicalised liberalism remained the dominant feature of *martiano* ideology. Often it is under-appreciated that liberalism in Latin American countries, and especially under colonial regimes, still contained radical and revolutionary potential in the late nineteenth century. An internationalism of language, an insistence on the exercise of individual judgement and the efficacy of individual actions, and an underlying generosity – all stood in sharp contrast with the wooden attitudes of the Spanish colonial administration in its last decades. Liberal vocabulary was, indeed, thoroughly diffused within Cuba by the 1880s. The spread of liberal ideas associated with the movements for Spanish American independence on the mainland were reinforced by occasional Liberal governments in Spain itself. Election campaigns to choose Cuban representatives in the Spanish Cortes during short-lived *aperturas* provided opportunities for a broadening of criticism of the colonial regime. That long before 1895 liberalism had won the intellectual argument in Cuba was evident from the failure by government ideologues to try to restate an authoritarian rationale in line with changing circumstances. The priorities of economic liberalism were absorbed by Cuban élites from the 1820s – the lowering of restrictions upon trade outside the empire, measures against Church wealth, the abolition of slavery and the unrestricted entry of British and US investment. So too, the main tenets of political liberalism had long been discussed. By the 1880s, they were the accepted and reiterated commonplaces of opposition and were integrated within popular mentalities, shaped and reshaped by the experiences of slave revolts, social banditry and the first, abortive war of independence.[48] Liberal language was by no means the monopoly of *independentistas*. Notions of liberty, justice and tyranny were resonant because they were shared with autonomists and annexationists. All three groupings resorted to the same web of assumptions and standard arguments, called upon a similar popular language, symbols and myths, and shared a sensitivity to the uses to which language could be put, even though they put the same concepts to opposite purposes.

The influence of Martí derived, in large measure, from his skill in putting familiar language to radical ends. He shared with his opposition predecessors and contemporaries an appeal to personal dignity and an emphasis upon a rupture with the complacencies of the colonial regime; he emphasised the fulfilment of the personality in a context of fraternity; he invoked a superior *patria* that would be brought about through civic virtue and dedication and a superior and simple morality with limited material aspirations. What, above all, distinguished Martí from his predecessors and from the annexationists and autonomists was his optimistic view of mass political participation. This was already becoming evident in his identification with co-operative mutualism among the first Mexican trade unions in 1875–6 and his support for early strike activity in the textiles and mining sectors.[49]

Martí rejected frankly élitist perceptions in which the politicisation of the 'humble classes' was an occasional and adventitious product of competition within the upper class; and he was unafraid of the risks of awakening popular over-expectations of government. Martí probably recognised the practical uses of such optimism, especially the pragmatic value of popular political participation in bringing about his vision of a *Cuba libre*. In the absence of patronage, sufficient resources to wage an effective war of independence could be raised only by acceding to popular demands for social change, and Martí looked to their satisfaction within a framework of class conciliation. Only through harnessing long-standing protest and a residual politicisation from an earlier period could independence be achieved.

## Martí and the integration of US experience

Long periods of exposure to the social consequences of industrialisation, urbanisation and mass immigration did little to undermine the assumptions and attitudes that Martí acquired in Spanish America and Spain. Both his reading of US authors and his observation of US society confirmed a stress in Martí's writing on harmony and reconciliation.

Thus it was entirely consistent with his previous positions that

Martí should admire the analysis of distress in a world of wealth contained in the writing of Henry George. Loath to abandon his past liberal attitudes Martí was attracted by George's endeavour to reconcile the *laissez-faire* liberalism of Smith and Ricardo with the socialism of Proudhon and Lassalle. George sought to distinguish monopoly profits from legitimate earnings of capital; and presented a policy of redistribution of land in order to achieve a more just society. He argued that over-concentration of private property was responsible for an enslavement of the labouring class, that leads to anarchy and despotism.[50]

A similar emphasis upon amelioration and social change without political violence was observed in Bellamy's critique of the US industrial system from which Martí drew heavily. Martí followed Bellamy in holding an Eastern-seaboard perception of US society. Both rejected an exclusive concern with material well-being, perceived an excessive individualism as inconsistent with patriotic spirit, held the industrial system responsible for poverty and stressed man's entitlement to an equal share in industrial production. Bellamy reflected and reinforced egalitarian versions of liberalism which rejected and sought to tame the emergent dominant form of corporate capitalism. Martí sympathised with Bellamy's pleading for the elimination of profit motivation and middlemen, the restoration of a spirit of service, and his invocation of equality of opportunity, the development of natural aptitudes, the practice of emulation as an incentive and the unification of the world in a single federal nation.[51]

The influence of Bellamy upon Martí was complemented by that of Emerson who embraced a 'pragmatic mysticism' that affirmed the primacy of the spiritual over the material, and who expressed a respect for Christianity – but not in its institutional expression – and a puritan emphasis on the integrity of individual religious experiences. Martí's priorities were indicated by the phrases he used to praise Emerson:

> poesía del espiritu humano . . . Castidad de expresión y sinceridad de pensamiento . . . una serena gratitud.[52]

> poetry of human spirit . . . Chastity of expression and sincerity of thought . . . a serene gratitude.

On the basis of both reading and observation, Martí advised wariness – neither an uncritical adulation nor total condemnation – towards the United States. He expressed admiration for heroism in the wars of independence, for the physical energy and material achievements of North Americans, for the popular clamour for reform, especially of electoral malpractices, and for the 'classical city' of Boston, a city of mystics and political agnostics, like Motley, Longfellow and Emerson.[53] On the other hand, Martí was sharply critical of the quality of justice, the spoils system and city-based politics; and he bewailed the philistinism of industrialists.[54] Martí was alert to the likelihood that, unrestrained, the commercial and financial dominance of Wall Street, which aroused the ire of US populists in the south and west of the United States, would shortly be transferred to Cuba, with similar adverse consequences for the small farmers, whom, like US populists, he envisaged as the bedrock of a radical democracy.

Exile in the United States was never responsible for a clearly articulated class politics in Martí. His thinking was pervaded by a literary humanism characterised by thought in images and a preference for analogies to the harmony of the family. His writing exhibited a conventional idealisation of the common interests and aims of the family, combined with a stress on the exemplary role of the paterfamilias, and values that echoed de Tocqueville – dignity, honour, decorum and the pursuit of happiness. He showed little interest in refining conceptualisation and a clear aversion to such concepts as ethnic distinction and class struggle.

This is not to assert that Martí was blind to the growing dimensions of class conflict. It is apparent that the bomb outrages at the Chicago Haymarket that marked the climax of a wave of labour unrest in the United States absorbed Martí's concern; and that their aftermath awakened Martí to the growing profundity and complexity of social stratification in the United States. After initially condemning the anarchist action, Martí came round to holding income-concentrating and profit-maximising businessmen responsible for both aborting a liberal vision of a harmonious society in which all social groups shared in prosperity and disrupting a previous confidence in the goodwill of a virtuous political leadership.

The fluidity of the class structure and the regionalisation of class formation in the United States and Latin America in the late nineteenth century probably precluded any more sophisticated analysis of class relationships in Martí's oeuvre. His priority – a *Cuba libre* – required, in any event, a class alliance. The independence struggle embodied a challenge to colonial assumptions that underlay a sharply pyramidal class structure that gave rise to explosions of social tension, which, in turn, provided a rationale for authoritarianism and externally imposed discipline. The independence leaders responded to popular demands that the boundaries of self-fulfilment should be pushed outwards, and took advantage – especially among émigré workers – of a decline in respect for the values sustaining a rigidly stratified society. Martí and his colleagues articulated persistent demands for full civil rights for the black and mulatto population, which, despite the legalisation of racial intermarriage in 1881, were still in 1890–1 denied. The multiracial cause was so deeply identified with the independence struggle that the belated endorsement by the Spanish government of the implementation of desegregationist legislation in 1894 made slender impact.[55] Martí's commitment to multiracialism, and to the view that a war that was both multiracial and national would have desirable levelling and equalising consequences, clearly had a profound impact upon a younger generation.[56]

A vocabulary of eclectic amalgams and pluralistic notions, shaped during his exiles, was useful to Martí in avoiding the rigidity of class appeal and in enlarging his support-base, so as to unite fragments of the Creole élite with mobile sectors of the labour force. Martí was determined to unite groups whose class combativity and ethnic militancy were intensified by an externally imposed status, especially caste consciousness, that long outlived slavery.

## Diagnosis and prescription for Cuba and Spanish America

Martí was a keen observer of the dramatic transformation in the international political and economic order that began in the last three decades of the nineteenth century. He wrote of the expansion of international trade and investment, and was anguished that while other countries like Argentina and Mexico diversified their export profiles, Cuba remained over-reliant on the same monocrop that dominated her external trade in the 1840s. Martí wrote too of international immigration. He showed a concern that chronic labour scarcity might defer the prosperity he envisaged for the continent; and, like contemporaries in the Southern Cone, he exhibited an interest in colonisation schemes in New Zealand.[57] Himself a victim of exile and forced migration, Martí was an early observer of the significance of intracontinental migrations and self-consciously exemplified patterns of transmission of radical ideas and their selective assimilation.

Martí's view of the continent was a view from the north. His generalisations about Latin (or, as he usually insisted, Spanish) America were shaped exclusively by an experience of Cuba and its northern republics. There is no evidence that Martí travelled further south than Venezuela. Among Spanish American republics, he had a particular admiration for Argentina. Rejecting stereotypes of Italian immigrants as organ-grinders, fruit-sellers and shoeshine boys, Martí extolled the merits of Italians as the industrialists, writers and actors who enriched and invigorated the economy and culture of Buenos Aires.[58] Martí's praise for Argentine enterprise in pushing back the frontier, and for the Argentine government in encouraging European immigration, fostering urban and rural settlement, and creating a business climate conducive to the efflorescence of banking and financial institutions, was unstinting in the 1880s.

Martí's perceptions of Argentina were, to a large extent, shaped by his characteristically Eastern-seaboard view of the United States. In his writings on the United States Martí showed little consciousness of the scale and character of frontier conflict. This unawareness was qualified only by an occasional reference to the urgency of allocating land to American Indians, both to compensate for past depredations and to divert them from belligerence to small-scale farming, where they could enjoy a share in the prevailing order and a stake in the market economy. Martí then projected this vision of a largely conflict-free frontier into Argentina, only in 1890 modifying his views a little in order to express some concern for the destruction of *gaucho* traditions. But these cautious revisions were not developed into any extended analysis of rural tensions in Argentina between *estancia* and *gaucho*, rural workers and landlords or even between large *estancieros* and small tenant farmers. Again, structural analysis was not evident in Martí.

Since internationally syndicated journalism was a principal way by which Martí extemporised an income, it reassured him to learn that his letters were popular writing.

Sin entrar jamás en denuncias ni censuras concretas, sino que – y esto me halaga más – mis simples correspondencias me han atraído el cariño y la comunicación espontánea de los hombres de mente más alta y mejor corazón la América que habla castellano.

I feel honoured that, without ever entering into specific denunciations or rebukes, my simple letters have brought me the spontaneous warmth and communication of the highest-minded and most tender-hearted men in Spanish-speaking America.

But he was perplexed that his letters, which by 1887 were published in twenty Latin American newspapers, had more success in the Southern Cone than in Mexico.[59] This perplexity indicated Martí's lack of awareness of comparative political and social structures: the potential readership for any journalism was larger in the Southern

Cone than in porfirian Mexico, owing to higher rates of urbanisation, higher levels of literacy and a political climate more conducive to the free exchange and publication of liberal ideas.

For Martí it was crucial that Cuba should not commit the error of over-mechanical emulation of European or North American examples. He warned against an over-concern with artifices, theories and the application of models that were out of joint with local circumstances. It was vital, he indicated, that Cuba should avoid repeating the errors of the earlier Hispanic American republics, but he suggested too that this was unlikely, since Cuba enjoyed a political maturity that was not evident on the mainland in the 1820s. Martí's stress on devising autochthonous solutions to Hispanic American and Caribbean problems was clearly expressed in the Manifiesto de Montecristi (1895), which can be read as a definitive statement of his mature political attitudes. It was essential to avoid repeating the mistakes committed in the 'republicas feudales o teóricas de Hispano-América', 'the feudal or theoretical republics of Hispanic America':

> el error de ajustar a modelos extranjeros . . . la concentración de la cultura meramente literaria en los capitales; el erróneo apego de las repúblicas a los costumbres señoriales de la colonia; la creación de caudillos rivales consiguiente al trato receloso e imperfecto de las comarcas apartadas; la condición rudimentaria de la única industria, agrícola o ganadera; y el abandono y desdén de la fecunda raza indigena.[60]

> the error of adjusting to foreign models . . . the concentration of a merely literary culture in the capitals; the mistaken fidelity of the republics to the seigneurial customs of the colony; the emergence of rival *caudillos* consistent with the mistrustful and imperfect treatment of distant provinces; the rudimentary condition of the monoculture, be it agricultural or livestock; and the abandonment and disdain for the rich indigenous race.

Patriotism and nationalism – *cubanidad* – were pervasive themes in Martí's writing. An early (1871) insistence on patriotic integrity was elaborated in his subsequent publications, and probably enhanced by the experience of exile.[61] Early too in his writings Martí identified the Cuban struggle for independence with those of the mainland Spanish American countries against Spain, of the United States against Britain, of Italy against Austria and of Spain against France.[62] According to Martí, patriotism was a purifying and a 'holy force' when it promoted human happiness, that was to be censured only when it was divisive of peoples.[63] For Martí, writing in 1892, the integral features of patriotism were

> la pasión republicana, la ansiedad de la acción, la unión de las energías, el orgullo de la virtud cubana, la fe en los humildes y el olvido de las ofensas, moverán, y nada más, nuestras plumas.[64]

> republican passion, desire for action, union of energies, a pride in Cuban virtue, a faith in the humble, and the forgetting of old scores; these sentiments, and only these, will move our pens.

For Martí, national redemption was closely tied up with race. In his early writings a negative stereotype of *mestizaje* can be seen, in which Spanish America suffered from a heritage of ethnic heterogeneity and its development was retarded by a blend of the absence of a work ethic among Spaniards and the passive resignation of Indians. But in his later publications, Martí evolved a positive stereotype, by which *nuestra América* enjoyed the peculiar advantages of *mestizaje*, that sprang from a fusion of the supposed positive qualities of the Indian, like patience and generosity, with those of the Spaniard, like courage and determination. *Mestizaje* conferred upon Hispanic America a degree of potential for national integration that was unthinkable in Asia or Europe, and would probably hold it in good stead against US penetration.

Martí rejected wholeheartedly the genesis of an aggressive foreign economic policy that crystallised in the Pan-American Congress of 1889–90 and the American International Monetary Commission of 1891. Indeed, just as the events of 1886–7 prompted a radicalisation of Martí's perceptions of the internal ordering of US society, those of 1889–91 crystallised his views of its external ambitions. Departing from the convention that a republic was incapable of imperial ambition, Martí saw incipient Pan-Americanism as a deviation from traditions of Bolivarian idealism and as an ill-disguised cover for an avaricious alliance of big business and politicians, determined to promote interests antagonistic to those of *nuestra América*, including the consummation of annexationist ambitions and the coercion of Hispanic American countries into severing ties with their European trading partners. Martí saw some cause for optimism in the exchanges, since aggressive US proposals evoked an unprecedented degree of Latin American unity, while sharp divisions within the US delegation over tactics and strategy became public knowledge.[65]

To perceive Martí as a fully-fledged economic nationalist would be to project ahistorical attitudes from a subsequent period. Martí was, in economics, a pragmatic liberal, who argued for the selective application of tariff barriers and trade agreements so as to protect nascent industry. Protection was justified in terms of the liberal notion that natural entities should be free to grow but sometimes require assistance in their early stages. Martí did not deviate from liberal conventions in prescribing a principally agricultural economy for Hispanic America, in arguing that Latin America enjoyed a comparative advantage in export agriculture, or in visualising nations of small farmers without extremes of income maldistribution.

In Mexico he was deeply hostile to proposals for a trade agreement with the United States, whose only beneficiary, according to Martí, would be the United States, because Mexico already enjoyed adequate access to her neighbour's markets and a small range of Mexican products would be exchanged for a large range of US manufactures and some foodstuffs.[66] He was equally adamant in rejecting porfirian railway concessions that he considered over-generous to US interests. Meanwhile, Martí was conventionally pragmatic in arguing against a continued over-reliance on the mining sector. His concerns were threefold: that Latin American economies were over-vulnerable to violent price oscillations and overseas competition; that profits were over-concentrated in the hands of a few entrepreneurs; and that mining was inconducive to the formation of industrious habits.

For Martí internationalism was not antithetical to nationalism. Following Bolívar, different ranges of nationalism and internationalism appeared in his writing. A Cuban nationalism that embraced both exiles and residents in the island was foremost in Martí's mind. He also addressed himself to *antillanismo*, a solidarity of Hispanic Caribbean nationalists. Martí displayed a general concern for the evolution of a Hispanic American identity that included the Hispanic Caribbean and peoples of Hispanic American origins in the United States. And, on occasions, he expressed a sense of kinship with patriots and nationalists in the colonial world as a whole.

*Antillanismo* long antedated Martí. A common cause brought Cuban and Puerto Rican nationalists together in New York as early as 1850.[67] Subsequently, in 1867, the Dominican ideologue and doctor, Ramón Betances, exiled in New York and Haiti, who wrote as *El Antillano* in the pro-Cuban and Puerto Rican independence publication *Voz de América: Organo de las antillas españolas* (1865–7), proclaimed an Antillean federation. A sense of shared problems was visible in the organisation of the Sociedad Republicana de Cuba y Puerto Rico (1865) and the Comite Revolucionario (1867), and also in collaboration in the abortive Lares insurrection of 1868 and the war of 1868–78. The war of Peru and Chile against Spain aroused among

Cuban and Puerto Rican nationalists hopes of mainland support for the completion of the independence struggle, which were briefly sustained by the Chilean mission of Benjamín Vicuña Mackenna. He advocated unsuccessfully a concerted naval attack by Colombia, Venezuela, Peru and Chile upon Spain at her most vulnerable points, namely her Caribbean colonies.[68]

As US expansion became more aggressive, solidarity became a more permanent theme. Martí and other Cubans expressed militant support for Dominican nationalists angry at compatriots who endorsed bids by US interests to acquire Samaná Bay in 1889.[69] More joint action was evident in the 1890s. Betances was made representative of the Partido Revolucionario Cubano in Paris. Hostos, for whom Martí expressed some affinity, as early as 1875, took a leading role in the formation in 1895 of a Sección Puertorriqueña of the Partido Revolucionario Cubano.[70]

Paul Estrade has offered the hypothesis that the most radical national consciousness (*prise de conscience*) to be observed in the colonial world in the last decades of the nineteenth century was visible in the Hispanic Caribbean. In Martí, Hostos, Betances and Luperón Estrade identifies a blend of democratic liberalism that stressed individual liberty and representative government, freedom of enterprise from external control and the importance of public instruction with a more radical emphasis on anti-racism, anti-imperialism and *antillanismo*.[71] Problems of external penetration by a dynamic US capitalism, which hardly touched Brazil till the 1930s or Argentina till later, were confronted by Cuba in the 1880s and 1890s, owing to the chronology of United States expansion. One further feature of *antillanismo* that merits attention is Martí's stress on the possibility of exploiting national bargaining leverage. The view that the Caribbean islands (and mainland nations) might exploit a disputed and unresolved external ascendancy to national advantage was mentioned but not developed by Martí.[72] He is imprecise about the circumstances in which *nuestra América* might explore opportunities for playing European powers off against the United States.

The internationalism of Martí was principally Hispanic American, but it came to embrace anti-colonial conflicts in other regions. Thus Martí identified with Egyptian resistance to British imperialism and Tunisian to French. His brief critique followed contemporary radical anti-imperialist thinking in Europe in emphasising the human and financial costs of imperial activism and in interpreting it as a demagogic distraction from domestic conflicts.[73] But the analysis was not taken further.

## *Martí and pragmatic politics*

A lofty literary scholarship that applauds the ideology and poetry of Martí fails frequently to acknowledge his consummate skill as a pragmatic politician. Martí was determined to turn patriotic commitment into an effective republican coalition in opposition, which, led from exile and building on past experience, would articulate aspirations of Cubans both abroad and in Cuba.[74] He aimed to raise funds both in the United States and Jamaica, through revolutionary clubs with mutual aid and possibly masonic overtones, in which differences of ideology, class, race and religion would be subordinate to national objectives. The clear objective of Martí was the rapid demise of the Spanish colonial regime and the establishment of a network of revolutionary clubs. Aiming to arrange the broad guidelines of a republican succession without entering into potentially divisive issues like the nature of its structure or the timetable for a transition to the republic, Martí set out to establish orderly procedures and processes in a loose and heterogeneous but durable coalition based on the sentiment of nationality and the principle of organised action.[75]

Martí considered the Partido Revolucionario Cubano (PRC) to be vital to the clarification of the aims, purpose and character of the independence struggle. He saw it too as a nucleus for a government in the independent republic of the future that devised a policy framework for peace. Recruitment practices and regular correspondence that nourished popular identification with the PRC were emphasised by Martí, because he believed a high level of popular identification to be essential to the health of the republic. He saw the PRC as valuable both in giving a future electorate experience of democratic participation and in accustoming the leadership to the notion of accountability to the entire party and not only to its paymasters.

Martí's attitude to annexationists was ambivalent. On the one hand, he attacked them on the grounds that their cause merely deferred the final triumph of independence;[76] on the other hand, he showed a pragmatic prudence in acknowledging the sincerity of some annexationists, and in entering into alliances with Creole businessmen impatient with the incorrigible Spanish rejection of proposals to dismantle archaic features of the colonial state. Protesting at the lack of congruence between economic structures and Spanish policies, segments of the Cuban business élites looked to further incorporation within the US economic orbit. Concerned that the ideal of a *Cuba libre* should not be sacrificed to transient interests, Martí acknowledged implicitly the tactical desirability of alliances with annexationists, of the propertied classes, who might be converted to the cause of independence. Martí nevertheless, in 1892, rebuked the timidity of the propertied classes:

> Y quién dice el proprietario tímido, me garantiza de que después del triunfo de la revolución, no continue yo padeciendo bajo los revolucionarios ambiciosos e impotentes, bajo un país de abogados sin empleo y de caudillos encabezados, lo mismo que padezco bajo este gobierno español de prostitución y simonía?[77]

And who, says the timid proprietor, gives me the guarantee that after the revolution, I do not continue suffering under ambitious and powerless revolutionaries, under a country of unemployed lawyers and *caudillos*, just as I suffer under this prostituted and nepotistic Spanish government?

Concerned that the ideal of a *Cuba libre* should not be sacrificed to transient interests, Martí was anxious that no schisms in and defections from the PRC should occur as a consequence of its being trapped in the narrowness of particular interests and regional or sectional differences.

Martí, the pragmatist, identified the opportunity to seize the political initiative in the early 1890s. Much earlier political debate had focused on the reform of the colonial state, the possibility of a measure of Creole political participation on a restricted franchise with strict property and literary qualifications, and the greater incorporation in decision-making of pressure groups, like the Economic Society, which represented strategic sectors and demanded that a dynamic direction be given to the Cuban economy. But by 1890 this debate was dead. Even conservative Creoles, for whom the maintenance of order, the pursuit of economic growth and the further propulsion of Cuba into the world economy, were the main priorities, acknowledged that the colonial compact was obsolete. The Economic Movement, formed from the Reformist Party and embodying the opinions of propertied groups without a direct interest in perpetuating the Hispano–Cuban connection in its established form, failed to put down roots and lost all momentum. Thus arose an opportunity for Martí and his allies to fill a political vacuum; thus too the tactical imperative of placating propertied elements alarmed that the programme of democratisation and the equation that Martí and Maceo drew between national independence and a multiracial society threatened their interests. So too there were compelling reasons for

Martí to reassure Spanish immigrants that they would not be victimised in a republican order.[78]

For Cuba Martí was determined not to repeat one problem he had encountered in both Mexico and Guatemala. Observing both countries from the optimistic and untypical environment of the liberal capital-city intelligentsia, he had failed initially to perceive the persistence and tenacity of *caudillismo* and *caciquismo* and the dangers posed to the radical tradition of republican virtue embodied in Lerdo by regional and local power structures whose principal linkages were personalistic and clientilistic.[79] Hence in Mexico (perhaps not in Guatemala), Martí was caught by surprise to discover that liberalism contained propensities for retrogression and military dictatorship.[80]

The clash of Martí with the *caudillista* features of the military leadership of Máximo Gómez threatened to demolish the civil–military *independentista* coalition. The apparently intemperate assertion of Martí that the Cuban struggle was not the 'exclusive property'[81] of any one leader has incurred the wrath of such scholars as Philip S. Foner, who is ungenerous to Martí and indicates insufficient awareness of the continental context of revolutionary idealism disintegrating into militarism, which Martí knew well:

> Unlike Maceo, who knew the need for strong authority in the revolutionary struggle from past experience and was inclined to overlook Gómez's dictatorial conduct, Martí saw in Gómez's behaviour an evil that had to be combatted before the revolutionary movement degenerated into a personal operation, divorced from the masses of the people . . .[82]

The evaporation of revolutionary commitment into the politics of myopic self-interest in the 1900s and into gangsterism and thuggery in the 1930s and 1940s justified Martí rather than Foner, when Martí placed his overwhelming stress upon the imperative of sustaining a unified national struggle and of

> impedir que las simpatías revolucionarias en Cuba se tuerzan y esclavicen por ningun interés de grupo, para la preponderancia de una clase social, o lo autoridad desmedida de una agrupación militar o civil, ni de una comarca determinada, ni de una raza sobre otra.[83]

preventing Cuban revolutionary feelings from being twisted and enslaved by any group interests, the hegemony of a social class, or the excessive authority of military or civilian groups, of specific regions or of one race over another.

In this struggle autonomism had no part. For Martí it was never an
option or even a short-term expedient or transitional phase. The
pragmatic generosity that he extended to annexationists did not also
embrace autonomists. By 1894 it was clear to Martí that no middle
option between independence and colonial status existed, and it was
essential that there should be no recurrence of the familiar cycle of
concessionary promises by the Spanish government that detached
'moderate' elements from the *independentista* struggle, followed by a
reassertion of authority by Spain and its withdrawal of concessions.
Martí expressed a total lack of confidence in autonomism:

> La reacción autonomista, lejos de ponernos en mal, nos ha servido
> de bandera; aturdida está, y la seguimos aturdiendo: los que están
> con nosotros, con nosotros siguen: con los que pudieran estar con
> los autonomistas, nosotros no contábamos.[84]

> The autonomist reaction, far from doing us harm, has become our
> banner: it is puzzled and we puzzle it, and will continue to do so.
> Those that are with us continue with us; and we are not counting on
> those that could be with the autonomists.

## *Perspectives*

Martí displayed a radical idealism tempered by liberal pragmatism
placed at the service of a revolutionary cause. The objective of a *Cuba
libre* provided a steady and unshakeable impulse dictating Martí's
choices. Yet his vision of an independent Cuba was never completely
articulated. His suggestive observation in 1893 was never developed
further:

> Independencia es una cosa, y revolución otra. La independencia en
> los Estados Unidos vino cuando Washington, y la revolución
> cuando Lincoln.[85]

> Independence is one thing, and revolution another. Independence
> came to the United States at the time of Washington, and revolution
> in the Lincoln era.

Fully cognisant of the destructiveness of war ('Las guerras no son
cosas de bastidor y de merengue'[86] – 'Wars are not for the weak and
the feeble'), Martí envisaged a brief struggle terminating in
independence. Yet he miscalculated. The war was protracted. Its
destructiveness, recently analysed by Louis Pérez Jr, hastened the

process of decapitalisation of Cuban and Spanish planters and accelerated the penetration of incipient transnational enterprise.[87]

The revisionist historiography that seeks to demystify Martí still has numerous questions to answer. Were his prolonged absences from Cuba responsible for a misreading of conditions in the 1890s? How far did Martí underestimate the scale of penetration by US-based enterprises before war began in 1895; and was he over-optimistic in his view that circumstances were propitious to the efflorescence of an egalitarian pro-yeoman-farmer ideology? Did absence incline Martí to overestimate the level of multiracial solidarity among Cubans? Did he overestimate too the extent to which warfare served as an integrative and levelling experience for rural and urban workers, peasants, small businessmen, exiles and resident Cubans? Was it impossible, in view of the data available, for Martí to assess accurately either the degree of Cuban commitment to the independence cause or the stubborn tenacity and the adaptability of strategy and tactics of metropolitan Spain? Did he miscalculate upon an unrealistic level of Hispanic American material support? The limited resources facilitated by Eloy Alfaro of Ecuador, to whom Martí had been introduced in New York by Vargas Vila, did not obscure either the absence of substantial Venezuelan or Mexican support or the opposition of the ultramontanist Conservative government of Miguel Antonio Caro in Colombia, which, still at the onset of the War of the Thousand Days (1899–1902), idealised the authoritarian order of the Spanish colony and had given diplomatic backing to metropolitan Spain.

The problem of the particularities of the composition of the Partido Revolucionario Cubano merits close attention. Were PRC resources sufficient to co-ordinate a prolonged war? Were they overstretched by commitments to a Sección puertorriqueña? What was the significance of a shift within the PRC to the annexationist faction led by Tomás Estrada Palma after Martí's death? Recalling the occasions when Martí dwelt upon his own mortality, why did he not prepare an heir or a group of heirs to succeed him?

Of Venezuela, the leading Marxist historian, Germán Carrera Damas, has recently concluded,

El culto a Bolívar ha llegado a constituir la columna vertebral, en pocas ocasiones el universo, del pensamiento.[88]

The Bolívarian cult has come to be the vertebral column, and sometimes the universe, of thought.

Martí has occupied a parallel, though not identical, position, as

eponymous hero and spokesman for Cuba. Cuban revisionist writing
has inaugurated the trend to dispel propensities towards a *martiano*
hagiography. It can be confidently forecast that thorough scholarly
investigation of the thorniest questions surrounding Martí's career
will further restore his humanity and clarify his significance.

# 8 Void and renewal: José Martí's modernity[1]

IVAN M. SCHULMAN

To Noël Salomon: *in memoriam*

Contemporary readings of the last fifteen years of Spanish American modernism's texts reveal the intensely subjective as well as the more objective socio-historical perceptions shared by the nineteenth-century writers who faced the turn-of-the century 'revolución del pensamiento',[2] revolution of thought, with its anguished and dramatic social upheavals. The modernist writers of the period sensed the shadows and mysteries of their volatile age which created restless, precarious concepts of time, a feeling of being 'modern' ('moderno'), 'ancient' ('antiguo'), and at the same time, 'very eighteenth-century' ('muy siglo diez y ocho'), as Rubén Darío characterised himself in his *Cantos de vida y esperanza* (1905). These multiple temporal dimensions evidence the hybrid nature and the unstable character of modern man's being and existence. They also signal a pattern that surfaces with Spanish American modernism (*c.* 1875), coincides with the dawn of Spanish American cultural modernity, and grows with the expansion of the socio-political modernisation of the continent.[3] This modernisation – modernism and modernity – is, as Angel Rama has noted,

el conjunto de formas literarias que traducen las diferentes maneras de la incorporación de América Latina a la *modernidad*, concepción socio-cultural generada por la civilización industrial de la burguesía del XIX, a la que fue asociada rápida y violentamente nuestra América en el último tercio del siglo pasado, por la expansión económica y política de los imperios europeos a la que se suman los Estados Unidos.[4]

the whole range of literary forms that translate the various ways of incorporating Latin America into *modernity*, a socio-cultural concept produced by the industrial civilisation of the nineteenth-century bourgeoisie, to which our America was joined quickly and violently in the last third of the previous century, through the

153

economic and political expansion of the empires of Europe, to which the United States added itself.

The violence of this transformation created in many modernists the concept of a baneful fate, described by Martí in 'El poema del Niágara':

> no hay ahora mandrugo más denteado que un alma de poeta: si se ven con los ojos del alma, sus puños mondados y los huecos de sus alas arrancadas manan sangre.[5]

> there is no crust of bread more gnawed than a poet's soul: regarded by the eyes of the soul, his raw fists and the holes left by his torn-off wings spurt blood.

The metaphor *sangre* belongs to what Cintio Vitier has termed the 'future' voice of a modern writer in his daily struggle with the void of modern existence.[6] A poet in both prose and verse, a revolutionary in art and politics, Martí had a futurity of vision which allowed him to fathom unexplored poetic spheres and search the distant horizons of a collective experience which he then internalised and expressed as personal testimony. This visionary poet and seer, who shares in the tradition initiated by Baudelaire and Rimbaud, succeeded in grasping the essence of the social crisis of modernist reconstructions and deconstructions with such clairvoyance and intuition that even today his acumen astonishes us. For he understood, far better than his contemporaries, that his was an age of 'elaboración y transformación espléndidas', 'splendid elaboration and transformation', characterised, however, by a 'desmembramiento de la mente humana',[7] a 'fragmentation of the human mind'.

The terrifying sense of a social collapse and universal apocalypse was felt by him as a writer: he metaphorised it as blood (*sangre*) and counterbalanced it with an eighteenth-century hope for the regeneration of man and his universe, or as Martí expressed it metaphorically, the reconstructions generated by *la sangre nueva*. In examining Martí's works we may often discover elements that appear at variance with each other or even paradoxical. But these are signs of modernity that constitute the corner-stone of Martí's ideology, the axis of his political life, and the symbiotic nature of his revolutionary art. In his writings there coexist ideological and stylistic liberation, oneiric imagery, epistemological disintegration, linguistic experiments, existential solitude and anguish, classic style, creative self-reflection, new patterns of poetic rhyme and versification, faith in mankind, idealism fused with materialism, and an insistence upon re-examining and preserving traditional forms and styles of previous periods of Hispanic literature.

## A search for new forms

'Estrofa nueva', 'Rosilla nueva', (Martí), 'La vida nueva', 'Rumbos nuevos', (Rodó) are titles, gleaned at random, that symbolise Martí's ideological and aesthetic belief in an inexorable need for re-creations in the face of an existing world he viewed as crumbling and a coming world still in a state of gestation, with all the anguished uncertainties of an evolutionary process. As he observed in 1882:

> No hay obra permanente porque las obras de los tiempos de reenquiciamiento y remolde son por esencia mudables e inquietas; no hay caminos constantes, vislúmbranse apenas los altares nuevos, grandes y abiertos como bosques. De todas partes solicitan la mente ideas diversas – y las ideas son como los pólipos, y como la luz de las estrellas, y como las olas de la mar . . . La elaboración del nuevo estado social hace insegura la batalla por la existencia personal y más recios de cumplir los deberes diarios que, no hallando vías anchas, cambian a cada instante de forma y vía, agitados del susto que produce la probabilidad o vecindad de la miseria.[8]

No work is permanent, because works belonging to times of resettling and remoulding are essentially changeable and unstable; there are no steady paths, and one hardly has a glimpse of the new altars, large and open like forests. From all sides the mind is assailed by diverse ideas – and ideas are like polyps, and like the light from the stars, and like the waves of the sea . . . The forming of the new social state makes the battle for one's personal existence unsure and one's daily duties more difficult to fulfil, and these, because they cannot find broad highways, change their shape and their path with every passing moment, stirred up by the fright produced by the probability and the proximity of wretched poverty.

Darío called the 'new' spirits *raros*; these were the writers who experienced the agony, the social and cultural relativism, described by José Enrique Rodó in 1896:

> El movimiento de las ideas tiende cada vez más al individualismo en la producción y aún en la doctrina, a la dispersión de voluntades y

de fuerzas, a la variedad inarmónica, que es el signo característico de la transición. – Ya no se profesa el culto de una misma Ley y la ambición de una gloria que ha de ser compartida, sino la fe del temperamento propio y la teoría de la propia genialidad . . . Los imanes de las escuelas han perdido su fuerza de atracción, y son hoy hierro vulgar que se trabaja en el laboratorio de la crítica. Los cenáculos, como legiones sin armas, se disuelven; los maestros, como los dioses, se van . . .[9]

The movement of ideas is increasingly tending towards individualism in production and even doctrine, to the scattering of wills and forces, to non-harmonious variety, which is the characteristic sign of transition. – No longer is one and the same Law venerated or shared glory seen as the goal of one's strivings, but rather one has faith in one's own temperament and the theory of one's own genius . . . The magnets constituted by schools of thought have lost their power of attraction, and today are mere lumps of iron on which work is carried out in the laboratory of criticism. Cultural circles, like legions deprived of their weapons, are dissolving; the masters, like the gods, are disappearing . . .

The sense of a hecatomb exhausts modern man and leaves him dizzy, as Martí observed:

Con un problema nos levantamos, nos acostamos ya con otro problema. Las imágenes se devoran en la mente. No alcanza el tiempo para dar forma a lo que se piensa. Se pierden unas en otras las ideas en el mar mental . . . Antes las ideas se erguían en silencio en la mente como recias torres, por lo que, cuando surgían, se las veía de lejos: hoy se salen en tropel de los labios, como semillas de oro, que caen en suelo hirviente; se quiebran, se rarifican, se evaporan, se malogran . . . se deshacen en chispas encendidas; se desmigajan.[10]

When we rise from our bed we face one problem and by the time we go to bed we face another. Images are devoured in the mind. There is no time to give shape to one's thoughts. They lose themselves in one another in the sea of the mind . . . Before, ideas rose up in silence in the mind like strong towers, and for this reason, when they arose, they could be seen from afar: today they flock out from one's lips, like golden seeds falling on boiling ground; they break, they lose their intelligibility, they evaporate, they come to nothing . . . they break up in flaming sparks; they crumble away.

New times, 'unhinged' ('desquiciados') times, 'an almost universal imbalance' ('desequilibrio, casi universal'),[11] are the characterisations Martí uses to describe this turmoil in his novel *Amistad funesta* (*Lucía Jerez*, 1885), a work snubbed by its author, but seen today as strikingly original and modern, one in which the narrator/author alludes to the collapse of 'las antiguas vallas sociales',[12] 'the old social barriers', that in the 'blue countries' (those of Spanish America) has produced a new and vast class of aristocrats:

> aristócratas de la inteligencia, con todas las necesidades de parecer y gustos ricos que de ella vienen, sin que haya habido tiempo aún, en lo rápido del vuelco, para que el cambio en la organización y repartimiento de las fortunas corresponda a la brusca alteración en las relaciones sociales, producidas por las libertades políticas y la vulgarización de los conocimientos.[13]

> aristocrats of the intelligence, with all the needs of appearance and rich tastes that come from it, without there having yet been time, so quick has been the upset, for the change in organisation and sharing out of fortunes to correspond to the sharp alterations in social relations, produced by political liberties and the diffusion of knowledge to the common man.

In reading this passage one is struck by its similarity to another written twenty-five years later by Rodó on the economic transformation – the modernisation – of Latin American societies:

> Comenzaba en estas sociedades el impulso de engrandecimiento material y económico, y como sugestión de él, la pasión de bienestar y riqueza, con su cortejo de frivolidad sensual y de cinismo epicúreo; la avidez de oro, que, llevando primero a la forzada aceleración del ritmo del trabajo, como harto lento prometedor, y lo sustituía por la audacia de la especulación aventurera.[14]

> In these societies the impulse towards material and economic aggrandisement was beginning, and, suggesting by it, the passion for comfort and wealth, with their train of sensual frivolity and epicurean cynicism; the greed for gold which, bringing first of all the obligatory acceleration of the rhythm of work, like a sluggish and satiated man of promise, and replaced it by the audacity of adventurous speculation.

Martí understood the dynamics of a multifaceted modernisation in its historic contexts – both diachronic and synchronic: especially the effects of a protracted colonial experience compounded by the economic dysfunctions created in 'peripheral' countries by the eurocentric attempts of his day to replicate cultural models and social structures of the centres of power and influence, cultural as well as political.

In the nineteenth century Martí understood our contemporary views of false homologies:[15] as he pointed out, 'Somos en nuestros propios países, cabezas hispanoamericanas, cargadas de ideas de Europa y Norteamérica',[16] 'We, in our own countries, are Hispanic American heads imbued with ideas from Europe and North America.' And to this incisive thought he added that with a 'descosida e incompleta', 'loose and incomplete', education, a Spanish American 'no halla luego natural empleo en nuestros países despoblados y rudimentarios', 'does not find obvious employment in our unpopulated and backward countries' – countries that the Cuban wished to see progress, by taking advantage of their fertile soil.[17]

In Martí's *ideario* two modernities stand out, different and antagonic and yet related; they constitute the conflicting modernities M. Calinescu calls 'bourgeois' and 'aesthetic':

> At some point during the first half of the nineteenth century an irreversible split occurred between modernity as a stage in the history of western civilisation – a product of scientific and technological progress, of the industrial revolution, of the seeping economic and social changes brought about by capitalism – and modernity as an aesthetic concept. Since then, the relations between the two modernities have been irreducibly hostile, but not without allowing and even stimulating a variety of mutual influences in their race for each other's destruction.[18]

In Martí's works and in those of other contemporary modernists we frequently discover a defence of the doctrine of progress, the benefits of science and technology, the cult of reason and the ideal of liberty, elements of bourgeois modernity. But aesthetic modernity is also evident in its negative dimensions in Martí's critical attitude *vis-à-vis* the decadent values of capitalist, materialistic society, whose development the Cuban analysed in his reportage from the United States during some fifteen years, and evident in positive ways in his exaltation of humanistic idealism, morality, the cult of beauty, the sense of historical evolution and the contemporaneity of the past in the formation of nineteenth-century standards, in other words, the historic 'returns' – whether conscious or half-conscious – which are an integral part of modernist art in the first stages of Spanish American modernity.

## Martí and Spanish American modernity

Modernism, modern, modernity: three terms that designate the aesthetic and ideological revolution that developed in heterogeneous and unstable forms in a galaxy of writers – moderns/modernists – from 1875 on, first in prose and then in verse. Max Henríquez Ureña, the historian of Hispanic modernism, has observed that is difficult to assign an exact date to these terms, but he points out that:

> ya en 1888 el vocablo modernismo era empleado por Rubén Darío en un sentido general, equivalente a *modernidad* . . . al referirse al escritor mexicano Ricardo Contreras, en su artículo 'La literatura en Centro-América'.[19]

> already in 1888 the word modernism was used by Rubén Darío in a general sense equivalent to modernity . . . on referring to the Mexican writer Ricardo Contreras, in his article 'La literatura en Centro-América'.

Darío's *raros* – Western writers such as Poe, Leconte de Lisle, Verlaine, Moréas, Lautréamont, Ibsen, Martí – cultivated an art at odds with traditions, 'porque', in his judgement, 'los cánones del arte moderno no . . . señalan más derroteros que el amor absoluto a la belleza . . . y el desenvolvimiento y manifestación de la personalidad';[20] 'because the canons of modern art . . . have no other goals than absolute love for beauty . . . and the development and affirmation of personality'. This exaltation of the individual, and the consequent interiorisation of reality, held such sway among the artists of this period that, as Manuel Machado said, 'lejos de ser una escuela . . . el modernismo era el finiquito y acabamiento de todas ellas',[21] 'far from being a school . . . modernism was the be-all and end-all'.

The modernist/modern revolution established a definitive foothold as a tradition in Hispanic letters towards the end of the nineteenth century, but with the predictable metamorphic, proteic characteristics of western modernity. As a result, Darío, in 1906, alluded to modernism as a *movement of freedom*. And before this, Martí, in 1882, wrote with his usual clairvoyant sense of the 'future' as an epoch not only of continental but of universal experience:

> Esta es *en todas partes* época de *reenquiciamiento* y de *remolde*. El siglo

pasado aventó con ira siniestra y pujante, los elementos de la vida vieja. Estorbado en su paso por las ruinas, que a cada instante, con vida galvánica amenazan y se animan, este siglo, que es de detalle y preparación, acumula los elementos durables de la vida nueva.[22] [Emphasis added]

This is *everywhere* a time of *resettling* and *remoulding*. The century gone by swept away with a sinister and forceful anger the elements of the old life. Obstructed in its progress by the ruins, that at every moment are threatening it and becoming animate with a galvanic life, this century, which is marked by attention to detail and preparation, is accumulating the lasting elements of the new life. [Emphasis added]

Martí's idea of 'reenquiciamiento y remolde', 'resettling and remoulding', offers an antithetic vision – the void and the renewal – in the face of the fragility of faith and the philosophic doubts that most artists of the time experienced – in Latin America and Europe – with respect to the viability of the ideas inherited from the Renaissance and the Enlightenment. In Germany, Nietzsche wrote about the decline of cosmological values (1888):

A kind of unity, some form of 'monism': and as a result of this belief man becomes obsessed by a feeling of profound relativity and dependence in the presence of an All which is infinitely superior to him, a sort of divinity. 'The general good exacts the surrender of the individual . . .' but lo, there is no such general good! At bottom man loses the belief in his own worth when no infinitely precious entity manifests itself through him – that is to say, he conceives such an All, *in order to be able to believe in his own worth.*[23]

This disturbing uncertainty regarding traditions and essences, which we also discover in the works of such thinkers as Martí or Rodó, intensified the aura of confusion that had begun to develop in the period prior to the advent of modernism: i.e. the age of Latin America's national construction during which positivism reigned supreme. It was an age in which the roots of modernity are discernible, especially in the presence of a critical spirit, but one without the anguish, anxiety or overwhelming isolation that artists suffered after the advent of modernism. These are the years prior to the process of dismemberment of the modern Spanish American world, the years Bradbury and McFarlane identify in Germany with the *Wendepunkt* (the threshold) of modern Europe. During these years there prevailed

> a faith in social advance, a readiness to believe that to expose abuses was to invite annihilation, that to repudiate the conventional past was to clear the way for a healthy moral growth, for welcome ideals. Hard work, clear vision, courage, purposefulness – these were the keys to the future, to the evolution of new types of men, of society, of art.[24]

In a similar way, Spanish American leaders such as Andrés Bello, dismayed by the revolutionary frenzy (1810–25) and 'el estado de desasosiego y vacilación', 'the disquiet and vacillation', considered the existing political chaos of the post-Independence period of reconstruction a transitory moment. And, according to Bello, time and experience would rectify all errors. In the process 'las inclinaciones, las costumbres y el carácter de nuestros pueblos', 'the inclinations, customs and character of our people', would be discovered.[25] Bello's faith and confidence in man and in the triumph of reason belong to a universally shared feeling as evidenced by the consanguinity of his ideas with those of the *Wendepunkt* of German pre-modernity.

Elements of both periods – pre-modernity and modernity – pervade Martí's art and ideology. His writings are characterised by his belief in renewal of the shattered human spirit teetering on the brink of the void that for him yawned between the artist and the burgeoning bourgeois society with its materialist bent. Standing on the frontier that divided a dismembered world from a world in the throes of gestation, Martí, who was conscious of the definitive rupture of the old socio-cultural regime, looked into the future hoping to create a harmonious ideological construct with the remnants of tradition and the spirit of renewal, a construct which would be applicable to the social regeneration he envisioned for Cuba, Puerto Rico and Latin America. The breach produced between the artist and society, noted by Calinescu and described by Martí in several essays and chronicles, gives rise to a cultural crisis and to a de-centring, characteristic of periodic, recurring, profound transformations in history, which overwhelm and overturn styles of thought and writing in periods of crisis such as the Renaissance, the age of the baroque or the age of romanticism.[26] In Latin America, between 1815 and 1885, the first symptoms of such a socio-cultural disintegration appeared: that of modernism/modernity.

If we conceive of modernism in the light of its philosophic and socio-economic infrastructures, and if we consider it as a stage of modernity, then the period of its genesis and early flourishing should be viewed as one in which the concepts of revolution,[27] experimentation and continuous innovation prevail, but without aesthetic or ideological confirmity.[28] Conceived in this way, modernist art marks the inception of a continuous progression in art and literature towards cultural maturity and self-discovery with a multifaceted and sometimes contradictory aesthetic.

Art forms measured in terms of 'continual progression', whether they are called modernist or modern, suggest a periodisation that goes beyond the narrow historiographic limits of generations, schools or movements. Indeed, art forms so conceived favour a construct based on a 'period' concept, the very same notion espoused by Martí a century ago. In a similar way Juan Ramón Jiménez, without referring to the Modernist/Modern Art equation, established heterodoxic links between modernism and the art of the Renaissance, of romanticism, and of twentieth-century literature; that is, correspondences which involve periods before as well as after it.[29] He also rejected the generational theory with respect to the modern period,[30] and in its place settled on the concept of 'generations by epochs',[31] because it appeared to him that as time elapsed, people were going to pay more attention to the similarities than to the differences in modern literature.

This theory of periodisation, refined with three historiographic perspectives, has been advanced by Bradbury and McFarlane in defence of the basically 'devolutionary' character of modernist/modern literature:

> Cultural seismology – the attempt to record the shifts and displacements of sensibility that regularly occur in the history of art and literature and thought – habitually distinguishes three separate orders of magnitude. At one end of the scale are those tremors of fashion that seem to come and go in rhythm with the changing generations, the decade being the right unit for measuring the curves that run from first shock to peak activity and on to the dying rumbles of derivative *Epigonentum.* To a second order of magnitude belong those larger displacements whose effects go deeper and last longer, forming those extended periods of style and sensibility which are usefully measured in centuries. This leaves a third category for those overwhelming dislocations, those cataclysmic upheavals of culture, those fundamental convulsions of the creative human spirit that seem to topple even the most solid and substantial of our beliefs and assumptions, leave great areas of the past in ruins

(noble ruins, we tell ourselves for reassurance), question an entire civilisation or culture, and stimulate frenzied rebuilding.[32]

The second and third alternatives – dysfunctions, rejections, deconstructions as well as reconstructions – characterise the beginning of the age of modernism and of Spanish American modernity.[33] In it, starting with modernism, there is a reflection of

esa crisis de conciencia que generará la visión contemporánea del mundo. Todos los continuos se fracturan. Las seguridades de la concepcion renacentista . . .[34] que originó la moderna ciencia experimental, se relativizan o se invalidan.[35]

That crisis of conscience that will give birth to a contemporary vision in the world. All apparently whole, fragments. The certainties of the Renaissance . . . that lay behind modern experimental science are made relative or are invalidated.

The literature of modernism which in Spanish America initiates the successive stages of modernity is

a special kind of literature. We call it modern and distinguish it from the merely contemporary; for where the contemporary refers to time, the modern refers to sensibility and style, and where the contemporary is a term of neutral reference, the modern is a term of critical placement and judgment.[36]

But modernism doesn't establish its own single style; 'if it does, it denies itself, thereby ceasing to be modern'.[37] It is not a school or style in the traditional sense, but a sensibility to change, a critical attitude, a defiance of norms; the structures of modernity are open, polyhedric. And, in accordance with its multiple perspectives, its style is characterised in different ways in different literatures.

For David Lodge the hallmark of modern writing is metaphoric language,

In modern writing there are formal experiment, dislocation of conventional syntax, radical breaches of decorum, disturbance of chronology and spatial order, ambiguity, polysemy, obscurity, mythopoeic allusion, primitivism, irrationalism, structuring by symbol and motif.[38]

In Martí's writings, which mark the beginning of this process for Spanish American letters, expressionist prose comes to mind:

Tocó aquella noche en el piano Keleffy . . . ¿A dónde íbamos? Nadie lo sabía. Ya era un rayo que daba sobre un monte, como el acero de un gigante sobre el castillo donde supone a su dama encantada; ya un león con alas, que iba de nube en nube; ya un sol virgen que de un bosque temido, como de un nido de serpientes, se levanta; ya un recodo de selva nunca vista, dónde los árboles no denían hojas, sino flores; ya un pino colosal que con gran estruendo de gemidos se quebraba; era una grande alma que se abría.[39]

That night Keleffy played on the piano . . . Where were we going? Nobody knew. At one time it was a flash of lightning hitting a hill, like a giant's sword smiting a castle where he believes his lady to have been enchanted; at another, a winged lion, going from cloud to cloud; at yet another a virgin sun rising from a menacing wood as if from a nest of serpents; and then some part of a jungle never glimpsed by man, where the trees had not leaves but flowers; or then a colossal pine tree cracking to the mighty din of its groans; it was a great soul opening up.

The ideological and artistic roots of this literary modernity are tied to the Renaissance and the initiation of the interiorisation of life, a process that culminates in the exploring of distant horizons that lie beyond experiential or factic limits. Its seeds also belong to romantic culture or, at least, in its authentic, non-derivative forms it is linked with romantic writers who 'break loose from the classical-Christian tradition, but they do not surrender the wish to discover in the universe a network of spiritual meaning which, however precariously, can enclose their selves'.[40] In Martí's case the search for philosophic or ideological structures is centred on his political mission, the devotion to social revolution, and his concern with the quality of human existence. In other writers – Rodó, in his 'El que vendrá', for example – the renewal is defined in terms of a vague 'rebirth of an Ideal'[41] that would coincide with the appearance of an 'unknown god'.[42] But, in general, the early writers of the Age of Modernity

anticipate the preoccupation with psychic inwardness, by means of which the self is transformed into a cosmic center and mover, as this will later become characteristic of certain modernist writers; but they still seek to relate this preoccupation to transcendent values, if not sources, in the external world. For them the universe is still alert, still the active transmitter of spiritual signs.[43]

In Spanish America, in the second half of the nineteenth century, a modern artistic expression appears with enough intensity and consistency to establish a chronological milestone, the inception in the arts of a de-centring and of an increasing agony at a point in time when the economies of western capitalism are experiencing vigorous development. Martí, towards the end of the nineteenth century, exclaimed: 'Crece en mi cuerpo el mundo'; 'The world grows in my body.' And yet, at the beginning of the twentieth century, writers who were revolutionary in other regards, such as Mariano Azuela in *Los de abajo*, will follow more traditional, metonymic patterns: 'Y Camila rompió a llorar . . . Meciéndose en una rama seca, una torcaz lloró también';[44] 'And Camila broke into tears . . . And swinging on a dry branch a wild pigeon cried too.' From this brief comparison it is obvious that the process of interiorisation of the universe follows an uneven evolutionary pattern. The pre-modern perceptions continue to prevail and coexist in Spanish America with the signs of modernity.

How can we conceptualise the other chronological pole of modernity: that is, (un)finished modernity? Howe on this point declares that perhaps modernity represents a new phenomenon, *without* a conclusion and *without* any term of comparison in the western world.

> Modernism need never come to an end . . . The history of previous literary periods is relevant but probably not decisive here, since modernism, despite the precursors we can find in the past, is . . . a novelty in the development of western culture.[45]

Bell, on the other hand, from the perspective of the social sciences, formulates a theory of modernity based on the study of highly industrialised economies (the United States, the Soviet Union). Comparing these with Spanish American economies, he distinguishes between the modern and the post-modern, a theoretical statement according to which the post-modern involves 'a shift in the kinds of work people do, from manufacturing to services (especially human and professional services) and a new centrality of theoretical knowledge in economic innovation and policy'.[46] Needless to say, in Spanish America the economic structures have not reached the developmental level Bell requires for the manifestation of a post-modernist culture, especially a hedonist and apocalyptic culture which he associates with the anti-bourgeois spirit and moral freedom of post-modernism.

An anti-bourgeois liberation literature has indeed grown up in Spanish America but it has emerged in the face of disquieting economic inequalities which are not the mark of the post-industrial structures described by Bell. The anti-modern structures that come to mind are those of numerous indigenous and black communities whose presence forces us to meditate on the oppressions and repressions which belong to Spanish American *otredad*.[47] And with respect to this *otredad* Fernández Retamar would have us reflect on the enlightening clairvoyance of Bolívar's ideas.

nuestro pueblo no es el europeo, ni el americano del norte . . . más bien es un compuesto de Africa y de América, que una emanción de la Europa . . . Es imposible asignar con propiedad a qué familia humana pertenecemos.[48]

our people is not European, nor is it North American . . . It is an amalgam of Africa and America, rather than an emanation from Europe . . . It is impossible to define with accuracy to which human family we belong.

Therefore, in the period of national reconstruction as well as today, we must question the suitability of applying, *grosso modo*, socio-economic – fundamentally eurocentric – concepts such as those of Bell and his followers, based on an experience alien to Latin American conditions.

It is equally evident that in modernist literature, and especially in Martí's writings, the seeds of Spanish American modernity are to be found; they exist and bear fruit without recourse to foreign models or ideals.

## The first-fruits of poetic modernity: Martí's Ismaelillo

To innovate and to preserve, 'debasar' and 'rebasar':[49] these are the two cardinal verbal signs of Martí's modern aesthetics as well as the guiding principles of his poetic doctrine. He rejected the outmoded, petrified forms of expression – the void – and improved upon them by means of an artistic renewal. But to modernise did not imply burying the past but rather bringing the past into the present in an original, subjective and creative manner. By way of confirming this double-pronged process – a return to the past/the perception of a renewed present and future – amidst his many theoretical writings we read that

su objeto es desembarazar del lenguaje inútil la poesía: hacerla duradera, haciéndola sincera, haciéndola vigorosa, haciéndola sobria; no dejando más hojas que las necesarias . . .[50]

his aim is to liberate poetry from useless language: to give it sincerity, vigour and sobriety, to make it lasting: leaving no more than the necessary . . .

Opposing two types of literature, Martí points out the persistence in one type of hackneyed elements ('lenguaje inútil', 'hojas') and proposes the necessity (expressed with the repeated verb 'hacer') of replacing them in order to produce a lasting, sincere, vigorous, sober poetry. This revisionist and self-imposed process is built on an acratic foundation, one which defines the modernity of Martí's art and its inherent 'future' quality. In 'Estrofa nueva' (*Versos libres*) the poet places man at the centre of his destiny: 'De nuestro bien o mal autores somos / y cada cual autor de sí', 'We are the authors of our destiny and of our selves', a concept that in its aesthetic tangents contributes to the desacralisation and de-idealisation (of norms, precepts or codes) of art. He observes that:

> Ni líricos ni épicos pueden ser hoy con naturalidad y sosiego los poetas *ni cabe más lírica que la que saca cada uno de sí propio*, como si fuera su propio ser el asunto único de cuya existencia no tuviera dudas.[51] [Emphasis added]

> Poets, today, cannot with naturalness and ease be either lyrical or epic: *the only lyric resides in oneself*, as if one's own being was the only certainty. [Emphasis added]

The poets of *sangre nueva* should be subjective and proteic, not lyrical or epic. In Martí, today's reader discovers a rich imagination that

> se emancipa, cuando es preciso, de su comunidad lingüística: pasa por encima o por debajo de las palabras, mediante notas, melodías, ritmos, colores, líneas, imágenes, gestos, danzas.[52]

> frees itself, when needed, from its linguistic community. It rises above words, using notes, melodies, rhythms, colours, lines, gestures, images, dances.

Of these transgressions was Martí conscious? In the prologue to *Flores del destierro* he referred to his own poems as

> escritos en ritmo desusado, que por esto, o por serlo de veras, va a parecer a muchos duro. ¿Mas, con qué derecho puede quebrar la mera voluntad artística, [palabras ininteligibles] la forma natural y

sagrada, en que, como la carne de la idea, envía el alma los versos a los labios.

written in an unusual rhythm, and for this reason or because they are truly so, they would appear harsh to many. But by what right can mere artistic will [several unintelligible words] break the natural and holy form, in which as the essence of an idea, the soul sends poetry to the lips?

And, in a notebook he wrote:

Por lo menos, hacen falta dos signos:
Coma menor,,
por ejemplo:
'Juntos de noche, Hafed, juntos de día'.
Así indico que la pausa en *Hafed* ha de ser más larga que en *noche*: si no ¿cómo lo indico? ¿cómo estorbo que otro pueda leer: 'Juntos de noche, – Hafed, juntos de día, desluciendo el verso, y poniendo a Hafed en el segundo inciso, cuando quiero yo que esté en el primero?[53]

At least two signs are necessary:
A small comma,,
for example:
'Together at night, Hafed, together in the daytime'.
Thus I indicate that the pause after *Hafed* should be longer than after *night*: if not, how can I show this? How can I stop another person reading: 'Together at night, – Hafed, together in the daytime', making the line lose its force, and putting Hafed in the second part when I want him to be in the first?

To describe a poetry with such unorthodox co-ordinates requires an equivalent emancipation in the language of the critic, because in the Cuban's works, above and beyond words, we discover visionary hallucinations, overwhelming sorrows, igneous poetic space, sombre glimpses, space-time leaps whose qualities surprise us, because here we have a poet who stands on the threshold of the modern age, and who was 'el primero en dotar al verso de novedosos y artísticos paramentos verbales, infinitamente más bellos y variados que nada de lo que Bécquer le añadió;[54] 'the first one to give poetry new artistic verbal embellishments, infinitely more beautiful and varied than anything Bécquer added'. When he tried to describe his disquieting, volatile, dualistic poetic expression Martí was forced to transgress the linguistic conventions of his times with an expressionistic style:

Hay una clase de poesía que sale, como un río de sangre, del alma atormentada, y rompe por entre peñascos en su espantada fuga, y no abre sus ondas sino para dejar paso a clamores, y flamea al sol, que la acaricia imperturbable, con viva llama roja, y se mueve lentamente – como un agonizante. – Y hay otra que parece lira blanda, de cuerdas sonantísimas, – en cuyos flexibles alambres hallan acordes fuertes todos los vientos – los nivosos, como los alisios, – de la vida. Vaso de perfume; – no, para abrasante agua, cauce de piedras![55]

There is a kind of poetry that comes, like a river of blood, from the tormented soul, and gushes through crags in its frightened flight, and does not open up its waters save to allow clamourings to emerge, and flames in the sun, which caresses it imperturbably, with a bright red flame, and moves slowly – like a dying man – . And there is another that seems like a soft lyre, with most resounding strings, – in whose flexible wires chords are found by all the winds – those carrying snow, as well as the trade winds – of life. A phial of perfume; – no, for burning water, a bed of stones!

Fina García Marruz sees in his *Versos libres* painful syllabic groups;[56] and Cintio Vitier perceives the voice of a poet of light and movement that creates a baroque, dark, frothy, volcanic, abrupt and 'strange' world.[57]

These unusual qualities of his illuminated, dazzling[58] poetry define his first volume of verse, *Ismaelillo*, written in Caracas and published in New York in 1882. Conscious of the singularity of the imagery of the book – in large measure, oneiric – Martí felt the necessity of clarifying the process of its genesis to his friend Diego Jugo Ramírez:

He visto esas alas, esos chacales, esas copas vacías, esos ejércitos. Mi mente ha sido escenario, y en él han sido actores todas esas visiones. Mi trabajo ha sido copiar, Juro. No hay ahí una sola línea mental. Pues, ¿cómo he de ser responsable de las imágenes que vienen a mí sin que yo las solicite? *Yo no he hecho más que poner en versos mis visiones.* Tan vivamente me hirieron esas escenas, que aún voy a todas partes rodeado de ellas, y como si tuviera delante de mí un gran espacio oscuro, en que volaran grandes aves blancas. [Emphasis added][59]

I have seen those wings, those jackals, those empty chalices, those armies. My mind has been a stage, and on it all those visions have been actors. My work has been to copy, I swear. There is not one single line there coming from the mind. For how can I be held responsible for the images that come to me without my asking for them? *I have done no more than put my visions into verse.* Those scenes wounded me so much that I still go everywhere surrounded by them, and as if I had before me a great dark space, where great white birds were flying. [Emphasis added]

The visions of *Ismaelillo*, engendered by his absent son, erupt in the spatial dislocations where the original and abundant imagery of the poems floats and flies, disjointed in a 'dark space': 'Tú flotas sobre todo, / Hijo del alma!', 'You float above all / My beloved son' ('Hijo del alma'); '¡Un niño que me llama / Flotando siempre veo!', 'I always see floating / A child that calls me!' ('Sueño despierto'). The poet fuses dream and reality, reversing both forms of perception; these leaps of perception are seen in the constant flight of the son and his sudden, periodic and balsamic appearances, and at the same time, in the insistence of the poet/speaker regarding thé *reality* of his son's image. As the prologue-dedication declares:

Si alguen te dice que estas páginas se parecen a otras páginas, diles que te amo demasiado para profanarte así. *Tal como aquí te pinto, tal te han visto mis ojos. Con esos arreos de gala te me has aparecido.* Cuando he cesado de verte en una forma, he cesado de pintarte. [Emphasis added]

If somebody were to tell you that these pages resemble other pages, tell them I love you too much to abuse you thus. *I describe you here just as I know you. You have appeared to me with these festive trappings.* When I stopped seeing you in this way I ceased to describe you thus. [Emphasis added]

The poet, attentive to the images whose visit he awaits for poetic inspiration, dreams open-eyed day and night, and insists on the 'strangeness' (la 'extrañeza') of his verses – a reflection of an external reality not merely deformed but hostile. The son constitutes the centre of the father's concern: 'Espantado de todo, me refugio en tì', 'When frightened by everything, I take refuge in you'; 'Esos riachuelos han pasado por mi corazón. ¡Lleguen al tuyo!', 'These streams have run through my heart. Let them reach yours!' Thus the son becomes the 'pillow' (la 'almohada'), the inner court, the 'cave' and the depository of a world whose rhythm and character frighten and offend the father in his anguished solitude. The son is also Ismael; in the father's choice of the symbolic figure from Genesis, father and son become one and share the same fount of personal testimony and passion. The father hopes that the 'streams' (los 'riachuelos') of emotion and solace that have passed through his heart will reach his son's and serve to protect him against a corrupt and hostile material world.

By means of a process of inversion – a metamorphosis born of filial love – the father, while he conjures up the vision of his son, is reborn *in* him: 'Hijo soy de mi hijo / ¡El me rehace!', 'I am the son of my son / He makes me anew!' This identification of father and son orchestrates and unifies the metaphoric outbursts of *Ismaelillo*, a book of verse which is a musical concert with three motifs of chaotic, tender and anguished leaps: the poet / the son / the world. In the form of 'viajes', 'voyages', the poet-son crosses emotional and noetic spaces, freed from the ties of the traditional *logos*.

The travels of the seer ('el veedor') who rides 'horas luengas / sobre los aires', 'long hours / through the air' ('Musa traviesa') are multiple – to empyrean regions, to battles, to fields of martyrdom, caves, balls and sensuous scenes. With his son, interiorised by dint of the poet's insistent evocation – 'el blanco / Pálido ángel / Que aquí en mi pecho / Las alas abre', 'the white / Pale angel / That here in my breast / His wings opens' ('Amor errante') – the poet survives storms and sombre experiences: this is a 'confused world' ('mundo confuso') with its 'powerful armies' ('ejércitos pujantes'), 'dull temptations' ('tentaciones sordas'), 'voracious virgins' ('vírgenes voraces'), 'strong, soft, perfumed arms' ('brazos robustos, blandos, fragantes') and the 'yellow king' (el 'rey amarillo'). The world of 'transformaciones espléndidas', 'splendid transformations', evoked in 'El poema del Niágara', pleasing to the revolutionary, boils and creaks; it deafens and bites as it is contemplated by the poet-agonist. In consonance with this dualistic vision of the universe the son is Ismael, Jacob, the object of pleasure, love and tenderness, the absent child evoked with pain/joy, and, at the same time, a refuge for the father, a being made heart and soul, and, therefore, not only a *reflection* but the poet's very *existence*. Thus, *Ismaelillo*, more than a 'devocionario lírico, un Arte de ser Padre, lleno de gracias sentimentales y de juegos poéticos', 'a lyrical book of devotions, an Art of being Father, full of sentimental graces and poetic games' – Darío's idea[60] – represents a voyage in the etymological sense of experience, a voyage towards the mournful world of modern life: 'las entrañas del vacío'/'el impulso renovador'; void and renewal.

Side by side with the snowy wings of the son and the numerous symbols of pure, ideal love, the vision of the son/father erupts, converted by means of the hostility of 'new life' ('nueva vida') into a 'naked warrior with bird's wings' ('desnudo guerrero de alas de ave'). By virtue of this double vision, *Ismaelillo* and *Versos sencillos*, traditionally considered to be books that represent the quiet, serene side of Martí's poetry must also be considered works that express struggle, conflict and the search for renewal. Moreover, in *Ismaelillo* it is not the solar vision that prevails, but the father's terror when confronted with modern life. In this prologue-dedication the poet directs his first words to the son, and employs the adjective 'frightened' ('espantado'): 'Hijo: espantado de todo, me refugio en tí', 'My son: frightened by everything, I take refuge in you.' And if later on he speaks of the 'fiesta' ('life') he prepares for the son, he knows that he will have to travel along the path through the 'cave' ('cueva'), the 'murky cavern' (lóbrego antro'), and the 'shadow' ('sombra'). The poet senses that 'quiere el príncipe enano / Que a luchar vuelva', 'the little prince wants me / To go back to the fight' ('Príncipe enano'). Life ('fiesta') is a struggle, which in critical moments takes on an apocalyptic quality:

> Clamor óigase, como
> Si en un instante
> Mismo, las almas todas
> Volando ex-cárceres,
> Rodar a sus pies vieran
> Su hopa de carnes:
> Cíñame recia veste
> De amenazantes
> Astas agudas: hilos
> Tenues de sangre
> Por mi piel rueden leves
> Cual rojas áspides:
> Su diente en lodo afilen
> Pardos chacales . . .
>
> ('Tábanos fieros')

Let us hear the outcry, as if in a single moment the newly freed souls had seen its fleshy garb drop to its feet. Clothe me with the primitive attire of sharp and menacing horns. Let thin threads of blood run down my skin like scarlet asps; brown jackals, sharpen your fangs on mud . . .

The destruction of the world – its de-basing – besieges the poet. On the one hand he evokes scenes of hecatomb with a rhythm filled with staccato vibrations, which announce imminent catastrophe:

> Detona, chispea,
> Espuma, se vacía
> Y expira dichosa
> La rubia champaña . . .
>
> Y lirios se quiebran
> Y violas se manchan.
>
> ('Tórtola blanca')

Golden champagne explodes, fizzles and froths, escapes and happily dies . . .

And the lilies of the valley are trampled on, and the violets stained.

On the other hand, there is the joy of the constant unexpected appearance of the son (the counter-theme of reconstruction and renewal) whose presence is accompanied by a serene, crystalline cadence:

> Suavemente la puerta
> Del cuarto se abre,
> Y éntranse a él gozosos
> Luz, risas, aire.
>
> ('Musa traviesa')

Smoothly the bedroom door opens, and happily come in light, laughter and fresh air.

These are two universes that Martí unifies by means of a transformational construct; from the lower depths – 'antros' – we ascend – to 'nidos de ángeles':

> Y con ella [la luz madre] es la oscura
> Vida, radiante,
> Y a mis ojos los antros
> Son nidos de ángeles!
>
> ('Musa traviesa')

And with her [the mother light] is the dark, radiant life. And in my eyes, the dens become like angels' nests.

In other verses Martí describes the inhabitants of the earth, using metaphors ordered according to descending values: proof of the testimony of an existential observer at the same time encouraged and disappointed, an idealist and a pragmatist:

> Seres hay de montaña
> Seres de valle,
> Y seres de pantanos
> Y lodazales.
>
>         ('Musa traviesa')

There are beings of the mountains, Beings of the valleys, Beings of the swamps And beings of the mud-flats.

The poet-seer who embraces both worlds (terrestrial and empyrean) conceives human experience as the product of imagination and reason, harmonised. For himself, nevertheless, he reserves the role of the martyr, symbolised by spilled blood, because as he sees it, the duty of man is '¡Rasgarse el bravo pecho, / Vaciar su sangre', 'To rip open the valiant breast, to drain its blood'.

'Hay que llevar sangre nueva a la literatura',[61] 'New blood must be brought to literature,' he exclaimed in another place, and pointed out that

> La literatura de nuestros tiempos es ineficaz, porque no es la expresión de nuestros tiempos. ¡Ya no es Velleda, que guía a las batallas; sino especie de Aspasia![62]

The literature of our time is inefficacious, because it is not the expression of our times. It is no longer Velleda, guiding the battle, but a kind of Aspasia!

The motif of the *void*. Yet, on the other hand,

> La literatura que anuncie y propague el concierto final y dichoso de las contradicciones aparentes . . . no sólo revelará un estado social más cercano a la perfección, sino que, hermanando felizmente la razón y la gracia, proveerá a la Humanidad, ansiosa de maravilla y de poesía, con la religión que confusamente aguarda desde que conoció la oquedad e insuficiencia de sus antiguos credos.[63]

The literature announcing and spreading the word about the final and blissful coming-together of apparent contradictions . . . will not only reveal a social state nearer to perfection, but will, by happily joining reason to grace, provide Humanity, anxious for marvels and poetry, with the religion that it confusedly awaits from the time that it recognised the hollowness and insufficiency of the ancient creeds.

The motif of *renewal*. Two modernities thus present themselves in the work of a modern writer of the nineteenth century, who in his lifetime foresaw the future. His works, therefore, constitute *necessary* texts, necessary in our uncertain, chaotic universe.

# 9 Order and passion in *Amistad funesta*

## NISSA TORRENTS

*Amistad funesta* was published in New York in 1885 under the pseudonym of Adelaida Ral in the bimonthly magazine *El Latinoamericano*. It is the one work of Martí's large output that has attracted the least critical attention. Although not a complete achievement, the novel is a powerful melodrama, written in an often startling poetic prose that shows surprising narrative freedom.

It was Martí's only novel, and he wrote it to earn a little money pending the solution of his disagreements with the military rebels of the Cuban rebellion; disagreements that had, temporarily, removed him from active politics.

### Martí and the novel

Written in seven days, the novel is dedicated to Adelaida Baralt who had commissioned it for the magazine. Martí's dedication poem plays down his possible achievement, and the adoption of a woman's pseudonym to hide his identity points to his attitude towards the genre and, possibly, towards women.

Paraphrasing Th. Sergeant Parry, who wrote that the novelist's subject had to be 'something better than life', Martí wrote that there should be 'two kinds of novel, those that paint life and those that, by presenting higher ideals, try to improve it'.[1] Both types of novel had a legitimate place, but mere entertainment was insufficient and degrading, he added. The question arises as to the reason Martí adopted the pseudonym of 'Adelaida Ral'. Was it because the novel was considered a woman's genre, inclined to frivolous subjects and favouring 'love' themes that belittled the author's intention and converted Juan Jerez into 'a mere beau when he had been conceived by the novelist for higher and higher enterprises and greater feats'? Martí was ill at ease with a genre based on fiction, in never-heard dialogues from non-existing people and in fabricated situations. 'The joys of artistic creation can never compensate for the pain of living in a prolonged fiction',[2] wrote Martí in his introduction for a planned publication of the work in book form, under the title *Lucía Jerez*. He tried to atone for his 'sin' by producing 'clean' fiction that could be read by any young girl, but also by contributing to the creation of a

176

Latin American novel, based on Latin American themes and characters – the plot is taken from a contemporary event – reflecting Latin American nature and customs. It is, from many points of view, an 'exemplary' novel which reflects Martí's ethics and aesthetics and his ideas of nationhood in magnificent prose, abounding in metaphor.

Martí complained that the publishers of his time only favoured light themes and rejected nobler subjects and exalted heroes as unreal and in bad taste, but he believed that those heroes were necessary in the mediocre times in which he lived. The contemporary demand for surface 'realism' was unheeded by Martí who preferred the poetic prose that would permit him to express his daydreams in simple but close metaphors, often self-referential, searching to reveal inner emotions, his love for the simple, his awareness of living in troubled times and his desire for personal resurrection and national independence.

*Amistad Funesta* is structured around two short chapters and one long final chapter that comes to a sudden and melodramatic end. The use of highly symbolical language sets the novel apart from the prevalent realism. It is a language that favours antagonistic images: black and white, blue and black, flowers and snakes; the language and the imagery of his poetry modified by the needs of his vehicle. The structure is reminiscent of the theatre, both in its chapter layout – first, second and third acts – and in the independence of situations that recall the tableaux form.

## Martí and his characters: the men

Many critics have seen the personality and the ideas of the author in the character of Juan Jerez; but I believe that Martí is to be found in the majority of the novel's characters, both the desirable and the undesirable, and that the genre that made Martí so apprehensive, reveals fears he may have preferred to keep hidden.

Juan Jerez is a paragon of virtue, defined by his lack of self-interest, high aims, the rejection of material values and, significantly, by a desire, so often stated by Martí, to be a loser and a martyr, a lover of his nation and a defender of the poor. Juan Jerez has a burning desire for purity, a caressing voice and a rich store of tenderness, qualities very close to Martí's heart but which, conventionally, are perceived as feminine and which amount, within the novel's context, to a break with accepted modes of male–female representation. Unlike Martí, Juan is rich and his generosity does not have to be tested in the market place. A lawyer, practising 'a deceitful profession, perniciously widespread among us',[3] he overcomes the shortcomings of his profession by dedicating his skills to fight for the cause of the oppressed, thus earning the author's highest accolade: 'He did not appear to be a lawyer of our times, but one of those troubadours who, fed up with their songs, had known how to convert their lyre into a sword.'[4] Juan, like Martí, is a poet who will know, when the time comes, how to become a soldier, but who in these mediocre times echoes his creator's frustrations: 'His pale face showed the nostalgia for action, the shining illness of great souls, whom duty or bad luck had reduced to menial tasks.'[5] A crusader, he is uncompromising about principle and belongs to 'the select race of those that do not work for success but against it'.

Juan considers his intelligence to be like a priest's vocation and although his is a lay priesthood, his duty towards the faithful is a total commitment which implies that the highest treason is *la trahison des clercs*, so common 'in our small nations'.[6] This betrayal is not just the outcome of personal greed and desire for power but of the wrong educational system, inherited from the metropolitan power and patently inadequate for the new nations which Martí liked to describe as 'blue', a positive colour.

Martí considered that a literary education, in new countries which did not have a reading audience that could pay for the privilege, was pernicious: 'From the cultivation of intelligence spring expensive tastes, as natural among Hispano-Americans as the colour pink in the cheeks of a fifteen-year-old girl.'[7] Aware of the cultural dependency of *nuestra América*, Martí believed that the intelligentsia, deprived of a 'natural' field of activity, would be tempted either to outright corruption or to empty political rhetoric.

Juan Jerez, whose inner virtue shines in 'a high and unknown light', is too near those knights errant that publishers disliked and Martí, to satisfy the requirements of his order, reluctantly turned him into a lover.

Había cedido, en su vida de libros y abstracciones, a la dulce necesidad, tantas veces funesta, de apretar sobre su corazón una manecita blanca. La de ésta o la de aquella le importaban poco; y él, en la mujer, veía más el símbolo de las hermosuras ideales que un ser real.

He had surrendered, in his life of books and abstract thoughts, to the sweet need, so often proved fatal, to hold against his heart a little white hand. It did not matter whose hand it was because he could only see in woman a symbol of imagined beauty and never a real being.[8]

Falling in love or even contemplating a relationship with a woman is seen as 'surrender', a degradation of man's lofty standards that could prove to be fatal. Real woman supposes a confrontation with the concrete – as opposed to the abstract which may prove a source of inspiration to '[the poet] who in his miraculous breast / the deeper the wound / the better the song'.[9]

Juan Jerez can only 'love the pure and perform great feats':

Poeta genuino, que sacaba de los espectáculos que veía en sí mismo, y de los dolores y sorpresas de su espíritu, unos versos extraños, adoloridos y profundos, que parecían dagas arrancadas de su propio pecho, padecía de esa necesidad de la belleza que como un marchamo ardiente, señala a los escogidos del Canto.

A genuine poet, his strange, pained and profound verse stems from a contemplation of self. His poems are like daggers torn from his breast. He suffers from that thirst for beauty that is the mark of those chosen for the song.[10]

Martí not only tells us about the source of his poetry, daggers and song, but also, when writing about Juan's need of a 'strange and violent desire for martyrdom',[11] predicts his future, a prediction that encompasses the complex desires that marked his path.

The shining knight, the poet, the patriot, the wilful loser is also the child of St Paul and St Augustine. For the author–narrator and for his personage, women are either pure spirit – Ana, near death, fickle; Adela, unsure of herself – or fatal – Lucía, a poisonous vessel of passion. Like St Paul, Juan believes that 'the body is not for fornication, but for the Lord'[12] and that man must 'flee fornication. Every sin man doeth is without the body; but he that committeth fornication sinneth against his own body.'[13] The assumption is that woman is the temptress and man the tempted. St Paul further tells the faithful that if chastity cannot be upheld, 'Let them marry: for it is better to marry than to burn',[14] advice that is echoed in Martí's words about 'the sweet need, so often proved fatal' to hold a woman's hand.

Juan's intense purity follows St Paul's words: 'It is good for a man not to touch a woman.'[15] Juan rejects all contact, except the pure kiss on the forehead, and perceives his fellow human beings as contaminated by impurity. Juan adheres closely to St Paul's precepts: 'Nevertheless he that standeth stedfast in his heart, having no necessity, but hath power over his own will, and hath so decreed in his heart that he will keep his virgin, doeth well.'[16]

Martí's own preoccupations are clearly reflected in Juan's, resulting in a curious reversal of accepted codes. In the novel, more concern is shown for the purity of man than for that of woman, who is seen as the main threat. Even Ana, the dying artist, in spite of her 'priestess-like soul'[17] feels aroused by man while Juan never responds to a woman's body, intent only on her spirit.

Only extreme youth saves woman from her own sexuality:

Estaban las tres amigas en aquella pura edad en que los caracteres todavía no se definen: ¡ay!, en esos mercados es donde suelen los jóvenes generosos, que van en busca de pájaros azules, atar su vida a lindos vasos de carne que a poco tiempo, a los primeros calores fuertes de la vida, enseñan la zorra astuta, la culebra venenosa, el gato frío e impasible que les mora en el alma.[18]

The three girlfriends were of that pure age in which personality is not yet defined. But, alas! it is in these markets that generous young men, looking for blue birds, usually tie their lives to beautiful vases of flesh which after just a short time, when first struck by the flushes of life, show the cunning vixen, the poisonous snake, the cold and insensible cat that dwells in their souls.

The blue birds of the young men's quest turn into lascivious snakes, poised for the bite. The familiar antagonic metaphor is formulated again: the purity of blue birds for men, the poisonous snake for women.

Juan is horrified when he is confronted with Lucía's sexuality. He wanted a symbolical woman, the repository of his pure love as shaped by his imagination; but he encounters 'Lucía in whom the flowers of her age hide the burning lava that, like the veins of precious metals, slithers in her breast'.[19]

As with St Paul, not even the married woman escapes condemnation. Juan Jerez talks about the repulsion he feels for a wife who offers her charms 'near the husband's work desk or her son's cradle'.[20]

The biblical echoes in Martí are thus not just the admirable ones that come from his lay rendering of the Beatitudes, qualities that adorn Juan Jerez, an outstanding example of meekness, purity, mercifulness, righteousness and acceptance of other people's vileness, but of St Paul's misogyny and of the curse that befell humanity after Eve's, apparently never to be forgiven, action. Eve, the friend of the snake, which is cursed by God above all animals, becomes the inseparable image of women in *Amistad funesta*; Eve, who lost

Paradise for all time and provoked the Creator into telling Adam: 'And I will put enmity between thee and the woman, and between thy seed and her seed.'[21] The battle of the sexes is written down at the beginning of humankind by its very Maker, and the curse is so powerful that it needed not only Christ the Redeemer but also the Virgin Mary to sanctify the family. But the virginity of Mary enhances all other women's guilt because it cannot be followed; Mary, the pure mother, untouched by man, is usually dressed in blue in western iconography and visited by a white bird – two of Martí's preferred metaphors for the favoured; Mary, who loves her son with the complete love that admits no sharing, a love that Martí also felt for his own son. In his tender love poem to his child, *Ismaelillo*, the intense relation is between father and son. No female shadows darken that pure love, which possibly shows an unconscious desire to be both father and mother, thus banishing the female and all her impurities from the supreme act of creation.

For Juan Jerez, woman should be flawless, the beautiful possessor of beauty, the natural perfume that exudes from the highest spirituality, the poet's mistress:

Por eso cuando creen que algún acto pueril o inconsiderado las desfigura, o imaginan ellos alguna frivolidad o impureza, se ponen fuera de sí, y sienten unos dolores mortales, y tratan a su amante con la indignación con que se trata a los ladrones y a los traidores, porque como en su mente las hicieron depositarias de todas las grandezas y claridades que apetecen, cuando creen ver que no las tienen, les parece que han estado usurpándoles y engañándoles con maldad refinada, y creen que se derrumban como un monte roto, por la tierra, y mueren aunque sigan viviendo, abrazados a las hojas caídas de su rosa blanca.[22]

This is the reason why when they [the poets] believe that some puerile or inconsiderate action disfigures them [women], or they imagine some frivolity or impurity [in women], they go out of their minds and feel mortal pain. They treat their mistress with the anger reserved for thieves and traitors. Having in their minds made women the repository of all the great and luminous desires they yearn for, when they seem to perceive that they do not possess them, they see women as usurpers, cheaters of refined evilness, and believe they crumble like a broken cliff. Then, they [the poets] die, even if they go on living, embracing the fallen leaves of their white rose.

The charitable lawyer has no pity for women. There is no forgiveness, no return from impurity. Man dictates the space woman inhabits, a static space – it is significant that Ana is practically immobile but Lucía cannot stand still – that precludes all initiative.

The novel is strewn with images of broken blossoms and torn handkerchiefs. They accompany the women while men like Juan recall St Francis and even Christ, when 'he follows barefoot children in the street until he knows where they live. Juan lifts from the streets, when others are not looking, the trodden flowers and carefully combs their petals before putting them outside the reach of people's feet.'[23]

Juan feels the sorrows of the world so deeply that he has aged prematurely. His love for his cousin, which he defines as 'a concession', helps in this process because she does not respond in an equally spiritual manner, but with fiery passion and a desire for the possession of the beloved.

But is this a 'concession' to woman or to his own, buried, sexuality that would be 'better married than burnt'? Juan Jerez is a much more ambiguous character than his exalted presentation would make the reader believe.

A poet and patriot, a man of great altruism, ready to die for his creed, he is the embodiment of Martí's ideal and the character's fears are as unconscious as those of his creator.

Apart from the homage to those Spanish republicans that sympathised with the Cuban cause, there is much of Martí in the character of Don Manuel. A political exile, forced to earn a meagre living in the New World, he is the loving father of a child, Manuelillo [resonances of Ismaelillo] who, like Martí's own son, encounters an early death. But Manuelillo is also a poet, pure and young, who dies with the premonitory vision of 'a palm on fire'. Cuba, like the fictional country of Manuelillo, is covered in palms, palms that were to be set on fire by the oncoming rebellion. Martí must have often feared that the fire would be started in his absence, and this was a painful fear.

The personage of Don Manuel allows serious discussion about the plight of the intellectual-client, in a society torn by internal contradictions that prevent the desired balance.

Estos tiempos nuestros están desquiciados, y con el derrumbe de las antiguas vallas sociales y las finezas de la educación, ha venido a crearse una nueva y vastísima clase de aristócratas de la inteligencia, con todas las necesidades de parecer y gustos ricos que de ella vienen, sin que haya habido tiempo aún, en lo rápido del vuelco, para que el cambio en la organización y repartimiento de las fortunas corresponda a la brusca alteración en las relaciones sociales producidas por las libertades políticas y la vulgarización de los conocimientos. Una hacienda ordenada es el fondo de la felicidad universal.[24]

We live through unsettled times. With the collapse of existing social barriers and the refinements of education, a new and very large class of aristocrats of the intelligence has emerged. They want to show off and have expensive tastes. But there has not been enough time, it has happened so rapidly, for social reorganisation and a more adequate sharing or riches, reflecting the sudden changes in social relations that stem from the new political freedoms and the spreading of knowledge. Properly balanced finance is the basis of universal happiness.

Don Manuel also allows Martí to speak about people and objects from the metropolis which he loves: Goya and Jovellanos – oases in a desert of unreason, a head of St Francis by Cano, Arabs and Romans in the coins found in his beloved Zaragoza where he studied, and Juana la Loca, the queen whose love for her husband led her to love him as a child.

Martí also shares much with Keleffy, the hypertense pianist, betrayed by his wife whom 'he thought he loved' but found to be 'like a cup without sound, a vase that did not respond to the harmonies of his soul'. Like Juan, the European pianist requires woman to be the repository of inspiration and beauty, pure and static, but instead he encounters a snake that constricts his imagination and prevents him from reaching the pure blue, the radiant light which is his goal: 'His music had an air of combat and torture that stopped it from reaching that equilibrium and harmonious proportion that are essential to durable works of art.'[25] Again, Martí's artistic ideals are spoken by one of the characters.

Something of the author can be detected in the apparently antagonic figure of Pedro Real. A winner, he is rich, tall, handsome and arrogant. A success with women, he is a hedonist of Celtic profile, for whom the pure Juan Jerez shows a curious fascination, even sympathy. The rogue is redeemed by love, a possibility which is not open to Martí's women characters; they either destroy love or are destroyed by it. 'Austere men feel in the company of high-spirited rogues the same fascination experienced by housewives who, incognito, attend a masked ball. There is in sin, when not excessive, a certain spirit of independence.'[26] Unusual words for Juan Jerez who cannot permit the slightest flaw in woman.

Juan's morbidity contrasts with the hedonism of Pedro when

talking about travelling – Juan shows a preference for Naples because his soul feels at ease in the town, as if it had reached its final destination, while Pedro exalts Paris and its rarefied pleasures. Juan longs for a pure, static woman while Pedro affirms:

La mujer es aquí una esclava disfrazada: allí es donde es la reina. Eso es París ahora: el reinado de la mujer. Acá, todo es pecado: si se sale, si se entra, si se da el brazo a un amigo, si se lee un libro ameno. ¡Pero eso es una falta de respeto, eso es ir contra las obras de la naturaleza! Porque una flor nace en un vaso de Sèvres, ¿se la ha de privar del aire y de la luz? Porque la mujer nace más hermosa que el hombre, ¿se le ha de oprimir el pensamiento, y so pretexto de un recato gazmoño, obligarla a que viva, escondiendo sus impresiones, como un ladrón esconde su tesoro en una cueva?[27]

Here, women are but slaves. In Paris, they are queens. The town is now the kingdom of women. Here everything is sinful. Whether they go out or come in, give their arm to a friend or read an amusing book. This is not respecting women! It is going against Nature! Because a flower is born in a Sèvres vase, must we deprive it of air and light? Because woman is born more beautiful than man, must we repress her thoughts, and, using sanctimonious prudery as an excuse, force her to live hiding her impressions as a thief hides his booty in a cave?

We know of Martí's disapproval of what he perceived as the excessive sexual freedom of North American women, and Pedro's free words are balanced by Ana's morality tale about an elegant young man who, having just broken a lily that had fallen to his feet, is contemplating in horror his own hands dripping with blood. Familiarity with Martí's imagery makes the symbols almost transparent: flowers cannot be cut, virginity cannot be tampered with.

## Martí and his characters: the women

In men, purity is a constant struggle because the beast nests in all our hearts, but in women it is a state, not a process, and as such, it does not admit change but only downfall.

The unusual division in the text between pure men and passionate women is responsible for the curious and complex situations that emerge between the characters who, irrespective of other contacts, are all involved with Leonor-Sol.

Her beauty is astonishing and exemplary. She looks 'like a Raphael

virgin, with American eyes and her waist is like the chalice of a lily'.[28]
An ideal American in the syncretism of her beauty, Sol is also pure, a
vase of mother-of-pearl. She is tender but also insensitive, blessedly
indifferent to others and willing to be led, attributes that the reader is
supposed to take as qualities because they adorn such perfect youthful
beauty. Sol, tender and beautiful, is not very intelligent and is happy
to lie at people's feet and listen, a precious empty vessel that will not
oppose men's fantasies.

She exacts confused responses from both men and women. Doña
Andrea, her mother, shares with Martí a passionate love for her child:

> De noche, Doña Andrea, que como a la menor de sus hijas la tuvo
> siempre en su lecho, no bien la veía dormida, la descubría para verla
> mejor; le apartaba los cabellos de la frente, y se los alzaba por detrás
> para mirarle el cuello, le tomaba las manos como podía tomar dos
> tórtolas, y se las besaba cuidadosamente; le acariciaba los pies, y se
> los cubría a lentos besos. Alfombra hubiera querido ser Doña
> Andrea, para que su hija no se lastimase nunca los pies, y para que
> anduviese sobre ella. Alfombra, cinta para su cuello, agua, aire,
> todo lo que ella tocase y necesitase para vivir, como si no tuviese
> otras hijas, quería ser para ella Doña Andrea.[29]

At night, Doña Andrea, who always slept with her as she was the
youngest of her daughters, as soon as the girl fell asleep, would
uncover her to see her better. She would brush her hair away to look
at her neck. She would take her hands, as if they were two doves,
and kiss them with care, caressing her feet and covering them with
slow kisses. She wished to be a carpet to be trodden on by her
daughter's feet, protecting them from pain. A carpet, a ribbon for
her neck, water, air, she wanted to be all to her, everything she
touched and needed, as if she had no other daughters.

It is not surprising that Sol's sisters are like shadows, unseen by
others.

The passionate feelings Doña Andrea has for her daughter are
transcribed in a lover's language, as if for Martí love had only one
language and there was no greater love than parental love.

It is the same Doña Andrea who mysteriously claims, 'If Manuel
[the father] was alive, you would not be so beautiful', and who, in
order to defend her daughter from Pedro Real, 'feels full of virile
strength'[30] and is also brought to near-suffocation by the thought of
her daughter living away from her.

The altruistic generosity of Juan Jerez, who has given money to Doña Andrea and decided not to visit the widow's household any more, in order to prevent malicious gossip, is contrasted with what is presented as the self-seeking gesture of the headmistress of Sol's school. Interestingly, she has no name or surname and is just known by her profession, 'la directora'. Does this lack of individual identity signal the emasculation of the feminine in women professionals? It is tempting to look for unstated motives in the harsh treatment of the headmistress, who, well aware of the dangers of beauty for a poor young girl, tries to protect Sol from social abuse. According to the author, her generosity stems from a desire to recover lost youth by being near the young and beautiful:

> Se aman y admiran a sí propios en los que, fuera ya de este peligro de rivalidad, tienen las mismas condiciones de ellos. Los miran como una renovación de sí mismos, como un consuelo de sus facultades que decaen, como si se viesen aún a sí propios tales como son aquellas criaturas nuevas, y no como ya van siendo ellos.[31]

> They love and admire themselves in those who, because they are not their rivals, have the same disposition as themselves. They look at them as if they were new versions of self, a consolation for decaying powers. They forget about their own reality and see themselves in the young.

Juan hides his generosity, the headmistress flaunts it. Only man can be generous, woman is moved by self-interest.

Adela, though a minor figure, shows Martí's indecision when confronted with a potentially intelligent woman. Intellectually curious, she is a nervous person but she is not impure. She listens with fascination to Pedro's words, to his tales of 'decadent' Paris, but her curiosity is redeemed by her interest in local affairs, by her conversations with Petrona Revolorio, an indigenous woman who acquaints Adela with the habits and customs of her people. Her character is sketchily drawn and it is difficult to see Martí in this voluble girl. Not so in Ana, the dying artist whose vibrant, passionate nature finds sublimation in art, and a rather drastic cure from possible temptation, in terminal illness.

Morbidity is given free rein in the portrayal of this young woman who at the beginning of the novel is already near death: a tragic condition that is described in favourable terms – 'Her pure spirit, so near death, was becoming even more lucid and refined.'[32] Her grave but unnamed illness gives her the 'rights of a married woman', that place her beyond desire. But does it? Would she not wish to be healthy for handsome Pedro? Is total sublimation of desire out of reach for even the purest woman?

Ana is the bird of death that contemplates her coming end like a journey, like a wedding. She is also the artist, touched by death, the mark of the chosen. Thanatos has triumphed over Eros but the language of victory is that of Eros, heightened, elegiac, luxuriant:

[Ana], como las tardes cuando se está yendo la luz, tenía el rostro a la vez claro y confuso, y todo él como bañado de una dulce bondad. Ni deseos tenía, porque de la tierra deseó poco mientras estuvo en ella, y lo que Ana le hubiera pedido a la tierra, de seguro que en ella no estaba, y tal vez estaría fuera de ella. Ni sentía Ana la muerte, porque no le parecía a ella que fuese muerte aquello que dentro de sí sentía crecientemente, y era como una ascensión. Cosas muy lindas debía ver, conforme se iba muriendo, sin saber que las veía, porque se le reflejaban en el rostro.[33]

[Ana], as when dusk covers the afternoon light, had a face which was both light and dark, and totally bathed in sweet kindness. She had no desires left, though she had wanted little from this world when she inhabited it. What Ana may have wished was not in this earth, maybe outside. Ana did not feel death coming, because what she felt growing within was like ascension. She must have been seeing very beautiful things as she was dying. Even if she was not conscious of them they were reflected on her face.

Death is a liberation from earthly desires and complexities, a flight towards those regions of perpetual blue and eternal light. The violent desire for death expressed by Juan is a reality in Ana who, like Martí, is an artist and whose nearness to death makes her into a lay saint. Her ideas of art reflect those of the author. Art and the artist are one and the resulting work, which is always disappointing, is the child of the creator, fragments of the self:

Porque desde que los imagino hasta que los acabo voy poniendo en ellos tanto de mi alma, al fin ya no llegan a ser telas, sino mi alma misma, y me da vergüenza de que me la vean, y me parece que he pecado con atreverme a asuntos que están mejor para nube que para colores.[34]

Because from the moment I conceive them to the end, I put so much of my soul into them that finally they are no longer canvases but my very soul. And I feel ashamed of showing them as if I was a sinner for daring to tackle subjects that are better left as clouds than turned into colour.

Martí is aware that his practice of art, intimate, profound, torn out of his entrails and his soul, is an exposure of self that borders on the obscene because, like the young virgin, other people's looks may soil it forever. Through Ana, Martí tells the reader that because art is not wholly necessary, it should not be practised unless it can be done to the utmost perfection.

Martí shares with modernity the frustrations about the materials of art but, more centrally, the frustration of the artist because of the gap between desire and actuality. Pure thought appears as infinitely superior to its material realisation. Only the artist knows his sources and the meaning of his symbols. Critics are but predators that feed on the genuine creator. The self-referentiality of art and the constant need to tell the reader about his ideas on art, further underline Martí's modernity. What distinguishes him is his concept of art as exemplary, an exercise of morality to improve humanity – though Cortázar can be seen in this light, as a late disciple.

Ana is also the vehicle through which Martí attempts to define what I could call 'a consumer culture for the expected and necessary national bourgeoisie'. The house in which the action takes place is, like Sol's beauty, syncretic. Not opulent, it looks lived-in and mixes European furniture with the naive expressions of belief that artisans inscribe in their simple ceramic household decorations. Martí believes that to dispel shadows, light and colour should be strong presences in houses – as they are in his writing. Good paintings by the solid, main-line painters of the nineteenth century – Madrazo and Fortuny – adorn the walls. The bookshelves abound in the work of artists who had either broken with their artistic past – Poe, introduced as new culture; Fitzgerald and the *Rubaiyat*; romantics like Musset – or exemplary works like *Wilhelm Meister*, the novel of measure and order, the 'epic' of the emerging bourgeoisie.

Ana and her friends, inhabitants of the desired *nuestra América*, drink [syncretic Hispano-Mexican] chocolate in native crockery which the author loads with symbolic meaning. American animal figures hold the cups: squirrels for young, active Adela; haughty quetzals for Ana, the artist; eagles for Juan; capuchin monkeys for Pedro; and elastic wild pumas for Lucía Jerez. The imperial and deadly connotations of the eagle are ignored in Juan's case but Lucía, who is first seen dressed in bright red, wearing no flower because the one she desires – a black rose – does not yet exist, is the puma, the snake, the monster with a woman's head that devours the roses in Ana's allegorical painting. A *femme fatale*, she destroys Juan's peace and Sol's life, acting as the unwitting hand that will prevent the young girl's loss of purity.

Full of untapped energy that will become destructive passion, Lucía is robust, demanding, a predator. Betraying the highest qualities of her sex, she ignores tenderness and her activity precludes the demure stance that so befits womanhood. Her hair is dark, abundant – a symbol of strong sexuality – and unruly, often falling and hiding her forehead which should be 'the mirror in which the lover looks at his own soul'.[35] But Lucía is not just a mirror that reflects man or a cup to be filled by his fantasies. In love with Juan from childhood, she wishes to possess him and to exclude others. From the very beginning of the novel the images that will accompany her are established: reds and blacks, flames and snakes. She represents the violence of passion which opposes the qualities of peace, sedentariness and serenity which are represented in the pure colours, blue and white, and in the irradiating light which depicts the kind and the tender.

The discovery of her own sensuality, which she does not reject, marks her personality. She daydreams that Juan has deposited a long and soft kiss on her hand. This symbolic dream 'filled her whole room with flowers. She thought that flames broke through the glass mirror and she closed her eyes, as they are always closed in moments of total happiness.' She falls into Juan's arms that delicately hold that body from which 'in that hour of birth, light seemed to spring'.[36] But this awakening to the erotic, cloaked as it is in highly sensual language, is to prove fatal, saddening Juan with its evidence of the impure and turning Lucía serious and apprehensive.

Her unnamed sexuality colours her vision and she develops a love–hate relationship with Sol's purity that will be fatal. At their first meeting, Lucía pins a rose on Sol's breast, a rose that after too passionate an embrace pierces the virgin's skin, drawing her young blood with its thorns. The highly symbolical scene, the piercing thorn and the maiden's blood, predict the end of the book in which the pistol in Lucía's hand fires the shot that pierces the virginal breast for ever, spilling all Sol's blood.

Sol, the empty, beautiful vessel, is fascinated by Lucía, who appears to awaken a dormant masochism. Lucía's powerful sexuality, her domineering presence, act curiously upon Sol's innocence:

Prefería ella (Sol) que Lucía la mirase, a que la mirasen los jóvenes mejor conocidos en la ciudad. [. . .] Pero Lucía se había entrado por el alma de Sol, desde la noche en que le pareció sentir goce cuando se clavó en su seno la espina de la rosa. Lucía, ardiente y despótica, sumisa a veces como una enamorada, rígida y frenética enseguida sin causa aparente, y bella entonces como una rosa roja, ejercía, por lo mismo que no lo deseaba, un poderoso influjo en el espíritu de Sol, tímido y nuevo. Era Sol como para que la llevasen en la vida de la mano, más preparada por la Naturaleza para que la quisiesen que para querer, feliz por ver que lo eran los que tenía cerca de sí, pero no por especial generosidad, sino por cierta incapacidad suya de ser ni muy venturosa ni muy desdichada. Tenía el encanto de las rosas blancas. Un dueño le era preciso, y Lucía fue su dueña.

She preferred (Sol) to be looked at by Lucía than to be looked at by the best known young men in the town. [. . .] Lucía had entered Sol's soul from the night in which she seemed to have felt some pleasure when the rose's thorn entered her breast. Lucía, ardent and despotic, sometimes submissive like a lover, rigid and frantic the next without apparent cause and, at that moment, beautiful like a red rose, unwittingly exerted a powerful influence in Sol's new and timid mind. Sol had to be led. Better prepared by nature to be loved than to love, she was happy to see those next to her contented, not because of a specially generous disposition but due to a certain inner ability to be either very happy or very unhappy. She had the charm of a white rose. She needed a master and Lucía had become hers.[37]

Their 'fatal friendship', detected by the alert eyes of Doña Andrea, Sol's loving mother, can only lead to an almost ritual blood-letting. Lucía, like an arbitrary goddess, will demand the blood of the virgin, the constant reminder of her own impurity. The good Ana and the innocent Sol have no place in this Earth where the beast in man is perpetually threatening, always ready to pounce on the unprotected. Lucía is moving in her passion, in the contradictions that tear through her woman's flesh, a carnal presence that is rejected by her beloved Juan.

Red is her colour, the colour of blood and of the female curse, a curse that she, being of flesh and blood, cannot exorcise; a curse which, deprived of a language to name it, she cannot come to terms with.

Robbed of tenderness because of her unrelinquished sexuality, Lucía kills the untested purity in Sol which she had been denied. Her crime is a crime of passion – her own, which she cannot control – and after the crime, she finds refuge, though not solace, in the loving arms of Ana, not those of Juan. Her passion has no place in the harmonious world which Juan desires.

*Amistad funesta* reflects Martí's values as clearly as his other writing, which is not surprising in a writer of such inner coherence. But it also reflects his fears. Maybe Martí was right in shunning the genre. In fiction the relevance of the unmentioned and the control over the written word are more elusive than in journalism and more revealing than in poetry.

The unnamed fears that the novel reveals do not, in any way, diminish the figure of Martí. On the contrary, they enhance it. A man of flesh and blood, a patriot and a great writer, Martí was torn by contradictory desires that humanised him, making him our brother, our contemporary.

# Concluding perspectives

CHRISTOPHER ABEL

In the early decades of the nineteenth century the Spanish colonial administration displayed a vigour and vitality that were visible in the official buildings of Havana. It was often an effective agency for promoting capitalist growth and was frequently responsive to the requirements of both Spanish and Cuban entrepreneurs. The colonial bureaucracy preserved one crusading objective, namely the reconquest of the lost mainland colonies, with Cuba as the springboard for their recapture. The legitimacy of the colonial regime lay in its capacity to provide both an orderly and peaceful framework for the pursuit of economic growth and a competent international diplomacy serving the needs of the export-sector Creole élite. The Creole élite, denied effective political participation, was placated by a tacit compact, by which the metropolitan government ensured a market for Cuban sugar-cane and provided peninsular troops to guarantee Creole prosperity and social ascendancy against the endemic threat of social conflict and race war.

By 1890 the position had altered irreversibly. The colonial administration was stagnant and archaic. It was widely perceived, in Spain as well as in Cuba, as a brake upon growth and lacking the will for self-reform. The self-confidence of the colonial administration sagged as the reality of Spain's diminishing role was increasingly apparent. After the total failure of Spain's attempted re-annexation of the Dominican Republic (1865), the ambition to recover the mainland empire was a discredited fantasy, cherished and propagated only by a small exclusive literary group in the metropolis. The colonial administration was exposed as structurally anomalous, a resource for predatory peninsular bureaucrats tempted by the short-term rewards of office and by opportunities to manoeuvre for long-term career advancement in Spain. A minority of committed reformers was thwarted by the combined strength of inertia and entrenched interest. The compact between the colonial power and the Creole élite, renewed after the first, abortive war of independence (1868–78), was clearly inoperative by 1890. The metropolitan market for Cuban sugar-cane was eroded by the first plantings of Spanish sugar-beet in 1882. Peninsular troops failed to police the island in the interests of

192

Creole capitalists. Widespread hiring by sugar-cane planters of private vigilantes indicated their lack of confidence in the capacity of the government to confront an explosion of banditry. A renewed emphasis upon the merits of white immigration (*blanqueamiento*) underlined Creole anxieties about the Colony's capacity to handle an ethnic *jacquerie*. Meanwhile, the Creole élite was antagonised by high levels of taxation to cover the war debt and by the failure of Spain to reach reciprocity arrangements with the United States, now indisputably Cuba's main trading partner, that met Cuban interests. Leading cigar manufacturers and merchants organised themselves in 1891 in the Movimiento Económico (the Economic Movement) which published a manifesto outlining Creole grievances.

The brief resurgence of Creole optimism about metropolitan intentions that was fuelled by the First Republic in Spain had by 1890 been dissipated. The colonial regime had exhausted its range of policy options and alternatives. Clumsy alternations between coercion and a tactically dictated leniency, between intransigent authoritarianism and tentative moves towards autonomism, served to antagonise the unconditional allies of the colonial government as well as to deepen the distrust of its opponents. A total loss of confidence in metropolitan intentions undermined the base for autonomism in Cuba, while forcing annexationist and *independentista* factions into an improbable pragmatic alliance.

The Colony was threatened by internal decomposition and the dissolution of the structures that supported it, when in 1891 it won a brief reprieve. The sugar-cane sector was revived by the Foster–Cánovas agreement, which permitted Cuba to share in the full benefits of the McKinley Tariff. But the boom proved temporary. The agreement was hastily reversed by the Wilson–Gorman Tariff Act, which, as world commodity prices tumbled, sharply curtailed Cuban access to US markets. The instant contraction of the export sector had immediate repercussions throughout the economy. The extent of Cuban integration into the US economy was fully visible; the incapacity of the Spanish government to influence decisions taken in Washington was manifest; above all, the unreadiness of the colonial administration to combat island-wide depression was exposed.

## Martí as politician

Martí and his allies enjoyed some advantages. The routine brutality and intermittent terror conducted by the colonial regime antagonised groups that might otherwise have acquiesced in it and kept alive a residual politicisation from an earlier period. The inefficiency of the regime angered progressive businessmen, who, through travel and reading, observed the advantages of pluralism accompanied by orderly procedures of government that pertained in some other parts of Latin America, and associated prosperity with republican government, technological change and European immigration. Cuba, which in the 1830s and 1840s was the country enjoying the continent's most impressive growth rates, was by the 1890s being overtaken by the republics of the Southern Cone, whose political and business élites engaged in debate in both Congress and a vigorous press. In Cuba no such institutions existed. The Economic Society provided an inadequate forum for planters, merchants and professionals to debate alternative economic policy options; and restrictions upon a free press obstructed the flow of vital business, as well as of political, information. Furthermore, while several other Latin American governments launched new public education programmes, a defective Cuban educational system, whose only purpose was to imbue an ideological conformity, delayed the emergence of new indigenous intermediate groups crucial to an effective capitalism – managers, technicians, accountants, engineers; and accelerated the import of foreign expertise to fill the gap.

Martí's political achievement lay in drawing together in one coalition diverse groups that had enjoyed some benefits from the colonial arrangements – some merchants and tobacco manufacturers – with others excluded from them – peasant farmers, pauperised ex-planters from the Oriente, labour activists (recently discussed by Jean Stubbs) in tobacco manufacturing, bandits, émigré workers (analysed here by Poyo) and others. Anxious that the cause of independence might be lost if divisions within Cuba worked to the interest of external forces, Martí worked to inject a sense of *cubanidad*. He was concerned especially that anger in the Oriente at the concentration of growth in the western provinces and a sense of abandonment by western-based colonial authorities should not be converted into a demand for a vengeful invasion of the west.

Harnessing a pervasive sense of economic, political and educational discrimination, Martí sought skilfully to reconcile a bewilderingly complex and fragmented opposition with energetic campaigning and a broad message of human optimism, and also to persuade wide sectors of opinion that, despite the apparent setbacks of the Ten Years' War and the *Guerra Chiquita*, these provided a useful basis of assimilated experience. Martí's prudence was evident in his emphasis upon the moral postulates upon which a republican *patria* was to be built and his downplaying of more precise and divisive issues, like the timetable for establishing a republic, the nature of its governance and its economic strategy.

As a political leader Martí worked under severe constraints. Exile, day-to-day oppression and numerous obstacles to the diffusion of information were reinforced by a tradition of autocracy and weak countervailing institutions. Meanwhile, the weak articulation of representative institutions and the absence of a strong municipal tradition made for a personalised attachment to political authority which bred *caudillismo*. Thus Martí outlined orderly procedures and processes for the Partido Revolucionario Cubano in order to forestall *caudillismo* and encouraged voluntary associations among exiled workers as means of gaining valuable participatory experience and as bases for future democratic action. He sought actively to superimpose qualities of tolerance, mutual respect and constitutionalism. Confronted by the imperatives of sustaining popular enthusiasm and the belief of his supporters in the reality of his aims, while lacking the funds to finance an elaborate apparatus, Martí had no alternative to an emphasis upon commitment to action. Indeed, commitment to action served as a surrogate for the practical ingredients of action.

The enduring impact of Martí was evident in his ideas, not in his political organisation. On his death the character of the Partido Revolucionario Cubano changed dramatically. Without Martí popular participation declined, the radical thrust in the party was blunted, and power shifted to conservative elements led by Tomás Estrada Palma, who saw independence and a US protectorate as preparing the ground for their goal of annexation. Co-ordination between the party and the radical generals in the field faltered; and the separatist momentum was diminished by conflicts between the provisional government, the expatriates and the military leaders – Máximo Gómez, Antonio Maceo and Calixto García. The recent writings of Louis Pérez Jr confirm the view that the pursuit of a separatist consensus was finally shattered by the divisive tactics of the US military occupation, which turned the 'responsible leadership' and 'better classes' against the rest of the Cuban populace, flattered the surviving *independentista* military leaders into consenting to the disbandment of the *ejércitos libertadores*, favoured the expatriate leadership at the expense of its domestic counterpart, courted former Spanish office-holders and ex-autonomists while excluding separatists, and promoted ethnic divisions both by denying black veterans access to the officer corps in the reconstituted Civil Guard and by imposing a male suffrage with strict property and literacy qualifications. Patriotic commitment and national sovereignty were compromised by the habit of requesting US mediation in internal disputes, by hasty steps to forestall proposals to enlarge economic ties with western Europe, by access for itinerant entrepreneurs to US citizenship and by the imposition of oaths of allegiance to the United States as a condition for holding public office. Only later, as Kapcia has shown, did Martí re-emerge as a symbol of defrauded expectations and lost unifying purpose, an exponent of an exuberant optimism qualified by a sombre perception of the present. But in the immediate post-war crisis of economic collapse and massive unemployment, political idealism evaporated in the pursuit of public office.

## Martí as journalist

Martí seized the opportunities posed by the evolution of a liberal press in Latin America. Certain processes that had occurred earlier in the United States were observed in several Latin American countries in the last decades of the nineteenth century. In particular, ephemeral broadsheets extemporised for electoral purposes were displaced by permanent newspapers, financed in large part by a growth of advertising connected with export-led growth, and frequently employing a modern imported printing technology. The consolidation of a daily press, aimed principally at an urban readership benefiting from an enlargement of the education sector, was welcomed by liberal élites both as an example of modern business enterprise and as an alternative medium to the pulpit.

Martí was shrewdly perceptive about the uses of journalism in the service of his cause – in popularising, amplifying and propagating a message, and in liberating readers from conventions, inherited truths and parochial perspectives. He recognised the uses of the press as a means of transmitting authentic information and as an instrument for moulding public opinion and instilling in it an elevated view of international events. Martí observed how, by acting as an interpreter of political processes in the United States for a Hispanic American readership hungry for information about its neighbour, he might acquire continent-wide influence, celebrity and a modest income, while simultaneously addressing himself to an insular public. Martí was perceptive in his estimation of his readers. Refraining from importing gratuitous private meanings to his work, he wrote with a mellifluous and direct style and made a confident use of immediately intelligible symbols and language. He saw too how the press could be used as a sounding-board, how his readers could be moved by moral outrage and evangelical notions, how they could be soothed by a carefully modulated reassurance.

The main themes of Martí's journalism both reflected his own shifting priorities and displayed an alertness to those of his readers. His early journalism from Spain exhibited more concern for day-to-day parliamentary politics, Church–state relations and international diplomacy than for social, and especially agrarian, issues. Later, writing from the United States, Martí began to place a greater stress on social questions, especially class conflict and hostilities between immigrant and resident workers in the cities: but, ironically, although Martí was the leading advocate of a small farmer democracy in Cuba, rural conflict in the United States was never more than a secondary theme of his writing.

## Martí as ideologue

Martí began from an optimistic perception of man and a view of morality in which moral ends constituted the springs of action. He believed strongly that freedom was axiomatic, that man was answerable to his own conscience and not to organised religion, and that the *patria* should embody a programme of moral values. Following traditions best represented by Machiavelli and Montesquieu, Martí was more concerned with the spirit of rulers than, like Hume, with the strength of institutions. And, in general, Martí showed more confidence in the populace than in its rulers. Repudiating the authority of an obsolete state and Church, Martí invoked the authority and responsibility of the parent and the schoolteacher. His emphasis upon leadership was qualified by his observations on societies where the citizenry enjoyed insufficient guarantees against the metamorphosis of leadership into *caudillismo*. Behind a stress on the spirit of rulers was an emphasis upon a perception of citizenship by which the citizen, through universal male suffrage, might act as a corrective to his rulers.

*Martiano* notions of liberation embraced an underlying assumption of abundance. Martí held that in Latin America, as in the United States, economic attitudes should not be predicated upon notions of scarcity, for scarcity was the consequence of personal rapacity or policy miscalculation. Martí looked, first, to the liberation of the self-regulating individual from forces, like the official Church, that stunted his talents; secondly, like Kossuth and Mazzini, to the liberation of the nation from external forces that worked against its interests; thirdly, to the liberation of small enterprise from big business. Thus, according to Martí, the individual would enjoy the opportunity to share in goods and services that would abound in a genuine process of liberation – a view that bore some comparison to those of Marx, but also had much in common with numerous liberal authors of the nineteenth century.

Contributors to this volume share the view that the ideas of Martí should be seen within their socio-historical matrix, and join in rejecting the superimposition of alien or subsequent ideologies upon Martí. Martí was neither a positivist whose vision barely strayed beyond the empirically verifiable, nor – as Schulman and Torrents underline – a literary humanist for whom the political was subordinate to the aesthetic. Though sympathetic – as Ibarra shows – to some aspects of socialism, Martí was not a socialist; nor was class struggle for him the secret of history. Martí did not formulate laws of motion of underdeveloped countries; nor did he attach to articulate conceptualisation the significance he gave to analysis and prescription. Because he was not a socialist, Martí never faced a Cuban version of the famous dilemma confronting Rosa Luxemburg; should a Polish national revolution take precedence over socialist revolution?

The ideas of Martí were securely anchored in the radical liberalism of the late nineteenth century that overlapped with features of both anarchism and socialism on such questions as welfare and mutual aid, fraternity and levelling. Martí combined the confidence in reason and rational discourse that pervaded contemporary liberal thinking with a passionate exasperation at their denial by the colonial regime in Cuba and Puerto Rico. He blended a stress upon personal regeneration that owed much to freemasonry with notions of the irrepressible need of the individual to express his personality authentically. Responsive to debates among competing strands of liberals, Martí sympathised unequivocally with radicals demanding remedial action to correct inequalities of wealth and income in capitalist societies against exponents of the view that all inhibitions to entrepreneurial freedom thwarted growth and had incalculable adverse social consequences. Opting for an open, participatory liberalism, Martí was unyielding in his repudiation of autocratic brands of liberalism that broadened the range of freedoms for selected entrepreneurs at the expense of other groups. Martí moved cautiously beyond fragmentary strictures upon the lack of *cultura* and complacent philistinism of industrialists to a total rejection of an ideology of possessive individualism, unfettered competition and beneficent cupidity. Martí rejected too notions of the automatic balancing of the pursuit of individual self-interest in the general interest.

Martí was more explicit in his vision of the international economy than in his view of the domestic economy. He came gradually to reject the main outlines of the international economic system, and was particularly outspoken in his advocacy of bimetallism as an instrument both of Latin American emancipation from metropolitan pressures and of the protection of the small farmer against international financial interests. Martí never fully elaborated his vision of the domestic economy. While foreseeing a transition towards a rational and organised freedom, Martí said little that was precise of the economic role of the post-colonial state, its relationship with private property or the regulation of foreign and domestic interests. Perhaps this lacuna can best be explained by Martí's main concern with considerations very specific to his time and place, especially the necessity of preserving a coalition of incompatibles while conducting the war; of holding together both radical elements that envisaged a war of independence as also a war of redistribution and conservative groups that looked to independence as the prerequisite of renewed export-led growth in conjunction with foreign interests.

One recurring theme of this volume has been the impact upon Martí of diverse ideological trends, how and from where he assembled the arguments to uphold and develop his visions of national independence and supranational solutions for the continent. In Martí's early writing a certain rudderlessness can be observed. This can be attributed in part to youth and inexperience, in part too to the suffocation by the authoritarian colonial regime of an intellectual tradition in philosophy, history, letters and law that had flourished earlier in the century. In one sense, Martí put this rudderlessness to good advantage. From his espousal in Spain of the mainstream of stock liberal formulae, Martí drew upon a broad, and ever-broadening, range of ideas. Hence he was never open to the charge made so frequently against Commonwealth Caribbean ideologues of a more recent period, that his thought-patterns were restricted by the horizons of a small-scale society, by, in a word, small-islandmindedness. Indeed, the precise opposite can be argued; that Martí, the exile in three continents, was open to ideas emanating from a greater diversity of sources than thinkers permanently located in one large-scale society, and was unusually receptive to ideas capable of assimilation into a different range of expectations from those for which they were devised. Particularly striking in Martí were his rejection of the mechanical emulation of other societies, and his capacity to filter ideas from experiences beyond Cuba and Latin America without losing sight of the imperative of founding his ideology upon authentic Cuban and Latin American experience.

Martí contributed to the continuing debate about a Caribbean identity. As Retamar, in this book, and Gordon Lewis and Paul Estrade, in other recent publications, have stressed, Martí shared with the Puerto Rican ideologue Ramón Betances, Dominicans like Gregorio Luperón and Eugenio María de Hostos, and the Filipino patriot José Rizal, an overwhelming sense of living in a period of irreversible change. They had in common an anti-colonial language and experience that drew upon western and southern European examples of national self-determination.

Observing the abolition of slavery in Cuba, the crumbling edifice of tradition, religion and education in the island and the expansionist drive of the United States, Martí perceived the 1890s as a decisive phase in the reshaping of international relations in the western hemisphere and the redefinition of race relations in the Caribbean. But perhaps Martí's most important contribution to the identity debate was his judgement that a particular identity could be reached only through continuous expressive experimentation and that the achievement of independence was only one step towards its crystallisation.

# Notes

## Chapter 1    The modernity of Martí

1   Rubén Darío, 'José Martí' (1895), in *Los raros* (1896) (Buenos Aires, 1952), p. 195.

2   José Martí, 'Tres héroes' in *La Edad de Oro* (1889), in *Obras completas* (Havana, 1963–73) (hereafter *O.C.*), XVIII, p. 304.

3   Martí, 'Fragmento del discurso pronunciado en el club del Comercio' (hereafter 'Fragmento'), (Caracas, 1881), in *O.C.*, VII, p. 285.

4   Martí, 'Discurso pronunciado en la velada de la Sociedad Literaria Hispanoamericana en honor de Simón Bolívar el 28 de octubre de 1893' (hereafter 'Discurso . . . Bolívar'), in *O.C.*, VIII, p. 241.

5   *Ibid.*

6   Martí, 'La estatua de Bolívar por el venezolano Cova' (1883), in *O.C.*, VIII, p. 175.

7   Martí, 'Discurso . . . Bolívar', p. 241.

8   *Ibid.*, p. 242.

9   Martí, *Ismaelillo* (New York, 1882), in *O.C.*, XVIII.

10   Darío recalls this event in *La vida de Rubén Darío contada por él mismo* (Barcelona, n.d.), p. 143.

11   Martí, 'Carta a Valero Pujol' (1877), in *O.C.*, VII, p. 111.

12   Martí, 'Lectura en la reunión de emigrados cubanos, en Steck Hall' (1880), in *O.C.*, IV, p. 202.

13   Martí, 'Fragmento', p. 284.

14   Martí, 'Discurso . . . Bolívar', p. 241.

15   Carlos Rafael Rodríguez, 'Martí y el nuevo Ayacucho', in *Casa de las Américas*, no. 138, May–June 1983, p. 47.

16   Roberto Fernández Retamar, 'Cuál es la literatura que inicia José Martí', paper given at VII Congreso de la Asociación Internacional de Hispanistas (Venice, August 1980), published in *Actas del Séptimo Congreso de la Asociación International de Hispanistas* (Rome, 1982), vol. I.

17   Fernández Retamar, '*La revelación de nuestra América*', in *Introducción a José Martí* (Havana, 1978).

18   Martí, Poem XXX, *Versos sencillos* (1891), *O.C.*, XVI.

19   Cited from J. E. Cairnes, *The Slave Power, its character, career and probable designs* (London, 1862) by Karl Marx, *Capital*, vol. I (intro. by G. D. H. Cole) (London, 1930), pp. 270–1.

20   Ricaurte Soler, 'De *nuestra América* de Blaine a *nuestra América* de Martí', in *Casa de las Américas*, no. 119, March–April 1980; and 'José Martí: bolivarismo y antimperialismo', in *Casa de las Américas*, no. 138, May–June 1983.

21   Paul Estrade, 'Remarques sur le caractère tardif, et avancé, de la prise de conscience nationale dans les Antilles espagnoles', in *Cahiers du Monde Hispanique et Luso–Brasilien, Caravelle*, no. 38, 1982.

22   Miguel Acosta Saignes, 'Cómo repudia una clase social a su Libertador', in *Casa de las Américas*, no. 138, May–June 1983.
23   Fernández Retamar, *Introducción a José Martí* (Havana, 1978), esp. pp. 35–47, 153–4; and 'Algunos problemas teóricos de una biografía ideológica de José Martí', in *Anuario del Centro de Estudios Martianos* (Havana), no. 2, 1979. The Centro de Estudios Martianos held in 1980 an international symposium on the theme *José Martí y el pensamiento democrático revolucionario*, contained in *Anuario del Centro de Estudios Martianos* (Havana), no. 3, 1980.
24   See especially Philip S. Foner, *A History of Cuba and its relations with the United States* (2 vols, New York, 1962–3), ch. 26; and John M. Kirk, *José Martí: Mentor of the Cuban nation* (Tampa, 1983), ch. 3.
25   Martí, 'Cartas de Martí' (1884), in *O.C.*, X, p. 84.
26   Martí, 'Cartas de Martí' (1886), in *O.C.*, XI, p. 19.
27   Martí, 'Cartas de Martí' (1888), in *O.C.*, XI, p. 437.
28   Martí, 'Carta de Nueva York' (1881), in *O.C.*, IX, p. 108.
29   Martí, 'Cartas de Martí' (1885), in *O.C.*, XIII, p. 290.
30   José Cantón Navarro, 'Influencia del medio social norteamericano en el pensamiento de José Martí', in *Algunas ideas de José Martí en relación con la clase obrera y el socialismo* (2nd edn, Havana, 1980).
31   Angel Augier, 'Anticipaciones de José Martí a la teoría leninista del imperialismo', in *Acción y poesía en José Martí* (Havana, 1982).
32   The most tenacious student of Martí's anti-imperialism, though not a Marxist–Leninist, was Emilio Roig de Leuchsenring, who began his work on Martí in the 1920s.
33   Cf. Francisco Pividal, *Bolívar: pensamiento precursor del antimperialismo* (Havana, 1977).
34   Martí, 'Impresiones de América' (I–III) (1880), in *O.C.*, XIX.
35   Letter to José Martí from Fausto Teodoro de Aldrey, 3 May 1882, in *Papeles de Martí (Archivo de Gonzalo de Quesada). III. Miscelánea, recopilación . . . por Gonzalo de Quesada y Miranda* (Havana, 1935), p. 41.
36   Letter to José Martí from Bartolomé Mitre y Vedía, 26 September 1882, *op. cit.*, note 35, p. 84.
37   Cf. Juliette Ouillon, 'La discriminación racial en los Estados Unidos vista por José Martí', in *Anuario Martiano* (Havana), no. 3, 1971.
38   Cf. especially Martí, 'Un drama terrible' (1887), in *O.C.*, XI.
39   As far as we know, Martí used the term 'imperialists' for the first time in 1883 in *La Nación* of Buenos Aires (*O.C.*, IX, p. 343).
40   Francisco Bilbao, 'Iniciativa de la América: Idea de un congreso federal de las repúblicas' (1856), in *La América en peligro: Evangelio americano: Sociabilidad chilena* (Santiago de Chile, 1941), p. 145.
41   Cf. Thomas F. McGann, *Argentina, Estados Unidos y el sistema interamericano* (Buenos Aires, 1960).
42   Darío, *op. cit.*, p. 198.
43   Martí, 'Congreso internacional de Washington' (hereafter 'Congreso') (1889), in *O.C.*, VI, p. 46.
44   Martí, 'La Conferencia Monetaria de las Repúblicas de América' (1891), in *O.C.*, VI, p. 160.

45 Martí, 'Nuestra América' (1891), in *O.C.*, VI, p. 19.
46 Martí, 'Congreso', p. 57. Martí writes of 'trying their systems of colonisation in free countries'.
47 Martí used this phrase frequently to refer to Latin America in general.
48 Martí, Poem III, *Versos sencillos* (1891), *O.C.*, XVI, p. 67.
49 Martí, 'Bases del Partido Revolucionario Cubano' (1892), in *O.C.*, I, p. 279.
50 Martí, 'La revuelta en Egipto' (1881), in *O.C.*, XIV.
51 Martí, 'Una distribución de diplomas, en un colegio de los Estados Unidos' (1884), in *O.C.*, VIII, esp. p. 383.
52 Martí, 'La revuelta en Túnez' and 'La guerra de Túnez y el ministerio' (1881), in *O.C.*, XIV.
53 Martí, 'Un paseo por la tierra de los anamitas', in *La Edad de Oro* (1889), *O.C.*, XVIII.
54 For example, in 1836, in 'Sobre el progreso y porvenir de la civilización', Michel Chevalier, then a Saint-Simonian who went on to lead a volatile political life, announced that 'the relating of the two civilisations, western and eastern' was, thanks to America, 'located between the two civilisations' and 'reserved for high destinies'. Thus 'the progress achieved by the nations of the New World is of the greatest importance to the general progress of the species', and will have, as one of several consequences, 'politically, the association of all nations, the equilibrium of the world', of which the European equilibrium is 'no more than a detail'.
55 Julio Le Riverend, 'El historicismo martiano en la idea del equilibrio del mundo', in *José Martí: pensamiento y acción* (Havana, 1982).
56 Cited by Miguel Acosta Saignes in *Acción y utopía del hombre de las dificultades* (Havana, 1977), p. 380.
57 Martí, 'El tercer año del Partido Revolucionario Cubano: El alma de la revolución, y el deber de Cuba en América' (1894), in *O.C.*, III, pp. 142–3.
58 Martí, 'Carta a Federico Henríquez y Carvajal, 25 de marzo de 1895', in *O.C.*, IV, p. 111.
59 Martí, 'Manifiesto de Montecristi, 25 de marzo de 1895', in *O.C.*, IV, pp. 100–1.
60 Martí, 'Carta a Manuel Mercado, 18 de mayo de 1895', in *O.C.*, IV, pp. 167–8.
61 Paul Valéry, 'La crisis del espíritu', in *Política del espíritu* (2nd edn, Buenos Aires, 1945), p. 23.
62 *Ibid.*, p. 24.

## Chapter 2  José Martí: Architect of social unity

This chapter is based on my doctoral dissertation 'Cuban émigré communities in the United States and the independence of their homeland, 1852–1895' (University of Florida, 1983). I would like to express my appreciation to David Bushnell, Ivan Schulman, Helen Safa, and Mariano Díaz Miranda who in a variety of ways made this article possible. Finally, appreciation is extended to the US Department of Education Fulbright-Hays Doctoral Dissertation Research Abroad Program for making my research in Havana possible and the University of Florida Manuel Pedro González José Martí Fund for travel funds to the London conference.

1　Gerardo Castellanos y García, *Motivos de Cayo Hueso* (Havana, 1935); Manuel Deulofeu y Lleonart, *Héroes del destierro. La emigración. Notas históricas* (Cienfuegos, 1904); José Rivero Muñíz, 'Los cubanos en Tampa', *Revista Bimestre Cubana*, 74 (January–June 1958), pp. 5–140; Juan J. E. Casasus, *La emigración cubana y la independencia de la patria* (Havana, 1953). For additional materials on the émigré communities that focus almost exclusively on their separatist activity see Aleida Plasencia (ed.), *Bibliografía de la Guerra de los Diez Años* (Havana, 1968); Biblioteca Nacional José Martí, *Bibliografía de la Guerra Chiquita, 1879–1880* (Havana, 1975) and *Bibliografía de la Guerra de Independencia, 1895–1898* (Havana, 1976).

2　John M. Kirk, *José Martí: Mentor of the Cuban nation* (Tampa, Fa, 1983), p. 4.

3　Kirk, *op. cit.*; José Cantón Navarro, *Algunas ideas de José Martí en relación con la clase obrera y el socialismo* (Havana, 1980); Ariel Hidalgo, *Orígenes del movimiento obrero y del pensamiento socialista en Cuba* (Havana, 1976), ch. 2.

4　Joan Marie Steffy, 'The Cuban immigrants of Tampa, Florida', unpublished MA thesis, University of Florida, 1975); L. Glenn Westfall, 'Don Vicente Martínez Ybor. The Man and his Empire: Development of the Clear Havana Industry in Cuba and Florida in the Nineteenth Century' unpublished PhD dissertation, University of Florida, 1977) and *Key West: Cigar City USA* (Key West: Historic Key West Preservation Board, 1984); Louis A. Pérez, Jr, 'Cubans in Tampa: From exiles to immigrants, 1892–1901' (hereafter 'Cubans in Tampa'), *Florida Historical Quarterly* (hereafter *FHQ*), 57 (October 1978), pp. 129–40 and 'Reminiscences of a *Lector*: Cuban Cigar Workers in Tampa', *FHQ*, 53 (April 1975), pp. 443–9; Gary Mormino, 'Tampa and the New Urban South: The Weight Strike of 1899', *FHQ*, 60 (January 1982), pp. 337–56; Durward Long, 'Labor Relations in the Tampa Cigar Industry, 1885–1911', *Labor History* (hereafter *LH*), 12 (Fall 1971), pp. 551–9 and 'La Resistencia: Tampa's Immigrant Labor Union', *LH*, 6 (Fall 1965), pp. 193–210; John C. Appel, 'The Unionization of Florida Cigarmakers and the Coming of the War with Spain', *Hispanic American Historical Review*, 36 (February 1956), pp. 38–49; Gerald E. Poyo, 'The impact of Cuban and Spanish workers on labor organizing in Florida, 1870–1900', paper presented at conference on 'The Situation of Black, Chicano, Cuban, Native American, Puerto Rican, Caribbean, and Asian Communities in the United States', Havana, Cuba, 4–8 December 1984, and 'Cuban Communities in the United States: Toward an overview of the 19th-century experience', in Mirén Uriarte-Gastón and Jorge Cañas Martínez (eds), *Cubans in the United States: Proceedings from the Seminar on Cuban American Studies, May 1984* (Boston: Center for the Study of the Cuban Community, 1984); Lisandro Pérez, 'The Cuban Community of New York in the Nineteenth Century', paper presented at LASA Congress, Albuquerque, New Mexico, 17–20 April 1985.

5    'Libro de índice de cubanos residentes en Nueva York – Documentos procedentes de la Junta Revolucionaria de New York, 1868–1878', Archivo Nacional de Cuba, Donativos y Remisiones (hereafter ANC, Donativos), Legajo 40, número 54; Cuba. Gobierno y Capitanía General, *Datos y noticias referentes a los bienes mandados embargar en la isla de Cuba por disposición del gobierno superior político* (Havana, 1870).

6    National Archives Microfilm Publications, 'Schedules of the Federal Population Census', Monroe County, Florida, 1870, 1880; and 'Schedules of the Florida Census of 1885', Monroe County, Florida, 1885. See 'Census of Manufacturers'.

7    See ch. 6 of Gerald E. Poyo, 'Cuban émigré communities in the United States and the independence of their homeland, 1852–1895' (hereafter 'Cuban émigré communities'), unpublished PhD dissertation, (University of Florida, 1983); and Susan Greenbaum, 'Afro-Cubans in Exile: Tampa, Florida 1886–1985', *Cuban Studies/Estudios Cubanos*, 15 (Winter 1985).

8    Gerald E. Poyo, 'The Anarchist Challenge to the Cuban Independence Movement, 1886–1890', *Cuban Studies/Estudios Cubanos*, 15 (Winter 1985). Information on the ideological debates and strikes during 1887–90 is included in the following newspapers: *El Productor* (Havana), *El Yara* (Key West), *The Tobacco Leaf* (New York), *Cigar Makers' Official Journal* (New York), and *El Español* (Havana). For additional information on anarchism see Aleida Plasencia (ed.), *Enrique Roig de San Martín: Artículos publicados en el periódico 'El Productor'* (Havana, 1967), and George Pozzetta & Gary Mormino, 'Spanish Anarchists in Tampa, Florida, 1886–1931' (unpublished paper, 1984).

9    José Martí, *Obras completas* (hereafter *O.C.*), 28 vols (Havana, 1963–73), I, p. 253.

10   Martí, *O.C.*, I, p. 254.

11   Martí had expressed his ideas about the requirements for a successful rebel movement to Máximo Gómez as early as 1882. See Martí, *O.C.*, I, pp. 167–71, and also pp. 253–4.

12   Martí, *O.C.*, I, p. 254.

13   *Ibid.*

14   Martí, *O.C.*, II, p. 255.

15   See Kirk, *op. cit.*, pp. 106–31 for a synthesis of Martí's social doctrines.

16   Martí, *O.C.*, I, p. 254.

17   Regarding Rivero's activities see the following: *El Productor*, 28 July, 1889; *El Yara* 13 September, 1889; José Rivero Muñiz, 'Esquema del movimiento obrero', in Ramiro Guerra y Sánchez *et al.* (eds), *Historia de la nación cubana*, 10 vols (Havana, 1952), VII, p. 278. Carbonell's socialist inclinations are evident in an article published in *El Porvenir* (New York), 2 April, 1890. He wrote, 'We are socialists . . . we accept the principles of socialism because we believe it is a beautiful doctrine that tends to vitalise society's interests and represents the disinherited through universal solidarity.'

18   Martí, *O.C.*, I, p. 272.

19    Martí, *O.C.*, I, pp. 275–6.
20    Martí's conflicts with the veteran political leaders are traced in Jorge Ibarra, *José Martí: Dirigente político e ideólogo revolucionario* (Havana, 1980), pp. 61–87, 116–23.
21    *A Martí* (Gato factory workers' presentation album) (Havana, n.d.); see the inscription by Ulises Parodi.
22    'La Convención Cubana', ANC, Donativos, Legajo 699, número 9; 'Acta de la Constitución del Partido Revolucionario Cubano, 5 de Enero de 1892', ANC, Donativos, Legajo fuera de caja 150, número 7. For background on Baliño see Instituto de Historia del Movimiento Comunista y de la Revolución Socialista de Cuba, *Carlos Baliño: Documentos y artículos* (Havana, 1976). Information on Borrego and Camellón is sketchy, but they arrived in Key West during the early 1870s, were active in patriot and local political affairs, and emerged as prominent leaders of the black community.
23    Martí, *O.C.*, I, p. 279.
24    *Patria* (New York). A list of the revolutionary clubs affiliated with the PRC in each locale appeared regularly in *Patria*.
25    Information on these labour activists is included in Poyo, 'Cuban émigré communities', ch. 7. For an interesting case study of an anarchist's transition from labour to patriot activism see Olga Cabrera, 'Enrique Creci: un patriota obrero', *Santiago*, 36 (December 1979), pp. 121–50.
26    *Cuba* (Tampa), 27 October 1894; 7 November 1896.
27    See Enrique Trujillo, *El Partido Revolucionario Cubano y El Porvenir: Artículos publicados en El Porvenir* (New York: El Porvenir, 1892), and *Apuntes históricos: Propaganda y movimientos revolucionarios cubanos en los Estados Unidos desde enero de 1880 hasta febrero de 1895* (*El Porvenir*, 1896), pp. 127–32.
28    *El Porvenir*, 2 April 1890; 3 February 1892; 18 July 1894.
29    *El Porvenir*, 18 July 1894.
30    Martí, *O.C.*, I, pp. 335–7.
31    *El Porvenir*, 15 August 1894. Here Trujillo is making reference to François-Marie Sadi-Carnot, President of the French Republic, who was assassinated by an anarchist.
32    José I. Rodríguez, *Estudio histórico sobre el origen, desenvolvimiento y manifestaciones prácticas de la idea de la anexión de la isla de Cuba a los Estados Unidos de América* (Havana, 1900), p. 284.
33    The situation in Key West from 1890 through 1894 is described in the following sources: Castellanos, *op. cit.*, pp. 287–9; *El Productor*, January–April 1890; *The Tobacco Leaf*, 27 July 1892; *El Porvenir*, January–March 1894.
34    Accounts of the strike are included in the following sources: Horatio S. Reubens, *Liberty: The story of Cuba* (New York, 1932), chs 1 and 2; Jefferson B. Browne, *Key West: The old and the new* (Gainesville, Fa, 1973), pp. 126–8; Castellanos, *op. cit.*, pp. 289–307; *El Porvenir*, January 1894; *The Tobacco Leaf*, February–March 1894.
35    Martí, *O.C.*, III, p. 31.
36    Martí, *O.C.*, III, p. 41.
37    Only two prominent Cubans in Key West challenged the PRC's position

with respect to the labour dispute; see Castellanos, *op. cit.*, pp. 293, 301. In New York, *El Porvenir* was sharply critical of Martí and the PRC for their handling of the crisis.

38  Martí, *O.C.*, III, p. 62.
39  For an interesting discussion of the activities of the PRC leadership in New York during the independence war, see Louis A. Pérez, Jr, *Cuba Between Empires, 1878–1902* (Pittsburgh, 1983), pp. 110–16, 132–5.
40  Pérez, 'Cubans in Tampa', p. 134; see *Patria*, 1895–8. Specific articles in *Patria* on Martí are included in the following issues: 20 May 1896; 24 February 1896; 19 May 1897; 27 May 1897; 21 May 1898.
41  *La Doctrina de Martí* (New York), 25 July 1896.
42  *Ibid.*
43  *La Doctrina de Martí*, 27 August 1896.
44  *El Vigía*, 21 August 1897.
45  *El Vigía*, 30 August 1897.
46  *El Vigía*, 11 December 1897.

# Chapter 3   Cuban populism and the birth of the myth

1  Oscar Pino Santos, *Cuba, historia y economía* (Havana, 1983), p. 220.
2  Maurice Halperin, *The Rise and Decline of Fidel Castro* (Berkeley, 1974), p. 6.
3  Ramón Eduardo Ruiz, *Cuba, the making of a revolution* (New York, 1970), p. 61.
4  *Ibid.*, p. 75.
5  Herbert Matthews, *Castro: A political biography* (London, 1970), p. 4.
6  K. S. Karol, *Guerillas in Power: The course of the Cuban Revolution* (London, 1970), p. 171.
7  Halperin, *op. cit.*, p. 7.
8  Francisco Fernández Santos, in Fernández Santos and José Martínez, *Cuba, una revolución en marcha* (Paris, 1967), p. xiii.
9  See, for example, Mario Llerena, *The Unsuspected Revolution: The birth and rise of Castroism* (Ithaca, 1978), p. 275 ('The ideological source of the 26th July movement is Martí').
10  Carlos Rafael Rodríguez, *José Martí, guía y compañero* (Havana, 1979), p. 51.
11  Ernesto Che Guevara, 'José Martí', in Centro de Estudios Martianos, *Siete enfoques marxistas sobre José Martí* (hereafter '*Siete . . .*), (Havana, 1978), p. 71.
12  Rodríguez, *op. cit.*, p. 53.
13  Since the concern here is specifically with the intellectual, bourgeois and petit-bourgeois *martianismo*, one must necessarily ignore the 'popular' *martianismo* which, ever since Independence, had existed in a very vibrant form, as a popular familiarity with the figure and general principles of Martí, sustained by schoolbooks, popular songs and *refranes*, poetry, commemorations and, lastly, the recounted experience of the thousands of veterans of Independence.

14    Nelson P. Valdés, 'The ideological roots of the Cuban revolutionary movement' (University of Glasgow, ILAS, Occasional Paper no. 15, 1975), p. 17.

15    By 1894, United States investments in Cuba already totalled US$50 million; figures from Jorge I. Domínguez, *Cuba: Order and Revolution* (Cambridge, Mass., 1978), p. 20. From 1913 to 1928, they increased by 536%, and in 1906 American-owned sugar mills produced 15% of the Cuban crop, a figure rising to 48.4% in 1920, and to 70–75% by 1928; figures from Dennis B. Wood, 'The Long Revolution: class relations and political conflict in Cuba, 1868–1968', *Science and Society*, vol. xxxiv, no. 1, Spring 1970, p. 9.

16    For example, in 1920 land held in reserve equalled the amount of land planted; Ruiz, *op. cit.*, p. 43.

17    The sugar price rose from 6.5 cents per pound to 22.5 cents between February and May 1920, but by December 1920 had fallen to 3.58 cents.

18    By 1920, foreign banks owned 20% of total Cuban deposits, while by 1923 that figure had risen to 76%; figures from Luis E. Aguilar, *Cuba 1933: Prologue to Revolution* (Ithaca, 1972), p. 43.

19    As one indication of this trend, by 1919 manufacturing employment had risen from 14.9% (1899) to 20%; see Rosalie Schwartz, 'The displaced and the disappointed: cultural nationalists and black activists in Cuba in the 1920s' (PhD thesis, Ann Arbor, 1981), p. 57.

20    *Ibid.*, pp. 31–2.

21    For the concept of 'enclaves' see, for example, Fernando Henrique Cardoso and Enzo Faletto, *Dependence and Development in Latin America* (Berkeley, 1979), pp. 26–7.

22    Hugh Thomas, *Cuba: or the pursuit of freedom* (London, 1971), p. 601.

23    By 1931, Cuba boasted a 71.7% literacy rate, and, under Machado, the level of school enrolment was the highest in Latin America, increasing particularly in the 1923–6 period; see Domínguez, *op. cit.*, p. 25.

24    D. L. Raby, 'The Cuban pre-revolution of 1933: an analysis' (University of Glasgow, ILAS, Occasional paper no. 18, 1975), p. 8.

25    Ruiz, *op. cit.*, p. 54.

26    For example, in 1903, Sanguily initiated a popular move in Congress to outlaw the sale of land to foreigners.

27    In 1901, the Convención Constitucional voted by 15–14 to accept the Amendment, subsequently, after American pressure, increasing that vote to 16–11; in 1909, the Liga Antiplatista was set up.

28    The Liberation Army had been disbanded in 1900 by the American Occupation authorities and was still institutionally weak.

29    Jules R. Benjamin, 'The *Machadato* and Cuban nationalism, 1928–1932', *Hispanic American Historical Review*, vol. 55, no. 1, February 1975, p. 66.

30    Jules R. Benjamin, '*The United States and Cuba: hegemony and dependent development, 1880–1934*' (Pittsburgh, 1977), p. 27.

31 Ortiz, for example, regretted universal suffrage and Mañach wrote of the importance of 'alta cultura'.

32 Other prominent contributors were Raimundo Cabrera ('Llamamiento a los cubanos', *Revista Bimestre Cubana*, xviii, 1923) and Emilio Roig de Leuchsenring ('La colonia superviva', 1925).

33 Raby, *op. cit.*, p. 19.

34 Of particular significance were the railway-workers' strike of 1924 and the sugar-workers' strike in 1925 (especially in the 'new' sugar areas).

35 Confederación Nacional Obrera Cubana.

36 Julio Le Riverend, *La República: Dependencia y revolución* (Havana, 1971), p. 206.

37 Cardoso and Faletto, *op. cit.*, p. 26.

38 Significantly, Rubén Martínez Villena, one of the student leaders, was prominently associated with the Movimiento.

39 The Protesta was made by thirteen academics against the controversial sale, by the government, of the Santa Clara convent and the presence of the Secretary of Justice at a meeting of the Academia de Ciencia. The thirteen included some of those subsequently active in radical politics, notably Martínez Villena, Francisco Ichaso, Juan Marinello, Jorge Mañach and José Z. Tallet.

40 Cited by Raúl Roa, *Retorno a la Alborado*, vol. 1 (Las Villas, 1964), p. 252.

41 José A. Tabares del Real, *La revolución del 30: sus dos últimos años* (Havana, 1973), p. 72.

42 Mella, FEU secretary, was rector, Tallet president and Martínez Villena and Roa on the staff.

43 Declaración del Congreso, in Roa, *op. cit.*, p. 254.

44 The Grupo Minorista was an intellectual and artistic grouping, which, based on the 'Social' magazine from 1927, advocated revision of values, development of an 'arte vernáculo' and new art and science, together with a general democratisation of society.

45 Tabares del Real, *op. cit.*, p. 70.

46 Written in Mexican exile in 1926 and published in 1927 as 'Glosas al pensamiento de José Martí'; see note 47.

47 José Antonio Mella, 'Glosas al pensamiento de José Martí', in Centro de Estudios Martianos, *Siete . . .*, p. 12.

48 Mella was, variously, secretary of the FEU, president of the Congreso, organiser of the Liga Antimperialista, active in the Liga Anticlerical and the Universidad Popular, and co-founder of the Communist Party.

49 Raby, *op. cit.*, p. 18.

50 Mella, *op. cit.*, p. 13.

51 The term *ideario* is used here, as indeed by Valdés (*op. cit.*, p. 12) because of the inherent difficulty of identifying a coherent body of *martiano* thought. For first, Martí's political thought and writings were extremely wide-ranging, making it difficult to detect a coherent pattern; secondly, they were often essentially polemical in nature, being frequently determined by the needs of propaganda, political organisation, or a particular audience; thirdly, they underwent a

significant change, from the early idealistic, romantic, almost conservative ideas to the later radicalised ideas, as a result of both experience and necessity. All of this made it, paradoxically, either easy or difficult to be truly *martiano*.

52    Not least among these 'relevant' concerns was the fear of militarism, a persistent issue in politics since 1902.

53    Schwartz, *op. cit.*, p. 114.

54    Raby, *op. cit.*, p. 10.

55    C. A. M. Hennessy, 'Roots of Cuban nationalism' ('hereafter 'Roots . . .'), *International Affairs*, vol. 39, no. 3, July 1963, p. 356.

56    Roa, *op. cit.*, p. 35.

57    A recent article has taken this regenerationalist theme still further; see F. B. Pike, 'Visions of Rebirth: the spiritualist facet of Peru's Haya de la Torre', *Hispanic American Historical Review*, vol. 63, no. 3, August 1983, pp. 479–516.

58    The Cuban ambivalence about, and search for, a national identity was in many respects the parallel of Andean *indigenismo*, Mexican *mestizaje* and the ideas of several Latin American cultural and political thinkers of the period.

59    After the dissolution and disarmament of the popular-based Liberation Army, Martí's fears of an emergent militarism in a power vacuum (in Latin America generally) had a particular echo in Cuba.

60    Roa, *op. cit.*, p. 103.

61    *Ibid.*, p. 182.

62    Carlos Ripoll, *La generación del 23 en Cuba* (New York, 1968), p. 75.

63    C. A. M. Hennessy, 'Latin America', in Ghita Ionescu and Ernest Gellner (eds), *Populism: its meanings and national characteristics* (London, 1970), p. 37.

64    For example, the brief recession of 1890–1, the effects of 1914–18, and the post-boom collapse of the 1920s.

65    Roa, *op. cit.*, p. 230.

66    Le Riverend, *op. cit.*, p. 211.

67    Roa, *op. cit.*, p. 235.

68    *Ibid.*, p. 235.

69    In 1921 he published, in *Cuba contemporánea*, 'sobre el problema económico y la reforma constitucional', and in 1927 'Con el eslabón'.

70    It is significant that, even in 1930, the student demonstration that resulted in the death of Rafael Trejo had intended, with deliberate symbolism, to march to Varona's house.

71    Growing out of the Peruvian student movement of 1919 and Haya's ideas of continental anti-imperialism and *indigenismo*, *aprismo* represented an attempt to 're-interpret' Marxism–Leninism in a Latin American context.

72    For example, Valdés, *op. cit.*, p. 17.

73    Universidad Popular Lastarria in Chile, and Universidad Libre in Buenos Aires.

74    Roa, *op. cit.*, pp. 122–3.

75    Aguilar, *op. cit.*, p. 75. Suchlicki also cites the Revolution as an influence on Mella, in Jaime Suchlicki, 'Stirrings of Cuban nationalism:

the student generation of 1930', *Journal of Inter-American Studies*, vol. 10, part 3, July 1968, p. 352.

76 Halperin, *op. cit.*, p. 4.

77 Arthur P. Whitaker and David C. Jordan, *Nationalism in contemporary Latin America* (New York, 1966), p. 156.

78 Shortly before this he briefly produced the anti-imperialist magazine *América Libre*.

79 Prominent among them were Eduardo Chibas, Aureliano Sánchez Arango, Carlos Prío Socarrás, Antonio Guiteras, Raúl Roa, Pablo de la Torriente Brau and Tony Varona.

80 For example, 22% of the 1933–4 graduates were lawyers, who, in their student years, with the combination of the Machadato and the economic crisis, must have viewed their employment prospects as minimal; figures from Niurka Pérez Rojas, *El movimiento estudiantil universitario de 1934 a 1940* (Havana, 1975), p. 33.

81 In 1931, the DEU programme called for laws against *latifundismo* and the sale of land to foreigners, and for the distribution of public land and recovery of foreign-owned land, nationalisation of public services, a national banking system and social reform. In 1933, the DEU Programme-Manifesto called for freedom of expression, updating of the Constitution, agrarian reform, a bureaucratic purging, specific educational reforms and social reform, electoral reform, new 'clean' parties, etc.

82 For example, a Comisión Universitaria had been designated to plan reforms and remove incompetent staff; significantly, however, the crucial demand of autonomy had been persistently resisted.

83 *Azúcar y población en las Antillas*, published in Havana, 1927.

84 Le Riverend, *op. cit.*, p. 206.

85 Declaration of the Ala Izquierda Estudiantil, cited in Olga Cabrera and Carmen Almodóbar (eds), *Las luchas estudiantiles Universitarias, 1923–1934* (Havana, 1975), p. 33.

86 Notably Sánchez Arango, Roa, de la Torriente Brau and Gabriel Barceló.

87 For example, Mirta Aguirre.

88 Suchlicki, *op. cit.*, p. 358.

89 Suchlicki (*ibid.*) wrote of the Ala activists as being from poorer, mostly provincial, homes, and as resenting the better treatment meted out to the more middle-class DEU prisoners in 1931.

90 Tabares del Real, *op. cit.*, p. 89.

91 *Ibid.*, p. 81.

92 This fact led Le Riverend (*op. cit.*, p. 273) to see proof of ABC's reactionary links.

93 Joaquín Martínez Sáenz, Carlos Saladrigas and Juan Andrés Lliteras. According to Suchlicki (*op. cit.*, p. 359) they were Harvard graduates.

94 The ABC Programme-Manifesto of 1932 included, for example, calls for the gradual elimination of *latifundismo*, restrictions on land acquisition by foreigners, agrarian co-operatives and social legislation, and specifically condemned American imperialism, foreign capitalism and corruption.

95   The programme also included a call for a corporate Upper House and restriction of suffrage to literates.
96   Tabares del Real, *op. cit.*, p. 103.
97   *Ibid.*, p. 101.
98   Antonio Guiteras, *Su pensamiento revolucionario* (Havana, 1974), pp. 90–1.
99   *Ibid.*, pp. 91–3.
100  *Ibid.*, p. 115.
101  *Ibid.*, p. 124.
102  *Ibid.*, pp. 103–4. The law of *sindicalización forzosa* was also Guiteras'.
103  *Ibid.*, p. 184.
104  *Ibid.*, p. 205.
105  The Reciprocity Treaty lowered American tariffs on 35 Cuban products (including a 20% reduction on sugar and tobacco), and the quota system at least guaranteed a continued, if not predictable, market.
106  The other side of the Reciprocity coin was that Cuban tariffs for 426, mostly manufactured, American products were similarly reduced.
107  Specifically Auténtico aspects were: expropriation of property for public interest or utility, State ownership of the subsoil, prohibition of the *latifundio*, limitation on landholdings, State role in the economy, and labour legislation. At the Constitutional convention the Auténticos counted the largest delegation.
108  While all industrial production, between 1930 and 1958, increased by 2.69% p.a., manufacturing production rose by 4.96% p.a.; figures from Jorge F. Pérez López, 'An index of Cuban industrial output 1930–1958' (PhD thesis, Ann Arbor, 1979), p. 81.
109  Francisco López Segrera, *Cuba: capitalismo dependiente y subdesarrollo (1510–1959)* (Havana, 1981), p. 241.
110  Le Riverend, *op. cit.*, p. 341.
111  Clearly, limitations of space preclude any detailed analysis of the complexities of the academic debate on populism, since opinions vary widely as to the origins, class nature, purpose, ideology and policies of the phenomenon.
112  Joven Cuba, ABC, DEU, PRC, and the Communists.
113  Domínguez, *op. cit.*, pp. 54–109, *passim*.
114  In 1939, the Party was legalised and the Communist-led union, CTC, tolerated; the Coalición Democrática Socialista included both Batista and the Communists, who then won six seats in the Constitutional Convention of 1939–40. In 1942, Marinello and Rodríguez even entered Batista's cabinet in the context of US–Soviet co-belligerence against Germany.
115  The Bonche Universitario was set up, by the Auténticos (in 1934), among secondary and university students, with the object of wresting control of the university from the Ala Izquierda, by strong-arm tactics, and was then used to press Auténtico influence in the unions. By 1937 the term *bonchismo* was in common usage. After 1940, it split into various, avowedly political, *pistolero* 'action groups', one of which, led by Manolo Castro, effectively ended the Bonche's domination in 1944.
116  Domínguez, *op. cit.*, p. 115.

117 Ladislao Gonzáles Carbajal, *El Ala Izquierda Estudiantil y su época* (Havana, 1974), p. 505.
118 Roa, Tallet, and Valdés Daussa.
119 Roa, *op. cit.*, p. 186.
120 *Ibid.*
121 Lionel Martin, *The Early Roots of Castro's Communism* (Secaucus, NJ, 1978), p. 29.
122 William S. Stokes, 'The "Cuban Revolution" and the Presidential elections of 1948', *Hispanic American Historical Review*, vol. 31, no. 1, February 1951, p. 70.
123 Valdés, *op. cit.*, p. 25.
124 By 1948, there had been no promised diversification, increased investment, racial legislation, Tribunal of Accounts, budget law, Civil Service reform, or many other of the promises in the 1944 electoral programme (see Stokes, *op. cit.*, p. 40, for the latter). Moreover, in both 1944 and 1948, the supposedly 'radical' PRC allied itself electorally with the reactionary Partido Republicano.
125 Stokes, *op. cit.*, p. 76.
126 In 1939, Cuban producers accounted for 22% of sugar production, but by 1952 this had risen to 55%. Pérez López, *op. cit.*, p. 22.
127 Hennessy, 'Roots . . .', p. 354.
128 For example, in 1952, Felix Lizaso published *Martí, místico del deber* while Jorge Mañach published *El pensamiento político y social de Martí* (1941) and *Martí, el Apóstol* (1944).
129 For example, in 1948, Blas Roca, of the Communist Party, published 'José Martí: revolucionario radical de su tiempo' (reprinted in *Casa de las Américas*, 1973).
130 In 1948, the two principal populist parties (PRC and PPC) between them won 62.25% of the vote.
131 American companies still controlled 40% of sugar production, 40 out of 161 mills, 7 out of the 10 largest agricultural enterprises, 2 out of the 3 oil refineries, 90% of telephones and electricity, and 50% of public railways. Between 1950 and 1958, US investments rose from $657 million to $1,000 million. Edward González, *Cuba under Castro: the limits of charisma* (Boston, 1974), pp. 62–3.
132 Between 1948 and 1958, manufacturing growth slowed to 2.7% p.a. Pérez López, *op. cit.*, p. 84.
133 Between 1931 and 1943, the urban population rose from 24.8% of the national total to over 54%, with a particularly significant rise in Oriente province; Schwartz, *op. cit.*, p. 52.
134 Significantly, both the Auténticos and the Communists lost votes in 1948.
135 The groups were numerous (at least nine major examples), the principal ones being: Movimiento Socialista Revolucionario (MSR) (led by Rolando Masferrer and Manolo Castro, who dominated the FEU from 1940 to 1946), the Unión Insurreccional Revolucionario (UIR) and Acción Revolucionario Guiteras (ARG). Between 1947 and 1948, the groups were responsible for 64 assassinations, 33 woundings, and 24 kidnappings; Nelsón P. Valdés and Rolando E. Bonachea, 'Fidel

Castro y la política estudiantil de 1947 a 1952', *Aportes*, October 1971, footnote p. 30.

136   The UIR, from 1946, acted as Grau's bodyguard, and Grau appointed MSR's Mario Salabarría as head of the Buró de Investigaciones, ARG's Fabio Ruiz as Chief of Police in Havana and UIR's Emilio Tró as Chief of Police in Marianao. In 1948, Masferrer was elected to the Senate and in 1949, Prío handed out 500 government bureaucracy posts to MSR and 200 to ARG.

137   In 1954, the turnout for Batista's patently fraudulent elections was 53%, compared to 80% in 1948.

138   According to Mauricio Solaún, 'El fracaso de la democracia en Cuba. Un régimen patrimonial', *Aportes*, no. 13, July 1969, p. 73, the *choteo* bred an attitude of rejection of traditional symbols of respect and authority and also an acceptance of patrimonialism and criminality.

139   Hennessy, 'Roots . . .', p. 354, refers to 'over 500 articles on Martí' being published in 1953 alone.

140   Carlos Rafael Rodríguez, 'Martí, guía de su tiempo y anticipador del nuestro', in Rodríguez, *op. cit.*, p. 19.

141   Most of the early 26 July Movement came either from Juventud Ortodoxa or García Bárcena's Catholic nationalist group, Movimiento Nacionalista Revolucionario.

## Chapter 4   Martí in the United States

1   José Cantón Navarro, *Algunas ideas de José Martí en relación con la clase obrera y el socialismo* (Havana, 1970), p. 117.

2   Henry James, *Portrait of a Lady* (London, 1972), p. 196.

3   Daniel R. Headrick, *The Tools of Empire* (New York, 1981).

4   Joseph A. Schumpeter, *Imperialism and Social Classes* (ed. Paul Sweezy) (Oxford, 1951), p. 14.

5   Rudyard Kipling, *From Sea to Sea* (London, 1900), vol. I, pp. 467–9.

6   V. G. Kiernan, *Marxism and Imperialism* (London, 1974), p. 109.

7   Kipling, *loc. cit.*

8   José Martí, *Obras completas* (hereafter *O.C.*) (Havana, 1961), XV, p. 85.

9   Martí, *O.C.*, XV, p. 82.

10   Martí, *O.C.*, X, p. 41.

11   Martí, *O.C.*, XXIV, p. 131.

12   Martí, *O.C.*, XII, pp. 122–3.

13   *Ibid.*, p. 144.

14   Martí, *O.C.*, XXIV, pp. 52–3.

15   *Ibid.*, p. 41.

16   *Ibid.*, pp. 145–6.

17   *Ibid.*, p. 135.

18   Martí, *O.C.*, XXIX, p. 150.

19   Martí, *O.C.*, XXIV, p. 162.

20   *Ibid.*, p. 166.

21   Martí, *O.C.*, XII, pp. 279–80.

22   *Ibid.*, p. 32.

23   Karl Marx and Friedrich Engels, *Letters to Americans 1848–1895* (ed. Trachtenberg) (New York, 1953), p. 157.
24   *Ibid.*, p. 163.
25   Martí, *O.C.*, XXIV, pp. 189–92.
26   *Ibid.*, pp. 197, 200.
27   *Ibid.*, pp. 201–2.
28   *Ibid.*, p. 210.
29   *Ibid.*, p. 216.
30   *Ibid.*, p. 216.
31   *Ibid.*, p. 225.
32   *Ibid.*, p. 227.
33   Martí, *O.C.*, XX, pp. 411–12.
34   Homer, *The Odyssey* (trans. Richmond Lattimore) (New York, 1975); quotations used in this paragraph are from IX, pp. 140–50.
35   Martí, *O.C.*, III, p. 49.
36   Roberto Fernández Retamar, *Introducción a José Martí* (Havana, 1978), p. 20.

## Chapter 5   Martí and socialism

1    G. D. H. Cole, *A History of Socialist Thought* (3 vols, London, 1953–6).
2    J. Ignacio Rodríguez, *Anexión de Cuba* (Havana, 1900), pp. 280–4.
3    Intervention de A. Herrera Franyutti, *En torno a José Martí* (Colloque International de Bordeaux, Bordeaux, 1974), p. 285.
4    Paul Estrade, 'Un socialista mexicano: José Martí', *En torno a José Martí* (Coloque International de Bordeaux, Bordeaux, 1974), p. 256.
5    José Martí, Obras *completas* (Havana, 1963–73) (hereafter *O.C.*), VIII, p. 285.
6    Martí, *O.C.*, XI, p. 158.
7    Martí, *O.C.*, IX, p. 322.
8    Martí, *O.C.*, XI, p. 20.
9    Martí, *O.C.*, X, pp. 84–5.
10   Martí, *O.C.*, VIII, p. 35.
11   Martí, *O.C.*, XII, pp. 506–7.
12   *Ibid.*, p. 70.
13   Martí, *O.C.*, X, pp. 62–3.
14   Martí, *O.C.*, VIII, p. 189.
15   Hans Otto Dill, *El ideario literario y estético de José Martí* (Havana, 1975), pp. 93–128.
16   Martí, *O.C.*, XV, pp. 387–92.
17   Martí, *O.C.*, XI, pp. 18–19. For Henry George, see *Progress and Poverty* (2nd edn, London, 1882).
18   Martí, *O.C.*, XI, p. 96.
19   *Ibid.*, pp. 187–8.
20   Karl Marx and Friedrich Engels, *Correspondencia* (editors' translation) (Buenos Aires, 1938), p. 296.
21   *Ibid.*, pp. 293–4.
22   *Ibid.*, pp. 275–6.

23   *Ibid.*, pp. 231–2.
24   Martí, *O.C.*, XI, p. 209.
25   *Ibid.*, pp. 145–6.
26   *Ibid.*, p. 175.
27   *Ibid.*, p. 178.
28   Marx and Engels, *op. cit.*, p. 262.
29   Martí, *O.C.*, XII, p. 427.
30   *Ibid.*, p. 377.
31   *Ibid.*, p. 378.
32   *Ibid.*
33   Martí, *O.C.*, XIII, p. 34.
34   Martí, *O.C.*, VI, p. 19.
35   Martí, *O.C.*, II, p. 255.
36   Martí, *O.C.*, IV, p. 325.
37   *Ibid.*, p. 168.
38   *Ibid.*, p. 156.
39   Martí, *O.C.*, III, pp. 304–5.

## Chapter 6   José Martí and his concept of the *intelectual comprometido*

1   José Martí, *Obras completas* (Havana, 1963–73) (hereafter *O.C.*), II, p. 380.
2   Martí, *O.C.*, XIX, p. 103.
3   *Ibid.*, p. 105.
4   Martí, *O.C.*, XV, p. 361. In the 'Apuntes' section of his *Obras completas*, Martí was eloquent on the need for spiritual comfort as provided by intellectual pursuits: 'Los pueblos inmorales tienen todavía una salvación: el arte. El arte es la forma de lo divino, la revelación de lo extraordinario . . . El ritmo de la poesía, el eco de la música, el éxtasis beatífico que produce en el ánimo, la contemplación de un cuadro bello, la suave melancolía que se adueña del espíritu después de estos contactos sobrehumanos son vestimentos místicos y apacibles augurios de un tiempo que será toda claridad.' *O.C.*, XIX, p. 17.
    'Immoral *pueblos* have still one salvation: Art. Art is the form of the divine, the revelation of the extraordinary . . . The rhythm of poetry, the echo of music, the blessed ecstasy that the contemplation of a beautiful picture produces in the soul, the sweet melancholy that fills the spirit after these superhuman contacts, are like mystical vestments and peaceful auguries of a time that will be all clarity.'
5   Martí, *O.C.*, V, p. 181. Fernández Retamar develops this line of thought with further examples: 'Even when he is talking about *los poetas de la guerra*, that were fighting in the battlefield for the liberty of Cuba, 'Firmaban las redondillas con su sangre' ['They sign their poems with their blood'] (*O.C.*, V, p. 529), he would not cease to be strict about specifically literary values. Martí would speak of 'la forma ingenua y primeriza' ['the naive and premature form'] of the output of those warrior poets that expressed warfare, friendship and love 'en rima o

romance, inferiores siempre, por lo segundón y mestizo de la literatura en que se criaron, a las virtudes con que en ellos se copiaban insensiblemente los poetas' ['in poetry or prose always inferior to the virtues they [the warrior poets] imitated from each other, because [the verse and prose] stemmed from a bastard and second-rate literature'] (*O.C.*, V, p. 230). See Roberto Fernández Retamar, 'Cuál es la literatura que inicia José Martí', *Anuario del Centro de Estudios Martianos* (Havana), no. 4, 1981, p. 31.

6 Quoted by Manuel Isidro Méndez in his 'Martí, Unamuno y Darío', republished in the *Anuario del Centro de Estudios Martianos* (Havana), no. 5, 1982, p. 292.

7 Martí, *O.C.*, XIII, p. 133. Writing in 1885, Martí studied the disappointing reality of North American life, and underlined the need to develop a basic spirituality: 'En este pueblo vasto de gente aislada y encerrada en sí, falta el trato frecuente, la comunicación íntima, la práctica y fe en la amistad, las enérgicas raíces del corazón, que sujetan y renuevan la vida. En este pueblo de labor, enorme campo de pelea por la fortuna, las almas apasionadas de soledad mueren.'

'Among this large population of isolated and inward-looking people frequent personal dealings are lacking. [So too are] intimate communication, the practice and faith in friendship, strong sentiments and deep feelings, that hold on to life and renew it. Among this hard-working people everything is a battlefield for riches, and passionate souls die of solitude.' *O.C.*, X, p. 226.

8 Martí, *O.C.*, XVI, p. 226.

9 Martí, *O.C.*, XV, p. 41.

10 Martí, *O.C.*, X, p. 189.

11 Julio Le Riverend, 'Martí: ética y acción revolucionaria', *Casa de las Américas*, vol. X, no. 57, Nov.–Dec. 1969, p. 48.

12 Martí, *O.C.*, VI, p. 351. Writing in 1883, Martí developed this aspect, indicating its relevance to bitter clashes then taking place between workers and capitalists: 'Hasta que los obreros no sean hombres cultos no serán felices . . . A los obreros ignorantes, que quieren poner remedios bruscos a un mal que sienten, pero cuyos elementos no conocen, los vencerá mal que sienten, pero cuyos elementos no conocen, los vencerá siempre el interés de los capitalistas, disfrazados, como de piel de cordero una zorra, de conveniencias y prudencias sociales.' *O.C.*, VIII, p. 352.

'Until the workers are cultured they will not be happy . . . The capitalist interests, disguised like a wolf in sheep's clothing by convenience and social prudence, will always defeat ignorant workers who want immediate solutions to evils that they feel but whose origins they do not grasp.'

13 Martí, *O.C.*, XII, p. 348.

14 *Ibid.*, p. 43.

15 Martí, *O.C.*, X, p. 299.

16 Martí, *O.C.*, VII, p. 122.

17 Martí, *O.C.*, XXII, p. 129.

18 Martí, *O.C.*, XIII, p. 333.

19 Martí, *O.C.*, XX, p. 518.

20    In his famous literary testament to Gonzalo de Quesada, written at Montecristi on 1 April 1895, Martí again played down the value of his work, noting 'De Cuba, ¿qué no habré escrito?: y ni una página me parece digna de ella: sólo lo que vamos a hacer me parece digno.' *O.C.*, XX, p. 478.
      'What have I not written on Cuba? Yet not one page seems worthy of her. Only what we are about to do seems worthy.'
21    Martí, *O.C.*, XVIII, p. 192.
22    Martí, *O.C.*, XXI, p. 227.
23    Ivan A. Schulman, 'Modernismo, revolución y pitagorismo en Martí', *Casa de las Américas*, vol. XIII, no. 27, July–Aug. 1972, p. 49.
24    Martí, *O.C.*, XVIII, pp. 279–92.
25    *Ibid.*, p. 289.
26    Martí, *O.C.*, X, p. 60.
27    Martí, *O.C.*, VI, p. 198.
28    *Ibid.*, p. 20.
29    'Mis amigos saben cómo me salieron estos versos del corazón. Fue aquel invierno de angustia, en que por ignorancia, o por fe fanática, o por miedo, o por cortesía, se reunieron en Washington, bajo el águila temible, los pueblos hispano-americanos . . . y la agonía en que viví, hasta que pude confirmar la cautela y el brío de nuestros pueblos; y el horror y vergüenza en que me tuvo el temor legítimo de que pudiéramos los cubanos, con manos parricidas, ayudar el plan insensato de apartar a Cuba, para bien único de un nuevo amo disimulado, de la patria que la reclama y en ella se completa, de la patria hispanoamericana – que quitaron las fuerzas mermadas por dolores injustos.' Martí, *O.C.*, XVI, p. 61.
      'My friends know how these poems came out of my heart. It was during that anguished winter when through ignorance, or fanatical faith, or fear or courtesy, the Hispanic American peoples met in Washington under the fearful eagle . . . [My friends know too] the agony that I went through until I could be sure of the caution and the energy of our peoples. [My friends know too] the horror and shame I experienced, legitimately afraid that we, Cubans, with parricidal hands, might help the demented plan to separate Cuba from the *patria* that claims her and whom she completes – from the Hispanic American *patria* – for the exclusive benefit of her new master in disguise.'
30    All quotations from *La Edad de Oro* are taken from the 1979 edition published in Havana by the Editorial Gente Nueva.
31    Martí, *O.C.*, XX, pp. 153–4.
32    Writing in 1969, Antonio Melis illustrated this mature approach by Martí to his young readers by comparing it to that of another great Latin American revolutionary: 'In *La Edad de Oro* he explained and commented on the great events in history and in art without falling into cheap sensationalism and paternalistic attitudes. 'Ya eres casi una mujer, y no se te puede escribir como a los niños contándoles boberías y mentiritas.' ['You are almost a woman and one can no longer write to you as if to a child telling you silly stories and little lies.'] These are words written by another great revolutionary, Ernesto Che Guevara, to his

daughter Hildita in 1966, words that well define the attitudes of Martí towards children.' See Antonio Melis, 'Lucha anti-imperialista y lucha de clases en José Martí', *Casa de las Américas*, vol. IX, no. 54, May–June 1969, p. 128.

33  Achilles, for instance, son of the sea goddess Thetis, is used by Martí to demonstrate the ills of the monarchy: 'todavía hoy dicen los reyes que el derecho de mandar en los pueblos les viene de Dios, que es lo que llaman 'el derecho divino de los reyes', y no es más que una idea vieja de aquellos tiempos de pelea en que los pueblos eran nuevos y no sabían vivir en paz.' Martí, *La Edad de Oro*, p. 37.

'Still today, kings claim divine right to rule, which is no more than an old idea from those times of struggle when peoples were young and did not know how to live in peace.'

34  *Ibid.*
35  *Ibid.*, p. 148.
36  *Loc. cit.*
37  Martí, *O.C.*, IX, p. 451.
38  Martí, *O.C.*, XI, p. 48.
39  Martí, *O.C.*, XX, p. 147.
40  Martí, *O.C.*, VII, p. 425.
41  In 'Tres héroes' he develops this concept: 'Libertad es el derecho que tiene todo hombre a ser honrado y a pensar y a hablar sin hipocresía. En América no se podía ser honrado, ni pensar ni hablar . . . En América se vivía antes de la libertad como la llama que tiene mucha carga encima. Era necesario quitarse la carga, o morir . . . En esos hombres van miles de hombres, va un pueblo entero, va la dignidad humana. Esos nombres son sagrados . . . Bolívar, de Venezuela, San Martín del Río de la Plata, Hidalgo de México.' Martí, *La Edad de Oro*, p. 13.

'Liberty is the right that every man has to be honest, to think and to speak without hypocrisy. In America man cannot be honest, nor can he think and speak . . . In America before freedom we lived like an overloaded llama. It was necessary to throw off the load or to die . . . In men like Bolívar of Venezuela, San Martín of the River Plate, Hidalgo of Mexico, thousands of men are represented. An entire *pueblo* is there, human dignity itself. Those names, indeed, are sacred.'

42  Martí, *O.C.*, IV, p. 170.
43  Martí, *O.C.*, XVIII, p. 14.
44  Andrés Iduarte has indicated, correctly, the importance of the impact upon Martí of his imprisonment. 'Martí spent six months of his seventeen years breaking stones under the tropical sun, with a chain attached to his feet – a barbaric punishment that forever marked him morally and physically . . .' See Iduarte, *Martí, escritor* (Mexico, 1944), p. 23.

45  Martí, *O.C.*, I, p. 45.
46  *Ibid.*, p. 50.
47  'Martí invigorated the creative role of the dispossessed and marginalised. He attacked the urban bourgeoisie as a class because they distanced themselves from the liberation struggles, preferring any anti-national solutions. He defined the aggressive future of imperialism and its

political, ideological and cultural representatives. Martí foresaw the decisive role that the independence of Latin America would play in detaining the imperialists. He showed how oligarchic corruption undermined democracy, through placing suffrage and national representation at the mercy of the wealth of big businessmen. Martí fought a singular battle against racism. He predicted that after independence in the republic it would be necessary to fight further for justice. He viewed with intelligent sympathy the anti-colonial struggle of other countries. He organised a party that was democratic in its base and popular in composition. He proclaimed that culture and even talent are neither private property nor the outcome of personal endeavour, but involve the service of the noble cause of human progress. Martí admired war poets, who did not always write good poems, but knew how to fight and how to die, creating a poetic life in its highest possible meaning.' See Julio Le Riverend, 'Palabras inaugurales' (Mesa Redonda en los Noventa Años del Partido Revolucionario Cubano), *Anuario del Centro de Estudios Martianos* (Havana), no. 4, 1982, p. 235.

48   Julio Le Riverend, 'Teoría martiana del partido político', *Vida y pensamiento de Martí. Homenaje de la ciudad de la Habana en el cincuentenario de la fundación del Partido Revolutionario Cubano. 1892–1942* (Havana, 1942), I, p. 88.

49   Martí, *O.C.*, I, p. 272. This is from the 'Resoluciones tomadas por la emigración cubana de Tampa el día 28 de noviembre de 1891', and was almost certainly drawn up by Martí.

50   Luis Toledo Sande, *Ideología y práctica en José Martí* (Havana, 1982), p. 94. The quotation he refers to is found in vol. V, p. 348, of the *Obras completas*.

51   Martí, *O.C.*, XV, p. 409.

52   Martí, *O.C.*, V, p. 272.

53   'Martí was essentially a revolutionary, and the rest was secondary. This statement can only shock those who even now have a poor and impoverishing idea of what it is to be a revolutionary. . . . A revolutionary is a man who wants to create a new world to be inhabited by a new man. To say that Martí was essentially a revolutionary is to affirm that he wished above all to transform reality in such a total manner as to be in agreement with what is just.' Roberto Fernández Retamar, *Lectura de José Martí* (Mexico, 1972), p. 15. Blas Roca develops this point and underlines the revolutionary nature of Martí's *obra*: 'From his leaflet *El presidio político en Cuba* until the very last works of his copious journalistic output, from his toast to Alfredo Márquez Sterling to his most fiery speeches during his emigration, all his work as a publicist, orator and poet, is pervaded by the denunciation of the public oppression of Cuba.' Blas Roca, 'José Martí: revolucionario radical de su tiempo', *Casa de las Américas*, vol. XIII, no. 76, Jan.–Feb. 1973, p. 16.

54   Martí, *O.C.*, XVI, p. 165.

55   Toledo Sande, *op. cit.*, p. 107.

56   Martí, *O.C.*, X, p. 288.

57   Writing on an exhibition of Vereschagin in 1889 he developed this concept further: '¡La justicia primero y el arte después! Hembra es el que

en tiempo sin decoro se entretiene en las finezas de la imaginación, y en las elegancias de la mente! Cuando no se disfruta de la libertad, la única excusa del arte y su único derecho para existir es ponerse al servicio de ella. ¡Todo al fuego, hasta el arte, para alimentar la hoguera!' Martí, *O.C.*, XV, p. 433.

'Justice first, Art afterwards! A man that wastes his time entertaining himself with the fineries of the imagination and mental elegance is no more than mere woman! When there is no freedom the only excuse for Art and its only right to exist is to be placed at the service of liberty. All strength, even Art, is needed to feed the fire!'

58  Martí, *La Edad de Oro*, p. 57.

## Chapter 7  Martí, Latin America and Spain

1  Julio le Riverend, 'Les années 1930 et le développement des sciences sociales' in *Les années trentes à Cuba: Actes du colloque international organisé à Paris en novembre 1980* . . . (Paris, 1982), esp. p. 104.

2  José Antonio Portuondo, 'Retratos infieles de José Martí', *Revista de la Biblioteca Nacional José Martí*, año 59, 3ra época, vol. X, no. 1, Jan.–Apr. 1968, pp. 5–14.

3  See especially Jorge Ibarra, *José Martí – Dirigente político e ideólogo revolucionario* (Havana, 1980).

4  Both Marxist and non-Marxist scholars agree that claims of exponents of Pan-Americanism to a lineal descent from Bolívar are largely unhistorical. See, for example, Miguel Acosta Saignes, *Bolívar: acción y utopia del hombre de las dificultades* (Caracas, 1983), esp. pp. 299, 320. Also David Bushnell, 'The Independence of Spanish South America', in Leslie Bethell (ed.), *Cambridge History of Latin America, vol III: from Independence to c. 1870* (Cambridge, 1985), pp. 95–156.

5  On US expansion, Philip S. Foner, *The Spanish–Cuban–American War and the Birth of American Imperialism* (2 vols, New York, 1972); T. Paterson (ed.), *American Imperialism and Anti-Imperialism* (New York, 1973); Lloyd C. Gardiner, Walter La Feber and T. McCormick, *Creation of the Modern American Empire – U.S. Diplomatic History* (London, 1973).

6  See Simon Collier, 'Nationality, Nationalism and Supranationalism in the Writings of Simon Bolívar', *Hispanic American Historical Review*, 65 (1983), pp. 37–64.

7  See, especially, John Lynch, *Simón Bolívar and the Age of Revolution* (University of London, Institute of Latin American Studies, Working Papers no. 10, 1983).

8  José Martí, *Obras completas* (27 vols, 2nd ed., Havana, 1975) (hereafter *O.C.*), XV, n.d., pp. 446–9.

9  See the valuable historiographical discussion in David Bushnell, 'The Last Dictatorship: betrayal or consummation', *Hispanic American Historical Review*, 65 (1983), pp. 65–105.

10  Martí, *O.C.*, 1893, VIII, pp. 241–50.

11  Martí, *O.C.*, 1895, IV, p. 88.

12  Martí, *O.C.*, 1892, IV, p. 303.
13  Ezequiel Martínez Estrada, *Martí, revolucionario* (2nd edn, Havana, 1974), pp. 134–5.
14  Martí, *O.C.*, 1881, XIV, p. 94.
15  *Ibid.*, pp. 79, 134.
16  See Cintio Vitier and Fina Garcia Marmiz, *Temas martianos* (Havana, 1969), p. 28.
17  Martí, *O.C.*, 1881, XIV, p. 67.
18  Joaquín Costa, *Oligarquía y caciquismo: Colectivismo agrario y otros escritos (Antología)* (ed. Rafael Pérez de la Dehesa) (2nd edn, Madrid, 1969) pp. 20–1.
19  Martí, *O.C.*, 1881, XIV, pp. 49, 188, 213–15.
20  *Ibid.* p. 69.
21  Angel Augier, *Acción y poesía en José Martí* (2nd edn, Havana, 1982), p. 242.
22  Paul Estrade, *José Martí – militante y estrategia* (Havana, 1983), p. 11–35.
23  This view was expressed by José A. Béguez César, *Martí y el Krausismo* (Havana, 1943).
24  On the impact of *Krausismo* in Spain, see especially Raymond Carr, *Spain, 1808–1939* (Oxford, 1966), pp. 301–4; on Martí's debt to *Krausismo*, see Luis Toledo Sande, *Ideología y práctica en José Martí – seis aproximaciones* (Havana, 1982), pp. 140ff, and a volume by Peter Turton (forthcoming, 1986) to be published by Zed Press, London.
25  The literature upon European romanticism is too vast to mention. J. L. Talmon, *Romanticism and Revolt* (London, 1965), pp. 135–65, provides a useful introduction. In Rubén Darío's words, the *versos libres* of Martí were 'versos de un hombre de libertad, versos del cubano que ha luchado, que ha vivido, que ha pensado, que debía morir por la libertad', 'verses of a man of liberty, verses of the Cuban that has struggled, that has lived, has thought and must die for liberty'. Cited by Angel Augier, *Acción y poesía en José Martí* (2nd edn, Havana, 1982), pp. 204–5.
26  Martí, *O.C.*, 1886, XX, p. 91.
27  See Antonio Melis, 'Lotta antimperialista e lotta di clasi en José Martí' in *Ideologie, Quaderni di storia contemporanea*, nos 5–6, 1968, pp. 100–20.
28  Martí, *O.C.*, 1871, I, p. 61.
29  Martí, *O.C.*, 1889, XX, p. 355.
30  Martí, *O.C.*, 1881, XIV, p. 100.
31  Martí, *O.C.*, 1891, XX, pp. 393–3; 1894, V, pp. 440–1.
32  Martí, *O.C.*, 1871, I, pp. 45–76. Here the pattern is set.
33  See, for example, Manuel Moreno Fraginals, 'Iglesia e imperio', *Revista de la Biblioteca Nacional José Martí*, vol. V, Jan.–Dec., 1963, nos 1–4, pp. 11–34; Miguel Figueroa y Miranda, *Religión y política en la Cuba del siglo XIX: El Obispo Estrada visto a la luz de los archivos romanos 1802–1832* (Miami, 1975).
34  Toledo Sande, *op. cit.*, p. 157.
35  Martí, *O.C.*, n.d., XIX, pp. 392–5.
36  Martí, *O.C.*, 1875, VI, p. 220; 1882, XXIII, p. 49.
37  Martí, *O.C.*, 1878, VII, p. 153.
38  Martí, *O.C.*, 1875, VI, p. 226; n.d., XIX, pp. 392–5.

39  José Canton Navarro, *Algunas ideas de José Martí en relación con la clase obrera y el socialismo* (Havana, 1981), esp. pp. 50–61.

40  Martí, *O.C.*, 1883, IX, p. 388.

41  Roberto Fernández Retamar, 'Desatar a America y desuncir al hombre' in *El partido revolucionario cubano de José Martí* (Havana, 1982), p. 84.

42  José Antonio Portuondo, 'Vigencia de latinoamericanismo de José Martí', *Cuba socialista*, año II, no. 4 (5), Oct. 1982–Feb. 1983.

43  'Manifiesto del Partido Socialista Cubano' in *El movimiento obrero cubano: Documentos y artículos: Tomo I: 1865–1925* (reprint, Havana, 1981), pp. 162–5; J. Rivero Muñiz, *El primer Partido Socialista Cubano-Apuntes para la historia del proletariado en Cuba* (Las Villas, 1962).

44  James Joll, *The Anarchists* (London, 1964), pp. 224–64.

45  See especially Raymond Carr, *Spain, 1808–1939* (Oxford, 1966), esp. pp. 440–55.

46  Temma Kaplan, *Anarchists of Andalusia 1868–1903* (Princeton, 1977); Juan Díaz del Moral, *Historia de las agitaciones campesinas andaluzas* (Madrid, 1967); Jean Becarud and Gilles Laponge, *Anarchistes d'Espagne* (Paris, 1970), pp. 9–52.

47  Joll, *loc. cit.*; Josep Termes, *Anarquismo y sindicalismo en España: Primera Internacional (1864–1881)* (Barcelona, 1982); José Alvárez Junco, *La comuna en España* (Madrid, 1971), esp. pp. 1–20.

48  Jorge Domínguez, *Insurrection or Loyalty: The breakdown of the Spanish American Empire* (Harvard, 1980).

49  Paul Estrade, *José Martí – militante y estrategía* (Havana, 1983), pp. 11–35.

50  See especially Henry George, *Progress and Poverty: An inquiry into the cause of industrial depression* (written 1877–9; 4th edn, London, 1882).

51  Edward Bellamy, *Looking Backward 2000–1887* (first published 1887; Boston, 1917).

52  Martí, *O.C.*, n.d., XIX, p. 355.

53  Martí, *O.C.*, 1881, IX, pp. 45, 88, 98; 1883, IX, p. 337.

54  *Ibid.*, pp. 64–85.

55  Verena Martínez-Alier, *Marriage, class and colour in nineteenth-century Cuba: A study of racial attitudes and sexual values in a slave society* (Cambridge, 1974), p. 41.

56  This is observed, for example, in Pedro Deschamps Chapeaux, *Rafael Serra y Montalvo, Obrero incansable de nuestra independencia* (Havana, 1975).

57  Martí, *O.C.*, 1883, VIII, p. 405; Donald Denoon, *Settler Capitalism: the Dynamics of Dependent Development in the Southern Hemisphere* (Oxford, 1983).

58  Martí, *O.C.*, 1882, XXIII, p. 224.

59  Martí, *O.C.*, 1887, XX, p. 112; *ibid.*, p. 85. In his journalism Martí was particularly effective and immediate in reporting direct speech. In his portrayal of courtroom drama he carefully contrived realism. See Martí, *O.C.*, 1881, IX, pp. 76–7, 148–50. He was effective too in light journalism on themes of general interest like the elevated railway in New

York and Berlin or the possibility of a Channel tunnel linking England and France: Martí, *O.C.*, 1882, XXIII, pp. 299–300.

60  Martí, *O.C.* 1895, IV, pp. 93–101.
61  Martí, *O.C.*, 1871, I, pp. 45–76; 1887, I, p. 199.
62  Martí, *O.C.*, 1873, I, pp. 93, 104.
63  Martí, *O.C.*, 1892, I, pp. 320, 329.
64  *Ibid.*, p. 323.
65  See especially Martí, *O.C.*, 1889, VI, pp. 46–62; 1891, VI, pp. 149–66.
66  See especially Martí, *O.C.*, 1883, VII, pp. 20–2.
67  Emilio Roig de Leuschenring, *Hostos y Cuba* (2nd edn, Havana, 1974), pp. 78–82.
68  Carlos M. Rama, *La independencia de Las Antillas y Ramón Emeterio Betances* (San Juan, 1980), esp. pp. 52–4.
69  Martí made three journeys to the Dominican Republic, celebrated in E. Rodríguez Demorizi (ed.), *Martí en Santo Domingo* (2nd edn, Barcelona, 1978), esp. p. 35. On related themes, see Christopher Abel, 'Politics and the economy of the Dominican Republic, 1890–1930' in C. Abel and Colin M. Lewis, *Latin America, Economic Imperialism and the State: the Political Economy of the External Connection from Independence to the Present* (London, 1985), pp. 339–66.
70  The outlooks of Martí and Hostos were similar. It remains unclear whether they exchanged views or reached analogous opinions independently. See Martí, *O.C.*, 1876, VIII, p. 54; Roig de Leuschenring, *op. cit.*, esp. pp. 76–82, 88; Carmelo Rosario Natal, *Puerto Rico y la crisis de la guerra hispano-americana (1895–1898)* (Hato Rey, 1975), pp. 79–98; Joaquin Freire, *Presencia de Puerto Rico en la historia de Cuba* (San Juan, 1966), esp. p. 107.
71  Martí, *O.C.*, 1889, VI, p. 160.
72  Paul Estrade, 'Remarques sur le caractère tardif, et avancé, de la prise de conscience nationale dans les Antilles espagnoles', in *Cahiers du monde hispanique et luso-brasilien, Caravelle*, no. 38, 1982, pp. 87–117.
73  Martí, *O.C.*, esp. 1881, XIV, p. 117.
74  On émigré co-ordination and tobacco workers, see Jean Stubbs, *Tobacco on the Periphery: A case study in Cuban labour history* (Cambridge, 1985), p. 109; Jean Stubbs, 'Dandy or Rake? Cigar-Makers in 1860–1958', in C. Abel and M. Twaddle (comps), *Caribbean Societies, Volume 1, Collected Seminar Papers No. 29* (Institute of Commonwealth Studies, London, 1982), pp. 17–25.
75  Martí, *O.C.*, 1887, I, pp. 18–19; and subsequent elaboration of 'Bases del Partido Revolucionario Cubano' and 'Estatutos secretos del partido', Martí, *O.C.*, 1882, I, pp. 279–80, 281–4; also I, pp. 436–9.
76  Martí, *O.C.*, 1892, II, p. 49.
77  *Ibid.*, p. 62.
78  Paul Estrade, 'Cuba à la veille de l'independance: le Mouvement Económique (1890–1893) I: Faits et Jalons pour son histoire', *Mélanges de la Casa de Velázquez*, Tome XIII (1977), pp. 385–424, and II: 'Bilan et essai d'interpretation'; Tome XIV (1978), pp. 357–80. See also Martí, *O.C.*, 1894, III, pp. 72–3.
79  Martí, *O.C.*, 1875, VI, p. 304; 1881, XIV, p. 57.

80 Ibarra, *op. cit.*, pp. 5–40. Writing in Mexico from the congenial surroundings of the *Revista Universal*, Martí seemed blind to the destructive impact of a spoils system and machine politics that undermined a liberal idealism; and he neglected consideration of the administrative apparatus – the competence of the accountancy system, the formation of essential data-gathering agencies – matters that were perhaps not the material of exciting journalism but were essential to the well-being and efficiency of the liberal state.
81 Martí, *O.C.*, 1884, I, p. 178.
82 Philip S. Foner, *Antonio Maceo – the 'Bronze Titan' of Cuba's struggle for independence* (New York, 1977), p. 121.
83 Martí, *O.C.*, 1887, I, p. 214; see also p. 217.
84 Martí, *O.C.*, 1894, III, p. 314.
85 Martí, *O.C.*, 1893, II, p. 196.
86 Martí, *O.C.*, 1890, I, p. 261.
87 Louis A. Pérez, Jr, 'Insurrection, intervention, and the transformation of the land tenure systems in Cuba, 1895–1902', *Hispanic American Historical Review*, 65, 1985, pp. 229–54.
88 German Carrera Damas, 'Simón Bolívar, el culto heroico y la nación', *Hispanic American Historical Review*, 1983, esp. p. 109, where Carrera Damas develops themes explored previously in his outstanding *El culto a Bolívar* (Caracas, 1964).

## Chapter 8   Void and renewal

1 This chapter was originally presented as an essay in Spanish at the 1983 seminar on José Martí, at University College, University of London. Its title was 'Las "entrañas del vacío" y "el impulso renovador": la modernidad de José Martí'. The phrase 'entrañas del vacío' comes from a verse by V. Huidobro; 'el impulso renovador' is from J. E. Rodó's 'El que vendrá'. In its revised English format this chapter represents a free translation from the original Spanish prepared with the editorial and secretarial assistance of Hernán Castellano Girón and Antonieta Olivares. We wish to express our indebtedness to them and to the Manuel Pedro González José Martí Foundation of the University of Florida Foundation for its support of the research and travel connected with the preparation and presentation of this essay.
2 José Enrique Rodó, 'Rumbos nuevos', in *Obras completas* (Madrid, 1967), p. 519.
3 See Angel Rama, 'La dialéctica de la modernidad en José Martí', in *Estudios Martianos* (Río Piedras, 1974), pp. 132–46.
4 Rama, *op. cit.*, p. 129.
5 José Martí, *Obras completas* (Havana, 1963–1973) (hereafter *O.C.*), VII, p. 229.
6 Cintio Vitier, 'Martí futuro', in Cintio Vitier and Fina García Marruz, *Temas martianos* (Havana, 1969), pp. 120–40.
7 Martí, *O.C.*, VII, p. 226.
8 Martí, *O.C.*, VII, p. 225.

9    Rodó, *Obras completas*, p. 153.
10   Martí, *O.C.*, VII, p. 227.
11   Martí, *Lucía Jérez* (Madrid, 1969), p. 110.
12   *Loc. cit.*
13   *Loc. cit.*
14   Rodó, *op. cit.*, p. 520.
15   See Rafael Gutiérrez Girardot, *Modernismo* (Barcelona, 1983), pp. 33–71.
16   Martí, *Lucía Jérez*, p. 70.
17   *Loc. cit.*
18   Matei Calinescu, *Faces of Modernity: Avant-Garde, Decadence, Kitsch* (Indiana University Press, 1977), p. 41.
19   Max Henríquez Ureña, *Breve historia del modernismo* (Mexico, 1954), p. 156.
20   Rubén Darío, 'Los colores del estandarte', in *Escritos inéditos de Rubén Darío* (New York, Instituto de las Españas, 1938), p. 123.
21   Manuel Machado, in *La guerra literaria*, as quoted by Ricardo Gullón, *El modernismo visto por los modernistas* (Barcelona, 1980), p. 130.
22   Martí, *O.C.*, IX, p. 325; emphasis added.
23   Friedrich Wilhelm Nietzsche, 'The Will to Power', in *The Complete Works*, ed. O. Levy (New York, 1924), XIV, p. 13.
24   Malcolm Bradbury and James McFarlane, 'The Name and Nature of Modernism', in *Modernism* (Harmondsworth, 1976), p. 41.
25   Andrés Bello, 'Las repúblicas hispanoamericanas' (1836), quoted in *Bello*, ed. G. Méndez Plancarte (Mexico, 1943), p. 83.
26   Federico de Onís, *España en América* (Madrid, 1955), pp. 175–81.
27   My adaptation of O. Paz's concept, expressed in 'El caracol y la sirena': 'La acción revolucionaria . . . es asimismo una restauración: la de un pasado inmemorial, origen de los tiempos', 'Revolutionary action . . . is in the same way a restoration: that of an immemorial past, the source of our times' *Cuadrivio* (Mexico, 1965), p. 22.
28   Manuel Machado considered anarchy to be the fundamental characteristic of modernism: 'No hay que asustarse de esta palabra pronunciada en su único sentido posible . . . para éste el modernismo es la cabellera de Valle-Inclán, para aquél los cuplés del Salón Rouge, para el otro los cigarrillos turcos, y para el de más allá los muebles de Lissáraga.' *La guerra literaria*, as quoted by Gullón, *op. cit.*, p. 129.
     'One should not be frightened of this word [anarchism], pronounced in its one possible meaning . . . for one person, modernism is Valle-Inclán's mane, for another the songs of the Salon Rouge, for a third Turkish cigarettes and for the rest the furniture of Lissáraga.'
29   Juan Ramón Jiménez, *El modernismo: notas de un curso (1953)* (Mexico, 1962), p. 102.
30   *Ibid.*, p. 237.
31   *Ibid.*, pp. 49 and 238.
32   Bradbury and McFarlane, *op. cit.*, p. 19.
33   Saúl Yurkievich equates modernity with Darío, especially his *Cantos de vida y esperanza*; see *Celebración del modernismo* (Barcelona, 1976), p. 25.
34   See Evelyn-Picón Garfield and Ivan A. Schulman, '*Las entrañas del*

*vacío': ensayos sobre la modernidad hispanoamericana* (Mexico, 1984), pp. 32–55.
35  S. Yurkievich, *op. cit.*, p. 18.
36  Irving Howe, *Literary Modernism* (New York, 1967), pp. 12–13.
37  *Loc. cit.*
38  David Lodge, 'Historicism and literary history: Mapping the modern period', *New Literary History*, 10 (1979), p. 550.
39  Martí, *Lucía Jérez*, p. 136.
40  Howe, *op. cit.*, p. 21.
41  Rodó, *Obras completas*, p. 154.
42  *Loc. cit.*
43  Howe, *op. cit.*, p. 21.
44  Mariano Azuela, *Los de abajo*, (Primera Parte, Capítulo XIV) (Havana, 1971), p. 68.
45  Howe, *op. cit.*, p. 13.
46  Daniel Bell, *The Cultural Contradictions of Capitalism* (New York, 1976), p. 14.
47  See Roberto Fernández Retamar, 'Nuestra América y Occidente', *Casa de las Américas*, no. 98, 1976, p. 40.
48  Retamar, *op. cit.*, p. 43.
49  *Debasar* and *rebasar* are two neologisms which Martí used to describe the nature of revolutionary change, in this case, with respect to the base or foundation of poetic expression.
50  Martí, *O.C.*, XXI, p. 168.
51  Martí, *O.C.*, VII, p. 225; emphasis added.
52  Karl Vossler, 'Formas gramaticales y psicológicas', in *Introducción a la estilística moderna* (Buenos Aires, 1932), pp. 84–5.
53  Martí, *O.C.*, XXI, p. 388.
54  Manuel Pedro González, in his preface to Martí's *Lucía Jerez*, p. 24.
55  Martí, *O.C.*, XXI, p. 225.
56  Fina García Marruz, 'Los versos de Martí', in *La Revista de la Biblioteca Nacional 'José Martí'*, 59, 1968, p. 20.
57  Cintio Vitier, *Los versos de Martí* (Havana, 1969), p. 34.
58  *Ibid.*, p. 11.
59  Martí, *O.C.*, VII, p. 271; emphasis added.
60  Rubén Darío, 'José Martí, poeta, I, II, III, IV', in *Antología crítica de José Martí*, ed. M. P. González (Mexico, 1960), p. 272.
61  Martí, *O.C.*, VIII, p. 282.
62  *Ibid.*
63  Martí, *O.C.*, XIII, p. 135.

## Chapter 9  Order and passion in *Amistad funesta*

1  José Martí, *Obras completas* (2nd edn, Havana, 1963–65) (hereafter *O.C.*), XVIII, p. 289.
2  *Ibid.*, p. 192.
3  *Ibid.*, p. 196.
4  *Ibid.*, p. 197.

5   *Ibid.*, p. 196.
6   *Ibid.*, p. 197.
7   *Ibid.*, p. 198.
8   *Ibid.*, p. 199.
9   Martí, *O.C.*, XVI, p. 115.
10  Martí, *O.C.*, XVIII, p. 199.
11  *Ibid.*, p. 200.
12  I Corinthians 6:13.
13  *Ibid.*, 6:18.
14  *Ibid.*, 7:9.
15  *Ibid.*, 7:1.
16  *Ibid.*, 7:37.
17  Martí, *O.C.*, XVIII, p. 202.
18  *Ibid.*, p. 195.
19  *Ibid.*, p. 201.
20  *Ibid.*, p. 199.
21  Genesis 3:15.
22  Martí, *O.C.*, XVIII, p. 240.
23  *Ibid.*, p. 249.
24  *Ibid.*, p. 221.
25  *Ibid.*, p. 231.
26  *Ibid.*, p. 207.
27  *Ibid.*, p. 209.
28  *Ibid.*, p. 213.
29  *Ibid.*, p. 226.
30  *Ibid.*, p. 243.
31  *Ibid.*, p. 226.
32  *Ibid.*, p. 266.
33  *Ibid.*, p. 250.
34  *Ibid.*, p. 212.
35  *Ibid.*, p. 203.
36  *Ibid.*, p. 201.
37  *Ibid.*, p. 247.

# Select bibliography

The contributors to this volume have used different editions of the *Obras completas* of José Martí. These include the editions of 1963–5 (28 volumes) and of 1975 (27 volumes). For further bibliographical material, see John M. Kirk, *José Martí: Mentor of the Cuban nation* (Tampa, Fa, 1983) pp. 181–98.

AGUIRRE, MIRTA, 'Los principios estéticos e ideológicos de José Martí', *Anuario del Centro de Estudios Martianos*, 1 (Havana, 1978), pp. 133–87.

ALVAREZ, B., 'La crise des années 30 à Cuba et les alternatives proposées par les divers secteurs politiques' in *Les années trente à Cuba. Actes du colloque international organisé à Paris en Novembre 1980* (Paris, 1982).

ARIAS, SALVADOR (comp. and author of prologue), *Acerca de la Edad de Oro* (Havana, 1980).

ARMAS, RAMÓN DE, 'José Martí y la época histórica del imperialismo', *Anuario del Centro de Estudios Martianos*, 3 (Havana, 1980), pp. 237–57.

——, 'La república cubana de Martí', *Casa de las Américas*, 13 (Jan.–Feb. 1973), pp. 44–50.

ARROM, JOSÉ J., 'Martí y el problema de las generaciones', *Thesaurus. Boletín del Instituto Caro y Cuervo*, 28 (Jan.–Apr. 1973), pp. 29–45.

AUGIER, ANGEL, *Acción y poesía en José Martí* (Havana, 1982).

BÉGUEZ CÉSAR, JOSÉ ANTONIO, *Martí y el Krausismo* (Havana, 1943).

BLANCO AGUINAGA, CARLOS, 'Sobre el concepto leniniano del término demócrata revolucionario', *Anuario del Centro de Estudios Martianos*, 3 (Havana, 1980), pp. 106–17.

CANTÓN NAVARRO, JOSÉ, *Algunas ideas de José Martí en relación con la clase obrera y el socialismo* (Havana, 1980).

——, 'Rasgos del pensamiento democrático y revolucionario de José Martí', *Anuario del Centro de Estudios Martianos*, 3 (Havana, 1980), pp. 91–105.

CARBONELL, NÉSTOR, *Martí, carne y espíritu*, 2 vols (Havana, 1951–2).

——, 'Un capítulo en la autobiografía de Martí', *Archivo José Martí*, 6 (Jan.–Dec. 1952), pp. 283–302.

CASAUS, VÍCTOR, 'El *Diario* de José Martí: rescate y vigencia de nuestra literatura de combate', *Anuario del Centro de Estudios Martianos*, 1 (Havana, 1978), pp. 189–206.

CASTRO, FIDEL, *José Martí. El autor intelectual* (Havana, 1983).

CENTRO DE ESTUDIOS MARTIANOS, *Trajectory and Actuality of Martí's Thought* (Havana, 1961).

DESCHAMPS CHAPEAUX, PEDRO, *Rafael Serra y Montalvo, obrero incansable de nuestra independencia* (Havana, 1975).

DESNOES, EDMUNDO, 'José Martí, intelectual revolucionario y hombre nuevo', *Casa de las Américas*, 9 (May–June 1969), pp. 115–21.

DUMOULIN, JOHN, 'El primer desarrollo del movimiento obrero y la formación del proletariado en el sector azucarero: Cruces, 1886–1902', *Islas*, Santa Clara, I, 48, 1975, pp. 3–66.

ESTRADE, PAUL, 'Martí, Betances, Rizal. Lineamientos y prácticas de la revolución democrática anticolonial', *Anuario del Centro de Estudios Martianos*, 3 (Havana, 1980), pp. 150–77.

——, *José Martí, militante y estrategía* (Havana, 1983).

——, *La colonia cubana de Paris, 1895–1898* (Havana, 1986).

——, *En torno a José Martí. Colloque international . . . Bordeaux* (Bordeaux, 1974).

——, 'Las huelgas de 1890 en Cuba', *Hommage des Hispanistes français à Noël Salomon* (Barcelona, 1979), pp. 251–71.

——, 'Remarques sur le caractère tardif, et avancé, de la prise de conscience nationale dans les Antilles espagnoles', *Cahiers du monde hispanique et luso-brésilien, Caravelle*, no. 38, 1982.

——, 'Cuba à la veille de l'independance: le Mouvement Economique', *Mélanges de la Casa de Velazquez*, Tome XIII–XIV, 1977–8.

FERNÁNDEZ RETAMAR, ROBERTO, *Introducción a José Martí* (Havana, 1978).

——, *Lectura de Martí* (Mexico, 1972).

FONER, PHILIP S., *Antonio Maceo* (New York, 1977).

——, *The Spanish–Cuban–American War and the Birth of American Imperialism*, 2 vols (New York, 1972).

——, *A History of Cuba and its relations with the United States* 2 vols (New York, 1962–3).

FORNET, AMBROSIO, 'De ingresos y talleres del siglo XX', *Revista de la Biblioteca Nacional José Martí*, 17:3, Sept.–Dec. 1975, pp. 87–96.

GARCÍA CANTÚ, GASTÓN, 'México en Martí', *Anuario del Centro de Estudios Martianos*, 1 (Havana, 1978), pp. 222–8.

GARCÍA GALLO, GASPAR JORGE, *Martí, americano y universal* (Havana, 1971).

GARCÍA MARRUZ, FINA, 'José Martí', *Archivo José Martí*, 6 (Jan.–Dec. 1952), pp. 52–86.

—— and VITIER, CINTIO, *Temas martianos* (1a serie) (Havana, 1969).

GHIANO, JUAN CARLOS, *José Martí* (Buenos Aires, 1967).

GÓMEZ, MÁXIMO, *Diario de campaña* (Havana, 1968).

GONZÁLEZ, MANUEL PEDRO, 'Aforismos y definiciones, o la capacidad sintética de Martí', *Anuario Martiano*, 4 (1972), pp. 27–50.

——, *Indagaciones martianas* (Santa Clara, 1961).

——, *José Martí, Epic Chronicler of the U.S. in the Eighties* (Chapel Hill, NC, 1953).

——, *Notas críticas* (Havana, 1969).

—— (ed.), *Antología crítica de José Martí* (Mexico, 1960), pp. 215–17.

—— and SCHULMAN, IVAN A., *José Martí: esquema ideológico* (Mexico, 1961).

GONZÁLEZ CASANOVA, PABLO, 'América Latina: marxismo y liberación en los planteamientos pioneros', *Anuario del Centro de Estudios Martianos*, 3 (Havana, 1980), pp. 194–217.

GRAY, RICHARD BUTLER, *José Martí: Cuban patriot* (Gainesville, Fa, 1962).

GRIÑÁN PERALTA, LEONARDO, *Martí, líder político* (Havana, 1970).

GUERRA Y SÁNCHEZ, RAMIRO, *Guerra de los diez años, 1868–1878*, vol. I (Havana, 1950), vol. II (Havana, 1972).

GUEVARA, ERNESTO (CHE), 'José Martí', in *Siete enfoques marxistas sobre José Martí* (Havana, 1978), pp. 69–76.

GUTIÉRREZ GIRARDOT, RAFAEL, *Modernismo* (Barcelona, 1983).

HART DÁVALOS, ARMANDO, 'Discurso en Dos Ríos', in *Siete enfoques marxistas sobre José Martí* (Havana, 1978), pp. 115–37.

HERNÁNDEZ PARDO, HÉCTOR, 'Raíz martiana de nuestra pedagogía', *Anuario del Centro de Estudios Martianos*, 1 (Havana, 1978), pp. 240–8.

IBARRA, JORGE, *Ideología mambisa* (Havana, 1967).

——, *José Martí: Dirigente político e ideológo revolucionario* (Havana, 1980).

——, *Aproximaciones a Clio* (Havana, 1979).

IDUARTE, ANDRÉS, *Martí, escritor* (Mexico, 1944).

——, *Sarmiento, Martí y Rodó* (Havana, 1955).

JIMÉNEZ, JUAN RAMÓN, *Notas de un curso (1953)* (eds R. Gullón and E. Fernández Méndez) (Mexico, 1962).

JIMÉNEZ PASTRANA, J., *Los chinos en las luchas por la liberación cubana, 1847–1930* (Havana, 1963).

JITRÍK, NOÉ, *Las contradicciones del modernismo: productividad poética y situación sociológica* (Mexico, 1978).

KIRK, JOHN M., *José Martí: Mentor of the Cuban nation* (Tampa, Fa, 1983).

LE RIVEREND, JULIO, 'Martí en la revolución de 1868', *Casa de las Américas*, 9 (Sept.–Oct. 1969), pp. 95–110.

——, *José Martí: pensamiento y acción* (Havana, 1982).

——, Raíces del 24 de febrero: la economía y la sociedad cubana de 1878 a 1895', *Cuba Socialista*, XI, 42, Feb. 1963, pp. 1–17.

——, *Economic History of Cuba* (Havana, 1967).

LEWIS, GORDON, *Main Currents in Caribbean Thought: The Historical Evolution of Caribbean Society in its Ideological Aspects, 1492–1900* (London, 1984).

LIZASO, FÉLIX, *Martí, Martyr of Cuban Independence* (translation by Esther Elise Shuler, of *Martí, místico del deber*) (Westport, Conn., 1974).

MALDONADO-DENIS, MANUEL, 'Martí y Fanón', *Casa de las Américas*, 13 (July–Aug. 1972), pp. 17–27.

——, 'Martí y Hostos: paralelismos en la lucha de ambos por la independencia de las Antillas en el siglo XIX', *Anuario del Centro de Estudios Martianos*, 3 (Havana, 1980), pp. 178–93.

MAÑACH, JORGE, *El pensamiento político y social de Martí* (Havana, 1941).

——, *Martí, Apostle of Freedom* (translation by Coley Taylor of *Martí, el Apostol* [1944]) (New York, 1950).

MARINELLO, JUAN, *Actualidad de José Martí: Martí, maestro de unidad* (Havana, 1943).

——, *José Martí* (Paris, 1970).

——, *José Martí, escritor americano* (Mexico, 1958).

——, *Once ensayos martianos* (Havana, 1964).

MÁRQUEZ STERLING, CARLOS, *Discursos leídos en la recepción pública del dr. Carlos Márquez Sterling la noche del 20 de octubre de 1938: Martí y la Conferencia Monetaria de 1891* (Havana, 1938).

——, 'José Martí y el pensamiento democrático revolucionario', *Anuario del Centro de Estudios Martianos*, no. 3, (Havana, 1980).

MARTÍ, JOSÉ, *Cuba, Nuestra América, los Estados Unidos* (edited by Roberto Fernández Retamar) (Mexico, 1973).

——, *El pensamiento político de Martí* (edited by Emilio Roig de Leuchsenring) (Havana, 1960).

——, *Inside the Monster: Writings on the United States and American imperialism by José Martí* (edited by Philip S. Foner) (New York, 1975).

——, *Our America by José Martí: Writings on Latin America and the struggle for Cuban independence* (edited by Philip S. Foner) (New York, 1977).

——, *On Education – Articles on educational theory and pedagogy and writings for children from 'The Age of Gold'* (edited by Philip S. Foner) (New York, 1984).

——, *José Martí en los Estados Unidos* (Madrid, 1968).

MARTÍNEZ ESTRADA, EZEQUIEL, *Martí, el héroe y su acción revolucionaria* (Mexico, 1966).

——, *Martí, revolucionario* (Havana, 1967).

MELLA, JULIO ANTONIO, 'Glosando los pensamientos de José Martí', *Casa de las Américas*, 13 (Jan.–Feb. 1973), pp. 5–9.

MERCHÁN, RAFAEL, *Estudios críticos* (Bogotá, 1886).

MINISTERIO DE LAS FUERZAS ARMADAS REVOLUCIONARIAS, *Historia de Cuba* (Havana, 1967).

MISTRAL, GABRIELA, 'La lengua de Martí' in *Antología crítica de José Martí* (edited by Manuel Pedro González) (Mexico, 1960), pp. 23–39.

ORTIZ, FERNANDO, 'La religión de Martí', *La Nueva Democracia*, 38 (1958), pp. 52–7.

——, 'Martí y las razas', in *Vida y pensamiento de Martí. Homenaje de la ciudad de La Habana en el cincuentenario de la fundación del Partido Revolucionario Cubano, 1892–1942*, 1 (Havana, 1942), pp. 335–67.

OUILLON, JULIETTE, 'La discriminación racial en los Estados Unidos vista por José Martí', *Anuario Martiano*, 3 (1971), pp. 9–94.

PÉREZ, LOUIS A., Jr, 'Cubans in Tampa: From Exile to Immigrants, 1892–1901', *Florida Historical Quarterly*, vol. LVII, 2, Oct. 1978, pp. 129–40.

——, *Army Politics in Cuba, 1898–1958* (Pittsburgh, 1970).

——, *Cuba Between Empires, 1878–1902* (Pittsburgh, 1983).

PICÓN-GARFIELD, EVELYN and SCHULMAN, IVAN A., *Las entrañas del vacío: ensayos sobre la modernidad hispanoamericana* (Mexico, 1984).

PICÓN SALAS, MARIANO, 'Arte y virtud en José Martí', in *Memoria del congreso de escritores martianos (Feb. 20 a 27 de 1953)* (Havana, 1953).

PORTUONDO, JOSÉ ANTONIO, *Martí, escritor revolucionario* (Havana, 1980).

——, 'Retratos infieles de José Martí', *Revista de la Biblioteca Nacional José Martí*, 3ra época, X, no. 1, Jan.–Apr. 1968, pp. 5–14.

——, 'Vigencia del latinoamericanismo de José Martí', *Cuba Socialista*, Año II, no. 4 (5), Dec. 1982–Feb. 1983, pp. 34–65.

POYO, GERALD E., 'Key West and the Cuban ten years war', *Florida Historical Quarterly*, CVII, 3, Jan. 1979, pp. 289–307.

——, 'Cuban Revolutionaries and Monroe Reconstruction Politics, 1868–1879', *Florida Historical Quarterly*, LV, 4, Apr. 1977, pp. 407–22.

RAMA, ANGEL, 'La dialéctica de la modernidad en José Martí', in *Estudios Martianos* (Río Piedras, 1974), pp. 132–46.

REYNA, EMILIO JORGE, *Martí. Monografías masónicas I* (Havana, 1964).

RIBEIRO, DARCY, *The Americas and Civilization* (New York, 1971).

RIPOLL, CARLOS, *'Patria': el periódico de José Martí, registro general (1892–1895)* (New York, 1971).

RIVERO MUÑÍZ, JOSÉ, 'Los cubanos de Tampa', *Revista Bimestre Cubana*, LIV, 1, Jan.–June 1958, pp. 5–149.

ROA, RAÚL, 'Rescate y proyección de Martí', in *Siete enfoques marxistas sobre José Martí* (Havana, 1978), pp. 19–36.

ROCA, BLAS, 'José Martí, revolucionario radical de su tiempo', *Casa de las Américas*, 13 (Jan.–Feb. 1973), pp. 10–21.

RODRÍGUEZ, CARLOS RAFAEL, *José Martí and Cuban Liberation* (New York, 1953).

RODRÍGUEZ DEMORIZI, EMILIO, *Martí en Santo Domingo* (2nd edn, Barcelona, 1978).

——, *Maceo en Santo Domingo* (2nd edn, Barcelona, 1978).

RODRÍGUEZ-FEO, JOSÉ, 'Martí en la Revolución', *Lunes*, 30 Jan. 1961, pp. 10–12.

ROIG DE LEUCHSENRING, EMILIO, *Martí, antimperialista* (1953), reprint ed. (Havana, 1961).

SALOMON, NOËL, 'En torno al idealismo de José Martí', *Anuario del Centro de Estudios Martianos*, 1 (1978), pp. 41–58.

SANGUILY, MANUEL, *José Martí y la revolución cubana* (New York, 1896).

SCHULMAN, IVAN A., *Símbolo y color en la obra de José Martí* (Madrid, 1970).

——, *Esquema ideológico de José Martí* (in collaboration with Manuel Pedro González) (Mexico, 1961).

——, *Martí, Darío y el modernismo* (in collaboration with Manuel Pedro González) (Madrid, 1969).

——, *Martí, Casal y el modernismo* (Havana, 1969).

SCHULTZ DE MANTOVANI, FRYDA, *Genio y figura de José Martí* (Buenos Aires, 1968).

SHELBY, CHARMION C., 'Mexico and the Spanish–American War: Some Contemporary Expressions of Opinion', in Thomas E. Cotner and Carlos E. Castañeda (eds), *Essays in Mexican History* (Austin, Texas, 1958).

SOTO, LIONEL, *La revolución de 1933*, 3 vols (Havana, 1977–8).

STUBBS, JEAN, *Tobacco on the Periphery* (Cambridge, 1985).

THOMAS, HUGH, *Cuba: or the pursuit of freedom* (London, 1971).

TOLEDO SANDE, LUIS, *Ideología y práctica en José Martí: seis aproximaciones* (Havana, 1982).

VILLAVERDE, CIRILO, 'La revolución de Cuba vista desde New York' in *Homenaje a Cirilo Villaverde* (Comisión Nacional Cubana de la UNESCO, Havana, 1964), pp. 23–49.

VITIER, CINTIO, *Temas martianos* (2a serie) (Havana, 1982).

——, *Lo cubano en la poesía* (Havana, 1970).

—— and GARCÍA MARRUZ, FINA, *Temas martianos* (Havana, 1969).

VITIER, MEDARDO, *Las ideas y la filosofía en Cuba* (Havana, 1970).

WESTFALL, L. GLENN, 'Don Vicente Martínez Ybor, the man and his empire: Development of the Clear Havana industry in Cuba and Florida in the nineteenth century' (unpublished PhD thesis, University of Florida, 1977).

# Index

Since all references are directly or indirectly addressed to Martí, his name is not included here. The Partido Revolucionario Cubano (PRC) listed here is the organization company founded by Martí. The later organization of the same name, founded in the 1930s, is referred to here by its more common appellation, *Auténticos*.